WATERLOO: THE DEFEAT OF NAPOLEON'S IMPERIAL GUARD

WATERLOO: THE DEFEAT OF NAPOLEON'S IMPERIAL GUARD

Henry Clinton, the 2nd Division and the End of a 200-year-old Controversy

Gareth Glover

FRONTLINE BOOKS

Waterloo: The Defeat of Napoleon's Imperial Guard
Henry Clinton, the 2nd Division and the End of a 200-year-old Controversy

This edition published in 2015 by Frontline Books,
an imprint of Pen & Sword Books Ltd,
47 Church Street, Barnsley, S. Yorkshire, S70 2AS

ISBN: 978-1-84832-744-3

CIP data records for this title are available from the British Library

Printed and bound by CPI Group (UK) Ltd, Croydon, CR0 4YY
Typeset in 10/12 point Palatino

For more information on our books, please email: info@frontline-books.com,
write to us at the above address, or visit
www.frontline-books.com

Contents

List of Maps

Acknowledgements

Any book of this complexity requires the help and assistance of others to come to fruition. In this regard I have been very fortunate in receiving the able and willing assistance of the staff at the John Rylands Library on my numerous visits to their Reading Room. I must mention in particular John Hodgson and Dorothy Clayton for their general support of the project and particular help to obtain images from the Clinton files.

With regard to the Beinecke Library in Yale University, I must offer my grateful thanks to Brian Dunnigan for helping me contact the right people, Karl Longstreth who helped me identify the Clinton maps and Anne Marie Menta for her help in providing reproductions of the Clinton material for my use.

Beyond this, the help and advice of the Napoleonic community in general has been gratefully received, particularly through the Napoleon Series Discussion site.

Finally I must as always thank my long-suffering but unbelievably supportive wife Mary and my two grown-up children Sarah and Michael who continue to inspire me. I must particularly thank Michael, who as a history graduate made an invaluable contribution to the book by proof reading it and making a number of suggestions which hugely improved the final version.

Preface

Sunset loomed, but the battle raged on; and through the thick haze of gunpowder smoke, occasional glimpses of the 'indestructible' Imperial Guard marching up the soft incline towards the chaotic remnants of the allied front line foretold imminent disaster.

Faintly at first, but slowly getting louder between the irregular discharges of cannon, musketry and the cacophony of battle, the massed ranks of drummer boys announced the attack with the rhythmic drum beat of the '*pas de charge*'.

'The crash of the Imperial drums, beating with the harsh unity that stamped them as the voices of veterans in war, woke me from my reverie and made my heart throb with their stony rattle. Never did I hear such drums and never shall again: there were years of battle and blood in every sound.'[1]

All seemed lost, the British Guards had fallen back in confusion before a second column of these whiskered veterans; this truly was the crisis of the battle.

But at such times, heroes forged of steel grasp their moment and snatch victory from the hands of fate. Colonel John Colborne coolly ordered his regiment in line formation to wheel its face to the left. His battle-scarred veterans obeyed without question and the 52nd Foot wheeled through ninety degrees with the precision of a training ground exercise. The movement was adeptly followed by the remainder of the brigade to garner their support.

Suddenly, through the smoke, the menacing column of French Imperial Guardsmen became visible directly to their front and still marching inexorably for the crest of the ridge ahead, seemingly oblivious to Colborne's men, now facing its vulnerable flank at short musket range.

Colborne recognised the perfect moment and called out for a crashing volley from his men. They did not let him down. The volley of a thousand lead musket balls struck the French column with such venom that it halted in its tracks, and those fortunate to escape injury turned to offer a confused but firm response.

Colborne's men did not hesitate to reload, but gave one lusty cheer and advanced immediately towards the shattered column in a determined bayonet charge. As the British infantry, so obvious in their deep red coats, advanced rapidly with grave determination to see the charge home, the French veterans were forced to make a snap decision, to stand or flee.

Some brave souls stood, but as always, the spirit of those furthest from the actual threat, at the rear and those on the right wing of the column, who were painfully aware of the threat but could not see or face it personally, broke first. The trickle of men fleeing instantly sapped the courage of the majority and soon turned the column into a fleeing mob.

The Imperial Guard had been defeated!

Such had never happened before, and as this news spread like wildfire through an exhausted French army, morale collapsed and they turned tail and fled *en masse*.

The light infantry brigade, led by Colborne's men, swept, across the field, destroying all semblance of order and any attempts to rally to offer further resistance. Defeat rapidly turned into inglorious rout.

Truly the Light Brigade had swept the field clear of the enemy and had won the battle for Wellington. Or so some historians would claim. But is it all true?

Indeed the absence of a mention of this glorious movement across the field in his despatch after the battle has caused controversy for two hundred years, between the 1st Foot Guards and the 52nd Foot in particular.

This book, using a mass of previously unpublished material regarding the exploits of the Light Brigade, and indeed the entire 2nd Division of which it was one of three brigades under the command of Sir Henry Clinton – will seek to put the record straight and not only apportion the glory fairly but also show the faults.

Little has been written about the exploits of this division during the Waterloo campaign beyond Colborne's movement. It is high time that their actions throughout the day, which certainly helped enormously to maintain Wellington's right wing during the mass cavalry charges, and also their vital support to the defenders of Hougoumont farm are told.

This is their story.

Introduction

So much has been written regarding the Battle of Waterloo and the campaign of 1815 that readers would be forgiven for thinking that there was nothing else to say. Incredibly, despite the millions of words published on this subject over the last two hundred years, this belief is far from correct. For far too long thousands of pages of primary source material from hundreds of eyewitnesses to the whirlwind events of 1815 have lain virtually ignored in the archives of Europe, until the last decade, when a dedicated group of individuals, including most notably John Franklin, Erwin Muilwijk and myself, have published a huge mass of this material, much for the very first time in the English language. This has forced every historian to seriously re-evaluate their understanding of this campaign and has shown that the story of the battle and campaign which we have grown up with has in many respects been misinterpreted or is quite simply wrong.

As part of this new understanding, I have recently published a revised history of the battle and campaign of Waterloo, incorporating all of this new evidence discovered throughout Europe, the Commonwealth and America,[1] entitled *Waterloo, Myth and Reality.*[2]

A very significant new source for this book was the voluminous papers of Lieutenant General Sir Henry Clinton, the son of the Sir Henry Clinton who commanded British forces during the War of American Independence and brother to Lieutenant General Sir William Henry Clinton, perhaps most unfairly known for the debacle in Eastern Spain in 1814.

The Clinton family clearly threw little away and there are literally hundreds of thousands of pages of documents written to or from Sir Henry Clinton and his brother William alone, preserved in two significant archives. I have been aware for a few years, of the no fewer than 130 archive boxes crammed with papers relating to the Clinton brothers, lying virtually ignored and un-catalogued at the John Rylands Library in Manchester. A few years ago, I spent many months regularly travelling to this library to search every single box for relevant material regarding the Waterloo campaign and photographed each individual page so that I could process all of this primary evidence at a more leisurely pace at my home in Cardiff. I completed this monumental task, to discover that I had over six thousand photographs of documents simply relating to Sir Henry Clinton during his time in Belgium in 1814-15 and during the subsequent occupation of France until 1818.

It soon became clear, however, that this was not the end of the trail. For I discovered that the Beinecke Library at Yale University also held papers not only from Sir Henry Clinton senior, but also much material regarding his two sons. It would seem that when the Clinton papers were auctioned in 1958, the collection was unfortunately split between these two major archives.

With some perseverance and a great deal of good will displayed by the staff at the Beinecke Library I was able to obtain photographs of over fifty more letters, two books of inspection reports and his daily diary, contained in four leather-bound booklets, all of which Henry Clinton wrote in the period 1814-16. The staff were also able to provide superb images of a number of maps relevant to the campaign which had actually been owned by Henry Clinton.

With a total of over ten thousand images of primary documents relating to the campaign, this has clearly become a major task, but one I have readily undertaken because of the breadth of the material and the unique insight this gives us of the commanders, units involved and their actions in this campaign.

Sir Henry Clinton was a very experienced officer, highly regarded by the Duke of Wellington and was uniquely placed to view the entire campaign and the build-up to it. He was appointed to serve as second-in-command to the relatively inexperienced Prince of Orange, who commanded the British army in Belgium alongside his own forces in the latter half of 1814.

Henry was primarily engaged in the regular inspection of all of the troops stationed in Belgium, from the remnants of the British units which had so recently failed to capture the fortress of Bergen op Zoom, together with the vast majority of the King's German Legion (KGL) who were in fear of being disbanded as part of the peace dividend, the new Hanoverian levies recently sent into Belgium and of course, not least, the Dutch and Belgian units of the fledgling Netherlands army. His honest reports regarding the abilities of the officers, the training and equipment of their men and the fair assessment of their failings are invaluable, allowing us to understand the true quality of this small army before news of the escape of Napoleon suddenly brought preparations for war back to the fore.

With this sudden change of events, Henry Clinton was again perfectly placed to be fully conversant with all of the works that were begun to make the Belgian fortresses secure from a *coup de main* and the efforts to bolster the army significantly. Orders were sent for every available regiment to proceed from both Britain and Canada,[3] and masses of recruits were sent from the depot battalions at home to bolster significantly the undermanned sister battalions stationed in Belgium. He was also perfectly placed to discuss the Prince of Orange's plans for defence and to make suggestions as to how these troops could be improved.

Henry Clinton was delighted to hear that his old commander, the Duke of Wellington, was to take command of this massively increased army in Belgium and that it was to be completely reorganised. He was appointed on 11 April 1815 to command the 2nd Division within this new organisation and with which he served throughout the ensuing campaign. He has left a frank and honest assessment of both his troops' abilities and their achievements.

This is the real point at which this story of the 2nd Division begins. This study of the 2nd Division in the Waterloo campaign builds on all of the information available regarding the troops that formed it and their subsequent actions during the campaign. This division comprised troops of the British Army, the King's German Legion and of the newly raised Hanoverian levies, and a true assessment of their worth and capabilities can now finally be made.

The division was stationed too far away to be involved in the Battle of Quatre Bras and only partially in the subsequent retreat, but was fully involved in the Battle of Waterloo, although most historians play down its role significantly, with one notable exception.

The role of the division in the battle is largely untold, with nothing said regarding their important roles in protecting Wellington's right wing, their part in the defeat of the great cavalry attacks or their invaluable support in the defence of Hougoumont, which may have collapsed without their aid.

It is only with the final crisis of the battle that Clinton's men suddenly come to the fore in the history of the battle, when his British light infantry brigade, or more specifically the 52nd Foot, are praised for their flank attack on the Imperial Guard and their leading of the subsequent final advance. But even here their laurels are contested, with the British Guards battalions claiming at least an equal part, if not the lion's share of the defeat of the Imperial Guard. Their part is therefore far from clear and it is high time that their achievements were rightly celebrated, unclouded by confusing counter-claims.

Recently, some historians, particularly led by Nigel Sale, have argued strongly that the exploits of the 52nd in defeating the Imperial Guard have been largely ignored and, because their exploits were omitted from Wellington's despatch, consequently a conspiracy theory has emerged. There is much sympathy for their claim regarding the granting of the laurels of Waterloo – including from this author, as will be seen. But it will also become clear that the cause for this omission and the real culprit of any conspiracy, if indeed there ever was one, was certainly not the Duke.

It is therefore clear that a full and unbiased account of the actions of Sir Henry Clinton's 2nd Division at Waterloo is now badly overdue and will provide the first in-depth, honest appraisal of Wellington's troops at Waterloo and of their real exploits.

Finally the division's prominent part in the advance and capture of Paris and the subsequent occupation of France has never been told with any real authority until now. Even as early as 24 August 1815 the formation of the division began to alter radically and it changed even further in the October when the Army of Occupation of France was formed. The force was to remain in France for three years until the end of 1818.

Therefore the main focus of this book will be on the 2nd Division as it actually was for a mere four months – but what a four months that was!

Gareth Glover
Cardiff 2014

Chapter 1

The Clintons

Any history of the 2nd Division during the Waterloo campaign must firstly look upon Sir Henry Clinton and his family and how he came to command the division throughout the campaign.

The earliest mention of the Clintons is when Geoffrey de Clinton was made Treasurer and Chamberlain to King Henry I and by the late 1200s their heir John de Clinton had been created 1st Lord of Maxstoke.[1] It is clear, however, that at this stage the Clinton family, although of noble Norman extraction, was far from a rich family; but a number of strategic marriages saw a steady improvement in both its standing and wealth.

A link with the upper echelons of the armed forces also began to strengthen significantly, beginning with Edward Fiennes Clinton (1512-85), who was Lord High Admiral to King Henry VIII's fleet.

By the eighteenth century the family was deeply entrenched within the upper strata of society, having risen through the Earls of Lincoln to the heady heights of Dukes of Newcastle.

Admiral George Clinton (1668–1761) will be readily recognised by most Americans as the Governor of New York, and his eldest son General Sir Henry Clinton (1738–95) is extremely well known to all Americans as the Commander-in-Chief of land forces in America during the American War of Independence. Sir Henry Clinton had married Harriet Carter in February 1767 and the couple had four children.

The oldest son, William Henry Clinton (1769–1846), became a General in the army and married Louisa Holroyd, the daughter of the Earl of Sheffield. Throughout the Waterloo campaign William remained in England, anxiously but vainly awaiting the summons to join Wellington's army.

The second child, Henry Clinton, is the man we are particularly interested in and we will look at his career in great detail shortly.

His sister Augusta eloped and married Henry Dawkins, who became an MP thanks to the influence of the Duke of Newcastle, but never really amounted to much; as Lord Herbert commented:

> Sir Henry Clinton ... being in bad circumstances, can allow his daughter little or nothing and Dawkins having so very large a family cannot allow his son above £600 a year and neither of their dispositions seems much adapted to rigid economy.[2]

The couple did, however, produce six sons and five daughters, two of the boys being closely connected to their uncle Henry during the Waterloo campaign.

Finally there was Harriet, who had married Harry Chester in 1799; he eventually became a Major General.

As can be seen, this was an extremely well-connected family by the time of late Georgian Britain.

Our Henry Clinton was born on 9 March 1771 in Weybridge, Surrey, and can only be described as a 'career soldier'. Following the premature death of his mother at the tender age of only twenty-six years-old, and with his father rather preoccupied by events in America, Henry was sent to Eton to join his brother. He left education three years later and Henry received his commission as an Ensign in the 11th Foot[3] on 10 October 1787. However, he soon received leave of absence and set off for France and Germany, where he toured with his brother William.

In October 1788 he volunteered to serve in the Brunswick Corps raised by an old friend of his father, General Riedesel,[4] who was acting with the Russian army in the Netherlands.

In March 1791 he gained rapid promotion by purchase, becoming a Lieutenant in the 1st Foot Guards and then a Captain in the 15th Foot[5] within a month. He then transferred back to the Guards in the ensuing October.

With the advent of war with France in 1793, Henry was appointed as an aide-de-camp to Prince Frederick, the Duke of York, and went on to serve under him in the disastrous Flanders campaign of 1794. He was promoted Brevet Major in April 1794 and on 10 May was wounded at Camphin during the Battle of Willems.

He was promoted to Lieutenant Colonel in the 66th Foot[6] in September 1795 and promptly sailed to join his regiment in the West Indies. Henry was present at the landing on St Lucia by General Sir Ralph Abercromby and the subsequent capture of Morne Fortune. In 1796 he exchanged back into the 1st Foot Guards and sailed from the Isle of San Domingo to join his regiment, but his ship was captured by a French cruiser and he was made a prisoner of war until the summer of 1797, when he was released (presumably by exchange of prisoners).

He was then appointed as aide-de-camp to Lord Cornwallis in Ireland and was present at the surrender of the French invasion force under General Humbert.[7] He was then attached to Lord William

Bentinck's mission with General Suvorov's Russian army and was present at the battles of Trebia and Novi in Italy in the summer of 1799.

Returning home, Henry found time to marry the Honourable Susan Charteris, who was three years his junior, the second daughter of Francis, the 7th Lord Elcho. Their marriage seems to have been a loving one, but they were not fortunate enough to ever have any children. Susan was clearly headstrong and she insisted in travelling with Henry to Switzerland in 1800 when he was appointed as a military assistant to William Wickham[8] and was then attached to the Austrian army in Swabia and was present at the Battles of Eugen and Moeskerch. Susan's attendance was not appreciated by Wickham, who later complained that she kept Clinton in bed when he should have been in battle.

He was appointed as Assistant Adjutant General in the Eastern District in June 1801, but in January 1802 he was appointed as Adjutant General in India, where he served until 1805. He was promoted to Colonel on 25 September 1803 and he and his brother were described by King George III at this time as soldiers of 'uncommon abilities'. While serving in India, where his organisational abilities were shown to great advantage, he also commanded the right wing of the army at the Battle of Laswari.

Henry was then appointed British military attaché to the Russian army of General Kutuzov in 1805 and as such was an eye witness at the Battle of Austerlitz. He returned home after the defeat of the Austro-Russian army.

He commanded the garrison of Syracuse in Sicily from December 1806 to November 1807, during which time he met and became a great friend of General Sir John Moore, famous for his light infantry training. Henry was promoted to Brigadier General in January 1808 and accompanied General Sir John Moore on his unsuccessful expedition to Sweden (where Moore was placed under arrest by the King of Sweden and was forced to flee and to sail away with his army).

On 21 August 1808, Henry Clinton landed in Portugal, having been appointed as Adjutant General to General Sir Harry Burrard who had just taken the command of the army in Portugal, but on the following day found he had a new commander, Sir Hugh Dalrymple. With the public furore following the signing of the Convention of Cintra, whereby the French army of Portugal, which had surrendered, was allowed to be repatriated to France in British ships, the senior officers returned home to face an inquiry and Henry was delighted to hear that his friend John Moore was to take the command.

Henry Clinton proved a very capable deputy but he did gain a reputation as a disciplinarian. According to one of Henry's victims, a Captain Cochrane, he 'loaded me with such a torrent of abuse as could not have been merited by the most "worthless" individual in the army'.[9]

In fact Clinton's charges against Cochrane of disobedience and neglect of duty appear to have been a counter to Cochrane's charges of Clinton's unreasonable conduct towards him. The action was ultimately unsuccessful.

Two days before the Battle of Corunna, which ended the campaign, Henry Clinton was taken ill with dysentery and his deputy, Colonel Anderson, took his place and it was he who was present when Moore was mortally wounded. Henry was, however, the first to take up his pen to defend Moore's conduct of the campaign when it came under severe criticism from some quarters.[10]

Before sailing for Sweden, Henry had also become a Member of Parliament in 1808, joining his brother William as the joint MP's for Boroughbridge, seats controlled by the patronage of the Duke of Newcastle. He continued his political career for ten years although it never became his primary focus, indeed according to Hansard he rarely attended Parliament and never took part in any debates.

Henry was promoted to Major General in July 1810 and he requested to serve abroad on campaign. His request was granted and he joined the army under the Duke of Wellington in the Iberian Peninsula in October 1811. He was first appointed to the command of the 6th Division on 9 February 1812. During the Battle of Salamanca, his division played a key role by defeating French General Clausel's counterattack and he was granted the rare privilege of an independent command on the River Douro whilst Wellington marched to take Madrid. He then led his division at the abortive siege of Burgos.

Absent from the Peninsula from January to June 1813 due to illness, he was made a Brevet Lieutenant General in April 1813. Returning in time to lead his division at the Battle of Vitoria, Clinton was made a Knight of the Order of the Bath.

He returned home again due to illness for a short time but did return to take part in the subsequent actions at the battles of Nivelle, the Nive, Orthes, Caceres, Tarbes and Toulouse. At the end of the Peninsular War he was made a substantive Lieutenant General and Inspector General of Infantry in England and was awarded the Army Gold Cross with one clasp, the Portuguese Order of the Tower and the Sword, and he was made Colonel of the 1st Battalion of the 60th Foot.[11]

In August 1814, Henry Clinton was appointed second-in-command to the Prince of Orange, who commanded the British, Hanoverian and Dutch-Belgian troops in the Netherlands. Later, when Napoleon escaped from Elba, Henry was very pleased to have the Duke of Wellington take command.

Henry Clinton was – as an inspecting officer should be - very unforgiving of the troops, and even the most minor failures were highlighted in minute detail. But he also was undoubtedly a very experienced officer with a strong command over his troops. His rigid insistence on total obedience to orders was renowned. He was uncompromising in enforcing regulations, and as such he would never be destined to be adored by his troops or regarded as the soldier's best friend, but he was admired. He was also a very conspicuous person on any battlefield, obstinately wearing his cocked hat across his head (like Napoleon) when the current military fashion was to wear the headgear pointing 'fore and aft'. The Duke of Wellington, no friend of fools, was very content to have Henry Clinton as a senior officer commanding one of his best divisions – this fact alone speaks volumes as to the abilities of the man.

In 1815 during the Waterloo campaign, Clinton led the 2nd Division, which Wellington posted in reserve behind his right flank. The 2nd Division included the 3rd British Brigade (Major General Frederick Adam), the 1st King's German Legion Brigade (Colonel du Plat), the 3rd Hanoverian Brigade (Colonel Hugh Halkett) and Lieutenant Colonel Gold's two artillery batteries (Bolton Royal Artillery (R.A.) and Sympher KGL). His troops helped to defeat and pursue Napoleon's Imperial Guard at the end of the battle. Following the battle Henry Clinton was granted the Austrian Order of Maria Theresa, the Russian Order of St George and the Order of William of the Netherlands, and on 9 August 1815 he was made Colonel of the 3rd Foot (The Buffs).[12]

Unfortunately, fate was not kind to Henry Clinton and he died in 1829 almost a recluse. This period of his life will be discussed later in this volume.

Chapter 2

Clinton's Command

The 2nd Division, as commanded by Lieutenant General Sir Henry Clinton at Waterloo, was only formed on the orders of the Duke of Wellington on 11 April 1815.

However, we are very fortunate that many of the units that were to form the 2nd Division were already established in the Netherlands for some considerable time before April 1815 and as such came under the experienced eye of Sir Henry Clinton at numerous regular reviews and inspections. His reports on these units are very frank and are most enlightening as to the troops' honest abilities, strengths and weaknesses. These reports provide a very different view of these troops and their commanders from the traditional version that is handed down, which is heavily coloured by their supposed actions during the Waterloo campaign.

But firstly we must explain how a number of British troops were already in Belgium in 1814, and how Sir Henry Clinton came to be in the position that is so useful to our investigations.

As the war, by a more or less combined Europe against Napoleon's France edged towards the final close in 1814, the French stranglehold on Italy, Germany and the Low Countries faltered. The Dutch populace began to rebel against their occupiers, who had controlled the country for more than two decades. The hereditary ruler, the Prince of Orange, who had been banished by the French twenty years earlier, was invited back to head the revolt. In fact he sent his son, now a British army officer, also confusingly referred to as the Prince of Orange. Military support by way of troops was also supplied by Prussia and Britain, and soon the weakened French forces were forced to abandon their hold on most of the country, concentrating all of their forces in the defence of the principal fortresses such as Antwerp and Bergen op Zoom.

A British force commanded by Sir Thomas Graham landed in Holland in early 1814 and eventually besieged Bergen op Zoom, but during a bungled assault, although the British infantry broke into the fortress, the defenders rallied and successfully captured the majority of the British troops within, expelling the rest. This ignominious episode occurred on 8 March and effectively ended all hope of the British force advancing into Belgium. Indeed even these fortresses were not relieved of their French garrisons until the general peace was signed on 30 May 1814.

With peace, most of the British units present in Holland were sent home or sailed to fight another war in America, where the young and ambitious United States continued unabated in its attempts to wrest Canada from the British.

However, a small British force was allowed to remain and this moved into Belgium into the area around Brussels. The troops remained in Belgium principally to maintain the peace whilst the fate of the Austrian Netherlands (i.e. Belgium) was decided at the Congress of Vienna. The Congress arbitrated in all such matters in an attempt to sort out the inevitable chaos resultant from twenty-two years of pan-European conflict.

The fledgling army of the Netherlands, along with the British forces remaining in Belgium, were commanded by the Prince of Orange, but the British government as always fretted over British troops abroad not being commanded by a British officer. In August 1814, Sir Henry Clinton was summoned to become second-in-command to the Prince of Orange, a post he accepted with some trepidation.

The British government envisaged Clinton's role as controlling the wild excesses of the Prince. The young royal, however, did not relish a 'minder' and he failed to discuss many of his plans with Clinton, simply using him as an 'Inspecting Officer' to drive up the standards and to attend to the training of his troops, many of whom lacked even the most basic military equipment and capabilities.

Henry Clinton was ordered to proceed to Belgium in August 1814, but his job began inauspiciously, as Clinton sailed for Belgium with no clear understanding of his actual role as second-in-command to the Prince of Orange. The confusion within the British government and the misunderstandings between them and the military establishment did not augur well. Indeed in a note Henry Clinton wrote in his diary dated 25 August 1814:

> On the 11th of July I was appointed to the Staff of Great Britain for the purpose of inspecting the infantry. On the 26th I received a summons to attend the Duke of York on the following day. His Royal Highness told me that it was the wish of government that I should be second in command of the army in Brabant in Holland in the chief command of which the Hereditary Prince of Orange was shortly to succeed Lord Lynedoch[1] ... The Duke of York as a motive for the choice of me was very flattering to me, that considering the youth of

> the Hereditary Prince it was wished that [I] should be upon the Staff in case any conduct of the army should require the adoption of coquettish measures & then desired me to call upon Lord Bathurst that day at 5 o'clock. Lord Bathurst merely said that he was glad I had accepted the service which had been proposed to me, told me that their motive in sending me was that I might assist in the disciplining of the army under the Prince of Orange & professed a desire that I might be ready to set off in a week, & I said I supposed I should receive particular instructions. To this Lord Bathurst assented. On 2nd August my appointment was officially ratified to me from the Adjutant General's office and soon after the expiration of ten days I sent to Lord Bathurst's office to report myself ready to proceed expecting always to be sent for or to receive particular instructions. I sent my horses on and applied for a passage for myself to Ostend, in the meantime I received an order through the Adjutant General to proceed to Brabant & to report to myself to the Hereditary Prince of Orange, I then wrote to Lord Bathurst saying I was only waiting his orders, on the 19th I received a note from [him] in answer to my letter, saying he had nothing at present to communicate to me. I mentioned to Major General Bunbury[2] on the following day how embarrassing to me to have had it stated that I was to be 2nd in command of the whole allied army and to assist in the discipline of it & yet to receive no particular instructions for my conduct, I said I did not wish to create difficulties, but that the post of 2nd in command [was] either a sinecure, or one of great importance. At the wish of the Adjutant General Bunbury said he assumed I was to command the British, but this the Duke of York had stated was not the intention of government. I then told him that I should lose no time in proceeding to the army, that I would endeavour to find out what was expected of me & having been taken from so important a post as that of the Inspector of Infantry, it ought to be for some object not less important & that I should use my best endeavours not to disappoint the government but that at present I know not at all what was the duty required of me.

Despite all the rush and confusion, Henry Clinton dutifully left London on 22 August to proceed to Ramsgate, where the transport ship *Hess* was waiting for him. Despite rough weather he was able to land at Ostend four days later by local skiff, whilst the transport did not dare attempt to enter the port to land his horses and carriage until two days later. Even then, the ship missed the entrance and beached but was able to discharge its valuable cargo at low tide when it was left high and dry by the falling tide. Clinton proceeded to Brussels in great haste and arrived there on 30 August. Here he was confronted by Sir John Colborne of the 52nd Foot, who was at that time acting as military secretary to the Prince of Orange and who simply informed him: 'that I had merely been notified as being upon the Staff of the Army & I found that the prince had not prepared any occupation for me.'[3]

Two days later in an interview with the Prince of Orange, Clinton was actually asked to recommend to the Prince what he should do with him. Clinton was quick to suggest how best he might be employed:

> I called upon the Hereditary Prince to ascertain what he expected of me in my capacity of 2nd in command, he with modesty representing his own inexperience desired to have my advice. I suggested that as General Alten[4] was appointed to command the Hanoverian, I might have the same appointment with the British, but the prince observed that this could be giving the only command he had & notwithstanding my representing that as commander of the army, such an appointment was giving away nothing, he remained fixed in his resolution & when I asked him how he preferred that I should be announced to the army in orders, he replied as 2nd in command. With regard to my duties he wished me to make very frequent inspections, and to attempt to establish discipline in the army & prevent those complaints of the inhabitants which were very frequent at present. I observed that there would be an awkwardness in my inspecting the Hanoverians, as General Alten had been appointed to command them, HRH however desired me to proceed upon the inspection of the troops & when I asked him if he would approve of my giving orders in remedying anything which might require it, he said that he wished in that case I would first report & recommend any measure to him & that he would give the orders, which would obviate any inconvenience in regard to General Alten. With respect to the British troops I observed that there appeared to me to be a great degree of relaxation in their discipline, to correct which in my opinion, it was necessary to improve the system of instruction. As regards to the duty of the officers, that considering the circumstances of his succeeding to the command of the army, it might be for him a very difficult task to draw together the aims of discipline; that I had always met [head on] the unpopularity attendant upon the practise of requiring officers to do their duty & that by giving directions for details upon this head I might relieve him from an inconvenient weight & that in conversation with the generals I might represent certain practises as having his approbation; to this he acceded.
>
> I do not see my course distinctly, or feel sanguine as to the success of what I propose to undertake.[5]

It is evident that this plan was made ad hoc and that neither felt fully at ease with the arrangement or was clear as to the specific individual responsibilities of Clinton. This would almost certainly – and in hindsight, definitely did – cause confusion and conflict. It was not a good start.

However, Henry Clinton turned his hand immediately with vigour to a rigorous programme of inspections of the various infantry regiments of all the different nationalities. This would allow him to see for himself the state of the various national contingents, the state of their equipment, their discipline and their ability to perform the intricate manoeuvres required in the field by formed troops, both at regimental and brigade levels. From these reports, a coordinated plan of improvement could be prepared and implemented.

Europe may well have been at peace for the first time in over twenty years, but Henry Clinton was not a man to shirk his responsibilities. His keen eye for detail and his uncompromising demands were certainly irksome to the officers and men of these battalions and he was disliked intensely for it. Nevertheless, his demanding standards undoubtedly improved the training and discipline of the troops, and their poor equipment gradually improved because of his unceasing tirades sent to those responsible for the supply of faulty, shoddy or poorly designed equipment. He may not have been a pleasant man to work with, but he did much to improve the weak units of all nationalities he found in Belgium. His pivotal role in preparing these largely inexperienced troops for war is certainly undervalued. He significantly improved their performance during the then unforeseen campaign they were to be so suddenly engaged upon ten months later.

But what forces did he encounter in Belgium in September 1814?

Troop Quality, Winter 1814-15

As to the British contingent in the Netherlands in the autumn of 1814, Henry Clinton found a very depleted force of some fourteen thousand troops, consisting of twenty battalions of infantry. These battalions, apart from three battalions of the Guards, which numbered in excess of six hundred men each, were generally weak in numbers, being second battalions or small single battalion regiments numbering on average no more than four hundred men each. There was also a small contingent of artillery and seven relatively strong regiments of King's German Legion and Hanoverian cavalry numbering over five hundred men and horses each. Of this total force it would seem that at any one time on average 15% or more were not fit for duty owing to sickness. This force was, however, slightly augmented in the September with the arrival of six battalions of the King's German Legion infantry from the south of France and the Mediterranean averaging over six hundred men each, whilst some British units left to return home.

Alongside these units, the Hanoverian 'Subsidiary Force' had recently arrived in Belgium, consisting of eight field (regular) battalions and fifteen landwehr (militia) battalions of about six hundred men each, totalling some fourteen thousand troops.

The future of Belgium, which had always been beholden either to the Spanish or Austrians, was far from clear, although some promises had been made in private to the Prince of Orange. The small Dutch army was reformed from the remnants of the experienced troops who had previously served under Napoleon, combined with volunteer units which had gained some limited experience during their late war of independence, but these were also liberally mixed with newly appointed volunteers. These were to be formed into twenty-two battalions of infantry, four regiments of cavalry and a few artillery units, amounting to some twenty-five thousand Dutch troops in all. But, as volunteers for army service were not as readily forthcoming as anticipated, two regiments of infantry from the German state of Nassau were added, German volunteers seemingly being much less scarce.

Meanwhile, no decisions on the army of Belgium could be finalised until the crowned heads of Europe decided on the country's future at the Congress of Vienna. Notwithstanding, the Hereditary Prince of Orange took measures to secure the country when the Austrian forces handed over responsibility to him and left. A number of Dutch units were put in garrison in Belgian towns and some attempts were made to form a Belgian army but with limited initial success.

There were therefore a total of some thirty-five thousand troops assigned to the Belgian provinces to maintain their defence – the majority of the Dutch army remaining in Holland – when Henry Clinton began his work.

In his very first day in the job he was to encounter a recurring problem: a lethal concoction of lethargy, war-weariness and plain slovenliness. This was always going to be a serious issue, as he recorded:

> I went to the parade of the Guards, on which was no officer above the rank of the adjutant; [who] also after waiting some time, at my inspection let the Guard march off without troop or any of the usual ceremonies. From neglecting these troops, officers and soldiers easily accustom themselves equally to neglect of the most important duties & there springs indiscipline, insubordination & all their attendant mischief.[6]

Very few of the British troops whom Clinton was to command later as part of the 2nd Division, apart from a few of the 52nd and 95th regiments, were actually in Belgium at this time. However, the King's German Legion troops and Hanoverian battalions were almost all already there and Henry was soon inspecting them. His records from this early period are enlightening as to the quality and quantity of these troops and their equipment.

The British Contingent

Henry Clinton began his tour of inspection at Tournai on 14 September, where he inspected the 2nd Battalion 52nd Foot consisting of 1 General Officer, 4 Captains, 18 Subalterns, 21 Sergeants, 12 Drummers and 213 Rank and File. As expected, he was very impressed with this veteran, although under strength, light infantry battalion:

> Lt Colonel Gibbs[7] the brother of the general, is the commander; this regiment has continued from the excellent system introduced by Sir John Moore, to enjoy a superiority above most regiments of our service, though composed of very young men mostly indeed recruits, it performed several movements in double quick time with great correctness, the pouches are of the proper kind, the arms, ammunition & accomplishments in good order, the packs well packed, the officers intelligent, in short the whole state showing a great deal of attention on the part of the officers to a very judicious system.[8]

On Saturday 17 September at Courtrai he inspected a detachment of the 3rd Battalion 95th Foot and recorded that this, along with a detachment at Mons, consisted of 2 Captains, 5 Subalterns, 3 Sergeants, 3 Buglers and 126 Rank and File, noting that they were: 'in excellent order, [but] none of these corps have their blankets.'[9] At this point the few British troops of the future division, although weak in numbers, were in fine shape.

The King's German Legion Contingent

The troops of the King's German Legion were generally held in high regard after their commendable performance in the Peninsular War. But there had been some difficulties in obtaining German recruits during the war and many other nationalities were at times incorporated into these battalions, with mixed results. Morale was also quite poor within the legion, as the end of the war was likely to lead to their disbanding in the near future. This left many fearful for their future, restless and disgruntled. This, unsurprisingly, affected discipline, and insubordination flourished. Henry Clinton noted the ill-feeling and varying quality of the battalions in his inspection reports.

He began by inspecting a troop of Horse Artillery of the King's German Legion[10] which he found in a good condition, noting only: 'In general nice limbering horses, men & horses in a good state.'

At Roeselare on 14 September, Clinton inspected the only four companies of the 2nd Battalion KGL which had yet arrived in Belgium. It consisted of 1 Field Officer, 3 Captains, 6 Subalterns, 3 Sergeants, 5 Drummers and 227 Rank and File. But he found that Lieutenant Colonel Beck,[11] who commanded this battalion, had declared himself unable to attend due to an unspecified wound,[12] and Major Breymann[13] actually commanded. For an experienced unit Henry Clinton was far from impressed:

> This detachment was very loosely put together, many of those present in the shape of servants &c did not appear & no officer could account for their men or answer the questions arising respecting their companies. The arms & accoutrements were not marked & though the arms were not in bad order they were not properly cleaned. These battalions consist of ten companies one of which is with the depot. These battalions had neither camp equipment. In ammunition these battalions have a regular company of light infantry armed with rifles. These men seem to be in also no one's orders, but to be instinctively to themselves & they require to be placed in the hands of some good drill.

Proceeding to Thielt on 24 September, here he inspected the 1st Line Battalion KGL consisting of 2 Field Officers, 5 Captains, 21 Subalterns, 37 Sergeants, 12 Drummers and 554 Rank and File, finding this battalion to be in much better shape, but short of weapons, recording that:

> This battalion is commanded by Lt. Colonel Bodecker[14] a steady old officer. It is composed of very serviceable men, many of whom have served several campaigns. The faults I observed were a looseness of the files and the knapsacks being ill packed & ill carried. The arms are not generally marked & they want practise in their movements. They want 58 stand of arms.

On the same day he also inspected the 3rd Line Battalion KGL at Deinze which consisted of 1 Field Officer, 5 Captains, 21 Subalterns, 31 Sergeants, 18 Drummers and 516 Rank and File. Henry found this battalion showing the same faults as the 1st Battalion, but in a much greater degree.[15] Their poor movements and equipment betrayed their years of garrisoning the Mediterranean islands:

> This battalion commanded by Lt. Colonel Wissell[16] is also a very serviceable body of men steady under arms and clean ... this battalion made some very awkward attempts to execute some of the most simple movements which I desired them to perform. The ammunition was taken from these troops upon their landing in England & none has since

> been furnished to them. They were supplied with canteens & haversacks, many of the former though now are not in a state for use.

Henry Clinton's concern regarding the poor shape of the KGL battalions caused him to pen a letter to the Quartermaster General (QMG), one Major General Sir Hudson Lowe, soon to become infamous as the gaoler of Napoleon on St Helena, requesting that they could be cantoned together to aid the necessary retraining:

> My dear General,
>
> In the present state of the several corps which compose this army, it is extremely desirable that they should as much as possible be under the immediate superintendence of their generals. Great advantage is to be derived by putting together a large body of troops under the eye of such an officer as Major General Mackenzie. The several battalions of the line of the German Legion are much in want of being brought together that order and system may be restored. ... If Tournai were vacated by General Gibb's Brigade, it would be a very good station for the 4 Line Battalions of the German Legion under General Hinuber[17] ... This young army would then be well placed for going on with its exercises.[18]

A week later, he inspected the 4th Line Battalion KGL[19] at Alost. It was composed of 2 Field Officers, 4 Captains, 26 Subalterns, 36 Sergeants, 10 Drummers and 516 Rank and File. Henry reported pretty positively that:

> Colonel du Plat[20] is the commander of this battalion, the arms and appointments are in good order with the exception of the pouches which are much worn, this battalion may well be brought forward as a proof of the good state in which a corps may be preserved by the establishing & maintaining a good system. In its exercise I observed the common fault, of the poor dressing of the point man previously to the companies wheeling into line, and an irregularity of pace in the double quick time.

The KGL battalions were clearly a mixed bag at that time, weak in numbers, poorly equipped and requiring a great deal of training to bring them back up to scratch.

The Hanoverian Contingent

Henry Clinton had much more to say regarding the newly raised Hanoverian troops, but although they undoubtedly required much training, he was generally very pleasantly surprised by the excellent quality of the recruits and their keenness to learn and desire to improve.

On 16 September at Oudenarde he reviewed the Osnabrück Militia.[21] It consisted of 1 Field Officer, 3 Captains, 15 Subalterns, 20 Sergeants, 8 Drummers, 16 Musicians and 510 Rank and File. His initial report on this battalion, although the men were clearly inexperienced, was extremely complimentary as to the zeal of both officers and men:[22]

> This is one of those corps which continues embodied contrary to the terms under which they have been raised. The commanding officer Major Count Munster has no experience as an officer and the battalion though composed of as fine a body of men as any I have seen except for any military purpose, there is every disposition in the officers & men to discharge their duty as is apparent by the manner in which they do what they understand and know to be their duty viz, the keeping in order all that is entrusted to their care. In no regiment of the British is the ammunition in the order in which it is in these newly raised & militia battalions. Their companies too are more complete, every man is distinctly & satisfactorily accounted for. It seems that the Hanoverian regulations for command differ materially from those of the English army and in some, where uniformity seems absolutely necessary to good order.

He was, however, less complimentary of Colonel Halkett[23] who commanded the brigade of which this regiment formed a part, recording that he was 'not at all qualified to render the service of which this battalion stands in need'.[24]

On the following day, Saturday 17 September, Henry Clinton was very busy and recorded, amongst a number of inspections, that he had inspected the Bremervorde Battalion of Hanoverian militia. He recorded it as consisting of 1 Field Officer, 4 Captains, 12 Subalterns, 16 Sergeants, 8 Drummers and 474 Rank and File, commanded by Lieutenant Colonel Schulenburg.[25] He was again complimentary about the raw material of the battalion:

> this battalion is very much of the same character with that at Oudenarde, the officers and men wanting every species of instruction to fit them for the field, but this regiment has an advantage over the others in the experience of the Lt. Colonel.[26]

In a further report he made on 29 September regarding the Quakenbrück Battalion of Landwehr,[27] he recorded that it consisted of 1 Field Officer, 4 Captains, 15 Subalterns, 18 Sergeants, 7 Drummers and 471 Rank and File. He found that they were a solid body of young men: 'This is though young a good & healthy new body of men commanded by Major Bulow,[28] their musquets are brown and arms & packs in good order'.[29] Henry also noted that this completed his first inspection of the Hanoverian battalions present at that time in Belgium, noting in general that:

> they contain materials for forming a fine army but they have everything to learn, the circumstance of their having a system of exercise different from that of the British army is attended with great inconvenience & will prevent the two armies from moving in the field with that precision which is desirable in all cases & in some circumstances to avoid confusion.

Following up this round of inspections Henry Clinton wrote a report regarding the Hanoverian troops on 30 September, itemising their needs both in training and equipment:

> Remarks upon the Hanoverian Levies
>
> Position of soldiers
> The men seldom stand square to the front & if their shoulders are so, the head is generally turned, this occasions great unsteadiness & is easily corrected.
>
> Looseness of the files
> Another cause of unsteadiness is in the intervals between the files, these must always touch lightly by the elbow, without for that purpose projecting the arm at all from the side. No movement in line, or by wheeling, can ever be correctly performed, without the files are properly closed.
>
> Closing of the intervals in line
> In order to close an interval, the soldiers are accustomed to face & march in file, this invariably occasions a loss of the alignment, & generally increases the evil it is intended to remedy. If troops should be required to march for any distance upon an alignment, it should be done by being thrown into column by wheeling backwards, but ordinary intervals arising from a loss of distance, are to be re-ordered by the side step, for which the officer commanding the division is to give the time, placing himself in front of & facing that flank of his division nearest the interval to be closed.
>
> Arms
> There are a great number of arms, the locks of which are not close to the barrel, in use powder would get between & soon damage the

stock. The arms should be marked without loss of time with the name of the regiment; the number of the company & of the soldier.

Accoutrements

Several of the pouches have suffered from neglect & not being properly cleaned & kept in order, many are furnished with a middle tin, which from the difficulty of moving it, is soon broken, & as they are of no use they had better be taken out altogether, the tin at the bottom will suffice to keep the pouch in shape.

Ammunition

In most of the battalions good care appears to be taken of the ammunition, this must be uniform & general, while limited to 20 rounds as at present, they should be kept in two packets of ten each & wrapped in fresh covers as often as this may be necessary to prevent the cartridges from being damaged. Nothing besides the ammunition is to be kept or carried in the pouch, the flints must be stowed in the pockets. In some of the battalions there are a number of small pouches incapable of containing about 20 rounds of ammunition, immediate application must be made for replacing these by such as are in general use.

Packs & Necessaries

The packs ought not to be larger than necessary to carry those articles which the soldier is required to have in his possession by the regulations of the army, the soldiers must be taught to pack them in the most convenient manner & it must be insisted that he has these in his pack whenever ordered to parade in marching order. In order to reduce what he has to carry to the most compact shape, the greatcoat is to be carried in the fold of the pack, unless that place should be occupied by a blanket in which case only, the greatcoat is to be rolled & strapped upon the pack.

No frames, in order to keep the pack in shape are allowed, those battalions which may have them must get rid of them.

The Hanoverian troops are not yet in a state to move in battalion correctly, any practise of this sort at present, would be only lost time. The first step towards their improvement ought to be the perfecting of the officers in the knowledge and practise of their several duties, beginning with that of the care of the soldiers entrusted to their charge. This includes the cleanliness and comforts of the soldiers, the preservation in good order of their arms, ammunition, accoutrements, clothing and necessaries, in short of everything which constitutes the efficiency of a soldier for service.

The next duty of an officer is the instruction of the soldiers in every branch of their duty for the performance of this, he must be perfected

> in all that a soldier is required to know from his position without arms, the facing, marching, wheeling, filing, oblique marching, the several platoon exercises to the most important of all, namely the duties of a sentry.
>
> When well acquainted with all these & the principles upon which they are to be performed, the officers must be accustomed (without the troops) to the exercise of marching, at certain given distances, and entering and marching upon alignments, to the changing of front in quick and double quick time, and they must be perfectly acquainted with all that soldiers can be required to perform in the field.
>
> When the officers shall have so qualified themselves, they may usefully and confidently commence the instruction of the soldiers in detail.
>
> It is not necessary that officers should perfect themselves in the whole of these requirements previously to their commencing the instruction of the soldiers. But before they proceed to teach the soldiers any one branch of their duty it is indispensable that the commanding officer is satisfied of their being duly qualified.
>
> It is very desirable that the troops should be able to perform, in the pace called double quick time (viz 150 paces of 36 inches in one minute) certain movements, but this must not be attempted until the soldiers, as well as the officers, have acquired the habit of moving at this rate with precision, to this end they must be practised to move to the front, and wheel, singly & in small squads upon ground on which the length of the pace is marked, while the time must be regulated by a plummet.
>
> In moving in double quick time the arms must not be allowed to swing, but the same care must be paid to the closeness of the files as when marching in ordinary time. When acting in battalion at the word 'double quick march' the arms are to be sloped.

Soon after, he was able to inspect the Salzgitter Battalion which had just marched into Lier on its way from Hanover to Brussels.[30] He was very impressed by the appearance of this battalion, given the distance it had marched:

> It is composed of very young men like most of the militia regiments but the battalion marched in good order, the only remarkable failure was in the packs having been left, & the commanding officer explained that as the march was a long one, he allowed the soldiers to put their knapsacks upon carts, they having paid for it, but the roads being a heavy mud and they had not been able to keep up with the troops. He added that it was the first instance in which he had allowed this indulgence.

He backed up these comments by writing to Colonel Colborne, regarding the results of his inspections:

> I have completed the inspection of the troops stationed upon the frontier & as far as this place & from the state in which I have found them, I have recommended that some change in their distribution should be made, in order that they may be more within the reach & under the eye of those whose duty it is to attend to their improvement & who are qualified for that duty from the want of some arrangement. General McHenry is an officer eminently qualified for forming troops, is stationed with only two companies of his division under his orders, he conceived that he had no authority to interfere with the proceedings of one of the young Hanoverian battalions quartered in the town with himself. I hope the Prince of Orange will approve of the suggestions which I have requested Sir Hudson Lowe to submit to him. A great deal remains to be done to bring all these troops into the order in which it is fit they should be, but the time & circumstances are very favourable. The Hanoverian levies are excellent materials, the men are of the best description & officers & all seem well disposed to receive instruction.
>
> It is very desirable however that Alten should without loss of time begin to direct the course which they are to pursue.[31]

Clinton also wrote to Horse Guards, the headquarters of the British Army, regarding the state of the troops in Belgium and advised them that he was generally pleased, although there was much to be done to bring them all up to standard. He did note with some concern, however, that the Hanoverian troops were being drilled with a significantly different drill book than the one used by the British army which, of course, had the potential to cause problems when the two forces were operating in the field together:

> My dear Torrens,[32]
>
> I am just retired to this place after making the inspection of the army under the command of the Hereditary Prince. Much is wanting to place the several corps of which it is composed in order. The defects are very different in different corps …
>
> The German Legion is in a pretty good state, the 1st Battalion of the line remarkably so, but the expectation of being disbanded has had an evident influence, which the example and authority of a good commander will counteract.
>
> The young Hanoverian levies are composed of the very best materials to form both soldiers and officers, but these are quite in their infancy. The first necessity here is to provide the means of instruction,

and in the first instance, these can be furnished to each of the brigades, it will be all that can be expected. The drilling of this army might have been expedited by placing the several corps in garrison with the British & German Legion; but they have a different system, which require that they should have their own instructors. This will necessarily occasion some delay, but the opportunity for forming troops is favourable, and I think in the course of the winter, this will become an efficient army ...

He also wrote to Major General Barnes, the Adjutant General, confirming that the Prince of Orange had acquiesced in his requests for the troops to be regularly sent out on long marches. They were to practise manoeuvres regularly, both at regimental and brigade level, to improve their movements:

Brussels, 7th August [October?][33]

My dear General,

In conversation with the Hereditary Prince of Orange yesterday, his Royal Highness expressed his approbation of the troops being required to make occasional marches.

In order to render this exercise useful in accustoming the troops to march with regularity, it will be necessary either in orders or by circular letters to the generals commanding divisions, to observe that although the troops are to be allowed to march at ease, viz, the officers may return their swords and the soldiers may trail or sling or carry their arms in any manner which they find convenient, the officers are never the less to remain with their divisions and one man on the pivot flank of each section or subdivision, according to the front of the column, must invariably preserve the wheeling distance, so that at the word, 'Attention', every man may spring into his place, and the column be ready to wheel into a connected line. That the soldiers upon the pivots of the front ranks are to march with attention, their arms shouldered, and to be relieved as often as shall be found convenient. It may also be proper to remind them that advanced & rear guards are always to be formed according to the strength of the corps, and that the troops are always to be in marching order. I think the distance should be from 6 to 10 miles and that these marches should not be made less frequently than once in each fortnight, either by regiment, brigade or otherwise as the commander of the brigade shall think fit. Besides this I think the troops should parade and mount guard in marching order one day in each week. H. Clinton.

Clinton also wrote home to demand better equipment for the troops, as regards to both their camp kettles for cooking – as the troops in Belgium had been allocated the heavy iron cooking pots which had long been discontinued in the Peninsula – and canteens or horns for use as their water bottle:

> My dear Gordon,
>
> If I am not mistaken it was regulated a few years ago, that the camp kettles to be used by our troops should be those of a small size, calculated to serve for 5 or 6 men and to be carried by the soldiers ...
>
> I find however that this army was furnished with the heavy kettles; in case therefore of our having to take the field an additional expense would become necessary; to provide for their permanent transport; and after all the troops would much oftener [sic] have to wait for, and sometimes go without their dinner.
>
> But as the light kettles constitute a part of our regulated equipment; I suppose if the overseer of baggage was to apply for them, they could be provided. Is this so?
>
> There is another part of our equipment which wants amendment and that is the canteen, that in use requires a degree of care and attention to prevent it's becoming useless, which it is not easy to obtain from soldiers, it is too bulky, of an inconvenient shape, and more capacious than is necessary. The horn which was in use so generally in Portugal and Spain, seems to obviate all these objections, if it does not contain so much as the canteen (it is for the most ordinary use made of them by the soldiers) to be preferred upon that account ...[34]

But, two months later, the replacement canteens had still not been issued to the troops and Clinton was required to write again:

> My dear Gordon,
>
> It is near a month since I received notice of the arrival of the canteens in this country, but they have not yet found their way to Brussels; however as it is no less the shape and bulk than the perishable nature of the canteens now in use; which it is desirable to improve, I send you a pattern of an horn such as a great proportion of our soldiers used during the service in Spain and Portugal. The only objection to which they are liable, is that they are not so capacious as the ordinary canteens, and this is an inconvenience which would only be felt when they might be required for carrying water, and for this purpose the camp kettles are more fit; they contain more than for the purpose of drinking, soldiers can have in their canteens, and they are lighter, of a far more convenient form, and is much more durable, that when once furnished to a soldier, he may

reasonably be required to preserve it without occasioning any further expense to the public, excepting in cases of accident.

I spoke to the Hereditary Prince concerning the camp kettles and as His Royal Highness also approves of the smaller kettle i.e. that of tin, calculated to serve for 5 or 6 men and to be carried by the soldiers, I hope an application will be made through the proper channels[35]

Throughout the autumn the troops were drilled regularly and Henry Clinton clearly saw continued steady improvement in the KGL units, but that a few officers were failing to improve with the rest. He also saw vast improvements in the Hanoverian battalions and, remarkably, he predicted that they would equal the KGL troops within three more months.

I enclose herewith some further remarks upon your brigade, I think it is in progress of improvement, but there is still much to be done, one or two awkward, ignorant or inattentive officers, both to the appearance of a regiment and [it can?] prevent the correct execution of a manoeuvre, this sometimes falls hard upon the rest, but not upon the commanding officer who is responsible for the efficiency of every part of his battalion and that all his officers are competent to the discharge of every part of their duty, and moreover that they do perform it with correctness. The Hanoverians have made great progress in their knowledge of moving, they will run your brigade hard in this respect in three months' time.[36]

With nothing to indicate a radical change of circumstances, only a few inspections were carried out during the harsh winter months. The only significant inspection during this period was that of the 2nd Battalion of the 52nd Foot in the January.

It is clear that Henry expected very high standards from such a renowned regiment and his criticisms were perhaps therefore more severe than they might have been of others. However the report did show that this second battalion had worsened since his previous inspection. It was still very weak in numbers, but was now poorly led and had become slovenly in appearance.

He records that the battalion now only numbered 1 Field Officer, 3 Captains, 10 Subalterns, 16 Sergeants, 12 Drummers along with 212 Rank and File:

This battalion has gained nothing since I saw it in the autumn, the pouches which are good, being for the most part supplied with the wooden boxes and the ammunition kept in the bottom of the pouch, there is some difficulty in getting at it; this would be extremely objectionable in the course of services, it is to be hoped that no

> prejudice, ignorances or apathy will prevent a better contrivance for carrying ammunition, being adopted. I was disappointed to see even these caps disfigured as in other ill commanded regiments. Colonel Gibbs is more indebted to the system established before he commanded the regiment than any exertion of his moderate abilities.[37]

Two days later he added in his diary:

> Although from the superior system established in the 52nd Regiment; and the general excellent composition of its officers, it has a great advantage over most corps. I had not the same reason to make this remark as I have had on former occasions. In such a corps no fault, no instance of the slightest inattention should be observable upon the most minute examination, the commanding officer himself appeared to require some little practise in moving the battalion.[38]

Henry also recorded in his diary that the KGL units were suffering a worryingly high level of desertion, or at least failure to return from their furloughs. As Clinton explained, the imminent disbanding of the legion and the fears that men whose time was not fully served would be transferred to units garrisoning the East Indies – a virtual death sentence for most – caused some of them to take matters into their own hands:

> The Hanoverians continue to desert or rather the German Legion, but the deserters are principally from amongst those whose period of service is not yet expired & who apprehend at the disbanding of the Legion that they will be drafted with other of our foreign corps & sent perhaps to the East Indies, but of 217 men which all as deserters from the infantry of the Legion between the 25th of November & the 25th of December General Hinuber [states] that 150 are men who having been allowed to go on furlough have not returned. It shows a want of management not to secure to the service of Hanover or Holland, this well-formed well taught body.[39]

With the first shoots of spring, Henry Clinton embarked on a second comprehensive round of inspections, which allowed him to fully gauge the improvements made by the various corps since the autumn. It is patently clear that some had done much better than others. He began his inspection tour on 7 March blissfully unaware that dramatic news would soon arrive.

The first battalion Clinton inspected was the 3rd Line Battalion King's German Legion which had performed poorly in the autumn. It now consisted of 3 Field Officers, 10 Captains, 24 Subalterns, 46 Sergeants, 11 Drummers and fewer men at 526 Rank and File:

> Although sixty or seventy men of this battalion have lately been discharged, it continues to be a very good body, this is one of the corps which belonged to the army of Sicily when Lord William Bentinck ordered the arms to be coloured & the good effect is visible, it is singular that any prejudice should prevent the adoption of this measure in the army. This battalion is in very serviceable order, though the commander Lt. Colonel Wissell does not appear to be very well qualified for the command, the officers wear caps which differ from the pattern ordered to be used by the army and so far set a bad example to the soldiers.[40]

But suddenly things changed completely and the world was turned upside down.

Chapter 3

Napoleon Returns

Napoleon Bonaparte, Emperor of the French, who had been defeated by the allies in 1814 and banished to the Isle of Elba, had landed on the coast of France at Golfe St Juan near Antibes on 1 March and had announced that he was marching with his band of one thousand men to reclaim the throne of France. Initially regarded as a madman and sure to fail, Napoleon had chosen his moment with skill, and the French royalist forces sent to block his path simply defected or melted away. Napoleon entered Paris on 20 March, King Louis XVIII fleeing to Belgium for a second stint of exile.

The news of Napoleon's relentless and seemingly unstoppable march on Paris caused panic in the Low Countries, traditionally the first victims of French aggression. On 17 March, the Prince of Orange released orders for all of the allied forces in the Netherlands to go onto a war footing:

> Head Quarters Brussels 17th March
> The army will immediately prepare to take the field.
>
> The heavy baggage of the British regiments and King's German Legion will be sent in depot forthwith to Ostend and that of the Hanoverian Corps to Antwerp, all sick unable to march in at the same time to be sent to these places.

Such an immediate response was designed to ensure that Napoleon, if successful in re-taking France, did not launch a pre-emptive strike before the fledgling Netherlands army and its allies were in a position to offer any defence. This was particularly essential until the border fortresses were made secure, garrisoned and re-armed with cannon.

Henry Clinton reported to Horse Guards on the state of the army and the immediate preparations for the defence of the country:

> My dear Torrens,
>
> ... the ... infantry of which this army is composed, consist more

> than one half of the Hanoverian levies and although these are excellent materials for forming an army, weak as they are in officers of any experience they certainly are not in a state to take the field as a separate corps. The most advantageous manner of putting this infantry together appears to be, by forming the divisions, of a brigade of British, one of the Legion and one of the Hanoverians, but as so large a proportion of the British are now necessarily employed in Antwerp and Ostend, the divisions will consist of a considerable majority of Hanoverians. In the present state of the Hanoverians, they would not, without injury to the consistency of the army, bear to form more than one third, the divisions ought therefore to consist of 2 brigades of British, and one of Hanoverians, at least for the present such a disposition seems indispensable. In the meantime it must be recollected that several of the battalions composing the army in this country have hardly sufficient numbers to take the field, most of them are below 400, so that after deducting the ordinary non effectives in the field they become mere skeletons.

He also wrote to Henry Calvert regarding the defence of the frontier towns and noted that the remainder of the allied army would assemble in the vicinity of Ath:

> The latest accounts from Paris have served to add to our anxiety without increasing the general alarm. The measures which have been taken here have been to reinforce the frontier towns whose works are to be repaired and to put the remainder of the army into convenient quarters for its assembly in the neighbourhood of Ath, if there is to be war we are in want of most of the materials for composing an army not excluding the article of soldiers. Some of our 2nd battalions are in tolerable order and in a state soon to become efficient if their ranks were only filled. The ... 52nd is a mere skeleton.[1]

But, soon it became clear that Bonaparte had achieved the seemingly impossible and captured Paris. Clinton remained convinced that Belgium was ill prepared to withstand an immediate attack:

> This morning the Prince of Orange received certain intelligence of Bonaparte having entered Paris on the 16th a few hours after the king had quitted the Tuilleries having taken the road to Rambouillet. This is one of the most extraordinary revolutions that the world ever witnessed. If Bonaparte feels sufficiently at his ease to leave Paris, it is not at all improbable that he will continue his rapid move & that he will find Belgium in so defenceless a state that he will have little difficulty in overrunning it.[2]

He was also highly critical of the Prince of Orange's orders to place some of the army directly on the line of the frontier where they would be very vulnerable to attack before they could retire onto their reserves:

> I learned from General Kielmansegge that the Prince of Orange ... had ordered him to advance his division & place it in villages close to the frontier, as this is objectionable as exposing the division to be beat in detail before it could fall back on supports & is also opening an offensive position & might hasten the beginning of hostilities, I determined to put some remarks upon the present composition & to send them for his perusal.[3]

In the report which he sent to Sir John Colborne for the perusal of the prince, Clinton made it clear why he believed having troops stationed too close to the front was a serious error:

> The line of the frontier cannot be defended, it ought therefore merely to be watched by a very light line of cavalry posts. The main body of the army so placed that in one march, it might be assembled near Ath but not nearer the frontier.
>
> ... It is certainly not the interest of Holland to provoke aggression, or to hasten the commencement of hostilities, which the assuming an offensive rather than a defensive attitude might do.[4]

The morale of the army improved dramatically, however, with the intelligence that the Duke of Wellington, who had been attending the Congress of Vienna, was to be sent to Belgium to take command of the army. Henry Clinton, who had worked closely with him throughout the Peninsular War, was delighted with the news:

> I found here to my satisfaction Sir C. Stuart[5] the English ambassador at the Hague & no less so that the Duke of Wellington was hourly expected from Vienna, his presence is greatly wanted to introduce system into the management of the movements of this little army. From the total want of some such management, the 52nd Regiment upon its arrival at Ostend ... was ordered at Ostend, to march to Nieuport.[6]

The news that the battle-hardened 1st Battalion of the 52nd Foot had arrived at Ostend was a significant reinforcement for the British army in Belgium. The battalion was ordered to march to join its 2nd Battalion in Adam's Light Brigade.

At the end of March, Henry Clinton received official notification that General Sir Rowland Hill, affectionately known to the soldiers by the sobriquet of 'Daddy Hill' due to his care of their welfare, was ordered out to join the army. Henry Clinton was, however, particularly happy that Hill, who was his senior, was on his way out. He also expressed his unbridled joy at hearing that the Duke was expected at Brussels in a few days to take command of the army:

> ... I hasten to beg you will express my gratitude to the Duke of York for this recollection of me upon the occasion of appointing Lord Hill to the Staff of this army ... There must of course be many senior officers appointed to this army, under whom I shall always serve with satisfaction. I am just returning to the army which with the exception of the troops destined to garrison the frontier places is concentrated about Ath. I hear & rejoice to hear that the Duke of Wellington is expected here on the 2nd, I wish he could find such an army as he left in the south of France.[7]

Following an inspection of the repairs to the defences of Mons, Henry Clinton found the works were not progressing well. He noted that the garrison consisted of the weak battalions of the 3rd, 4th and 8th King's German Legion and that:

> This day, the 52nd & 95th Regiments composing General Adam's Brigade marched from Tournai to Leuze, he had formed them in the streets in Tournai where having arrived very unexpectedly from Courtrai they had not got under cover, fortunately the weather is fine & warm[8]

Orders were issued by the QMG's office on 3 April for a further concentration of the army between Ath, Lens and Enghien. As Sir Hudson Lowe explained:

> Except one brigade of the German Legion at Tournai & one at Mons, with a battalion of the 95th at Leuze, the whole of the infantry which have been stationed in that vicinity will be now removed to Ath & Lens or to the area of those places.

These movements left few troops in the fortified towns which concerned the inhabitants who felt vulnerable to sudden attack: I had understood the inhabitants upon observing the march from Tournai of a large body of troops had expressed some alarm.[9]

Regarding the weak state of the line battalions of the KGL in numbers of men and the lack of experienced officers and NCOs in the Hanoverian units, Henry Clinton made a very practical suggestion as to how to remedy this to Sir Hudson Lowe:

> the right force in point of value from its competence is the German Legion and in many respects they are not at all inferior to our best troops, many of these battalions do not exceed 300 men and they are complete in officers to the establishment of 1,000 men, the 8 battalions of the legion are now considerably below 4,000 men, and not more than 3,000 have I believe agreed to re-enlist which would leave at the rate of 1 officer to 6 or 7 soldiers, if they could receive drafts they have well taught officers for at least 8,000 men. It seems that some arrangement here, advantageous to our cause might be made for drafting some of the battalions of Hanoverians into the legion, or else forming of the legion 3 battalions and applying the officers of the other 5 battalions to the Hanoverian army, the great deficiency of which is in officers and these are deficient no less in numbers, than in expertise, if however measures of this kind be not resorted to we shall miss an opportunity of doubling the number of our officers from the ranks as not at all in a state to be trusted alone, they are indeed hardly in [a] state to take the field. The officers have been allowed as I am informed, no bat & forage allowance of course cannot afford to purchase the means of conveyance so that whenever one of these battalions march, they are always followed by a number of country wagons for the baggage of the officers as well as for carrying their camp kettles which you know our soldiers carry themselves.[10]

Lord Rowland Hill arrived in Belgium in early April and immediately met with the Prince of Orange, but according to his aide Digby Mackworth, the meeting did not go well:

> Our journey to this place terminated last night at about 8 o'clock, and I immediately accompanied Lord Hill to the palace of the Prince of Orange, where, after waiting a considerable time the prince arrived, and had an interview with his lordship which lasted till past eleven. It appears that the prince has made himself unpopular in our army, and that the present situation has a little turned his head, nor have flatterers been wanting to make him believe that he is as great a general as some of the ancient princes of his house; which, judging from the present state of the army under his command, and from the mode in which everything is carried on by him, does not appear to be the case. He received Lord Hill with much cordiality in appearance but his lordship was not much satisfied with the interview he had with him. Delays and excuses were found where immediate action was required; and the only point in which Lord Hill succeeded with the prince, was the inducing him to withdraw the troops from the advanced position which they occupied between Tournai and Ghent.[11]

Henry Clinton was not a fan of the Prince of Orange and wrote home to his brother a very poor assessment of the Prince's military competence, which was not aided by the hopeless attempts of the British government to influence things from afar:

> The impolicy of appointing so incompetent a person to the command of an army had been now made apparent & the authors of this very injudicious measure have left all the mischief which it was calculated to produce, having given the Prince of Orange the rank of general in our service they cannot supersede him but by the person of Lord Wellington, without displacing him and so the army is exposed to all the danger of his inexperience, or to what is hardly less objectionable to the direction of people at home, who cannot be acquainted at the time they issue their orders, with what is to be the state of things at the time when their orders can be obeyed, but we have often seen that our present ministers show more activity in endeavouring to repair a mischief, than sagacity in guarding against it. They are warned that the Prince of Orange is wild & extravagant in his ideas for disposing of his army, they wait until he has done that of which they disapprove & perhaps with reason & then they issue their mandate for remedying the evil, by making him undo what he has done. He most injudiciously marched forward his army to the very frontier & by forced & harassing marches & counter marches & after things have been gradually recovering from that state for a week, the whole army is upon a sudden ordered to retreat, and assume a most cautious discouraging defensive posture or retiring posture. It is impossible for more to have been done to harass the troops, to excite the contempt of officers & to destroy the confidences which all were at first disposed to feel in the presence of our army. Our good fortune has been that the enemy has not been in a state to take advantage of our calamities & now the arrival of the Duke of Wellington will be considered as of now applying the remedy, as if he was not only the only general fit to command an army, but the only one capable of keeping it from falling into confusion.

Sir Frederick Adam reported on 4 April the state of the light brigade, which although in fine fettle, was still lacking some essential equipment:

> The 3rd Battalion 95th is complete in all respects.
>
> The 2nd Battalion still wants pack saddles for the carriage of the surgeons panniers. The 52nd are not complete either in pack saddles or horses. Each of these battalions have a wagon for their sick. The brigade is complete in wagons for the carriage of ammunition but the covers are not yet furnished by the commissary nor are all the tarpaulins

completed. The 52nd have not yet received their camp kettles & nor have they got entrenching tools. The 52nd are now so quartered that the companies are together.

2 companies at Ligne
4 between Moulbaix and Bliquy
4 In hovels St Amand & Villers.[12]

Henry Clinton had also begun to construct a chain of beacons to provide a rapid communication system in the event of an invasion and he suggested that this chain could easily be extended to Brussels:

> It might be of importance to establish a communication by signals between this place and Brussels, the preparation of telegraphs would be a work of some time but any particular events might be expressed by means of fire occasioning a thick smoke, so that in a few minutes you might be apprised of the actual advance of the enemy. I have given directions for preparing beacons for a communication of this sort as far as this place and I will request General Cooke to have eminent points fixed upon for the placing of beacons between this place and the high ground upon this side of Hal, from whence the upper part of Brussels and the steeples of St. Gudule[13] and the town house are distinctly visible.[14]

By the 7 April the communication by warning beacons was fully established in two lines:

> I have established a communication by beacons between the frontier, between Leuze & Conde, the most dangerous part of our frontier in its present state, and Tournai on one side & Ath on the other, so that I should be apprised excepting in foggy weather of any hostile move, at Ath, in a very few minutes.[15]

This was further extended to Enghien by 10 April. A series of inspections showed that the regiments which had been in Belgium since the previous autumn had improved markedly, but had still more to do. Henry Clinton's frustrations over the failure to supply them with adequate equipment was very evident:

> I have inspected minutely several regiments of the 2 divisions which have pro tempore been placed under my command. I find great improvement in most of those of which I have had a sort of superintendence since my arrival in this country, enough to prove most outstandingly how much might be done towards the improvement of this army if officers did not totally disregard this

Weekly State of the Infantry Force Serving in Flanders Under the Command of General His Royal Highness the Prince of Orange, Headquarters, Brussels, 1 April 1815
British & King's German Legion (showing only those units that became the 2nd Division at Waterloo)

Notes:

The 1st Brigade from states of 15th ultimo.

The 1st Battalion 52nd Regiment from disembarkation return.

2nd Battalion 52nd Regiment from state of 15th ultimo.

95th Regiments from state and disembarkation return.

71st Foot yet to arrive in Belgium.

	Brigades and Corps	Light Brigade 2nd Battalion 52nd Foot	1st Battalion 52nd Foot	Detachment 95th Foot	Major Gen Hinuber 2nd Brigade 1st Line Battalion	2nd Line Battalion	3rd Brigade 3rd Line Battalion	4th Line Battalion
Officers	Field Officers	1	1	2	3	1	3	2
	Captains	4	6	9	6	9	10	8
	Subalterns	12	28	28	28	26	25	27
	Staff	4	6	6	4	5	6	4
Quartermasters of Cavalry								
Sergeants	Present	22	55	67	44	46	43	45
	Present Sick	2		1	3	2		2
	Absent Sick				2	1		
	Command				1	2	4	2
	Prisoner of War							
	Total	24	55	68	50	51	47	49
Trumpeters & Drummers	Present	13	23	25	11	12	13	6
	Present Sick				1			1
	Absent Sick					1		
	Command					1		1
	Prisoner of war							
	Total	13	23	25	12	14	13	8
Rank & File	Present	232	824	837	399	425	523	423
	Present Sick	34		13	26	50	5	11
	Absent Sick	2		8	12	12	9	
	Command	2			32	15	12	31
	Prisoners of War				5	18		
	Total	270	824	858	469	520	549	465
Horses	Present							
	Sick							
	Command							
	Total							
Alterations	Men Joined			542			3	
	Men Dead							1
	Men Deserted				3	2	2	1
	Men Discharged						3	
	Men Given							
	Men Promoted					1		
	Men Reduced					1		
Commanding Officer / Station		Lt. Col. Gibbs / Leuze	Major Rowan / On march to Brussels	Col. Wade / On march to Leuze	Lt. Col. Bodecker / Tornai	Major Muller / Tornai	Lt. Col. Wissell / Mons	Major Reh / Mons

Weekly State of the Hanoverian Forces Serving in Flanders Under the Command of General His Royal Highness the Prince of Orange, Headquarters, Brussels, 1 April 1815 (showing only those units that became the 2nd Division at Waterloo)

		Brigades and Corps Malitia Battalion Salzgitter	Malitia Battalion Bremervorde	2nd Battalion Duke of York (Osnabrück)	3rd Battalion Duke of York (Quakenbrück)
Officers	Field Officers	1	1		1
	Captains	3	4	4	3
	Subalterns	13	13	13	12
	Staff	4	4	3	4
Quartermasters of Cavalry					
Sergeants	Present	18	19	20	20
	Present Sick		1		
	Absent Sick	1			1
	Command	2	2	2	1
	Prisoner of War				
	Total	21	22	22	22
Trumpeters & Drummers	Present	8	8	8	8
	Present Sick				
	Absent Sick				
	Command				
	Prisoner of war				
	Total	8	8	8	8
Rank & File	Present	545	598	547	524
	Present Sick	15	10	20	
	Absent Sick	22	2	16	32
	Command	8	6	12	2
	Prisoners of War				
	Total	590	616	595	564
Horses	Present				
	Sick				
	Command				
	Total				
Alterations	Men Joined			1	
	Men Dead				
	Men Deserted				
	Men Discharged	1		12	
	Men Given				
	Men Promoted				
	Men Reduced				
Commanding Officer / Station		Major Hammerstein / Lens	Lt. Col. Schulenburg / Tornai	Captain Schule / Tornai	Major B. Hunefeld / Tornai

> part, indeed the whole of their duty. I have made representation upon representation of what was wanting to repair the equipment of these regiments to … the furnishing a proper supply of the light camp kettles & horns for canteens instead of the objectionable wooden ones, these were supported by unanswerable reasons, Gordon approved of the kettles (regulated by a board) & desired me to send him a pattern home which I did. The subject on which I have of late had to send correspondence with Calvert was the browning the barrels & an improvement in the pouches for the preservation of the ammunition. When there was a question of taking the field I had reason to write to both & I expressed my hope that the troops coming from home (who have had nothing to do but to put themselves in order since they returned from France last year) might have new arms, improved pouches & the same for Gordon in what concerned his department. Calvert answers that orders have been given to the Ordnance for browning the barrels but he fears it has not been executed, but as for the pouches the general pattern had been regulated by a board of general officers, that it could not be altered without equal authority & that at any rate the present was not a time for changes. Gordon tells me that camp kettles are furnished but that the horns of the English cattle are not sufficiently large, this is a mistake, but he sends me in his correct style, a list of articles to be supplied to troops on embarking, they comprise, two very essential articles for troops in the field, namely camp kettles & bill hooks, I inspected the other day the 2nd Battalion[16] 55th just arrived from Dover & there was not one of these two articles in the whole battalion, though it had been regularly inspected … previously to its embarkation. How can it be expected that an army can be in order with such instances of want of energy & precision in officers constituting its main spring.[17]

He continued his programme of improvements with a request for the Hanoverian troops to be issued with the light camp kettles:

> It would be a great saving of transport if you would furnish the Hanoverians in the field with this sort of kettle, whatever fund would have to defray the expenses would not be of much consequence.[18]

This relentless drive for improved equipment and training was ultimately to reap great rewards.

Chapter 4

The 2nd Division is Born

The 2nd Division which fought at Waterloo was formed by a General Order dated 11 April 1815. It was to be commanded by Sir Henry Clinton and would form part of the 2nd Corps, which was to be commanded by Sir Rowland Hill. It is now time to look in detail at the experience of the various national contingents of the division, the individual battalions and their commanders.

The 3rd British Brigade Commanded by Major General Frederick Adam

52nd (Oxfordshire) Light Infantry, 1st Battalion;
Commanded by Brevet Colonel Sir John Colborne.

71st (Highland) Light Infantry, 1st Battalion;
Commanded by Brevet Colonel Thomas Reynell.

95th Foot (Rifles), 2nd Battalion;
(6 Companies) Commanded by Brevet Lieutenant Colonel Amos Norcott.

95th Foot (Rifles), 3rd Battalion;
(2 Companies) Commanded by Brevet Lieutenant Colonel John Ross.

Major General Frederick Adam (1781–1853)

Major General Sir Frederick William Adam was a veteran officer who had joined the army as an Ensign in the 26th Foot in 1795. He served in Holland, Sicily and the east coast of Spain, where he fought at the Battle of Castalla and the siege of Tarragona, being severely wounded at the latter.

In 1817 he was given the command of all troops in the Mediterranean and in 1824 he became Lord High Commissioner of the Ionian Islands.

In 1832 he was made Governor of Madras and he ended his career on the board responsible for army clothing.

He was awarded various honours: Knight of the Austrian Order of Maria Theresa, the Russian Order of St Anne, Knight Grand Cross of the Order of St Michael and Knight Commander of the Order of the Bath.

He died at the age of seventy-two, having suffered an apoplectic fit on the platform of Greenwich Railway Station.

52nd Foot (Oxfordshire) Light Infantry, 1st Battalion

The 52nd Foot was a two battalion regiment, both battalions of which saw significant service during the Napoleonic wars. Having been raised in 1741 to fight as conventional line infantry, they fought in the American War of Independence and then served in India. The regiment was transformed, however, by the light infantry teachings of Sir John Moore at Shorncliffe Camp in 1803. They were thereafter fully able to skirmish as light infantry or function as a line regiment as circumstances required. The 1st Battalion served in England until 1805, when it was sent to Sicily. In 1807 it was present at the siege of Copenhagen and then proceeded to the Peninsula, where it served throughout the rest of the war, seeing action at the battles of Vimiero, Corunna, Bussaco, Fuentes d'Onoro, Ciudad Rodrigo, Badajoz, Salamanca, Vitoria, Nivelle, the Nive, Orthes and Toulouse.

The 1st Battalion embarked at Portsmouth on 4 January 1815 to fight in North America and it arrived at the Cove of Cork on 20 January. By sheer luck, the fleet assembled here was significantly delayed in sailing by tremendous storms and contrary winds. This gave time for urgent messages, recalling these troops to arrive, and thus allowing the 1st Battalion to arrive at Ostend on 31 March in time to participate in the Waterloo campaign. The battalion marched to Grammont, where it joined its 2nd Battalion on 7 April. Here they were able to complete the General Order[1] that all effective men in the 2nd Battalion were to be transferred to the 1st Battalion. The officers, non commissioned officers and men unfit for service were ordered home with the 2nd Battalion. In consequence of this order nine sergeants and 224 rank and file were transferred to the 1st Battalion; however, twenty-six sergeants, eight buglers and 284 rankers transferred the other way, being deemed unfit for active service. The 2nd Battalion was then immediately sent home.[2]

The battalion was therefore a very experienced one, although it did receive significant drafts from its less experienced 2nd Battalion when it was sent home from Holland in 1815 prior to the Waterloo campaign. However, this meant that it was an extremely strong battalion in simple numbers and was also unique in being composed of only men deemed fully fit for active service.

Brevet Colonel Sir John Colborne (1778–1863)

Colonel Sir John Colborne had joined the army as an ensign in the 20th Foot in 1794. He served in Holland and Egypt, and then in Italy, where he was present at the Battle of Maida. He then fought in Portugal and Spain throughout much of the war and served on the Staff (as Military Secretary) of Sir John Moore who held a very high opinion of Colborne. He was present at the battles of Corunna and Albuera before transferring to the 52nd. He also took part in the siege of Ciudad Rodrigo, where he was badly wounded, and returned home for a period of convalescence. On his return he commanded the battalion at the siege of San Sebastian, and the battles of the Bidassoa, Nivelle, the Nive, Orthes and Toulouse.

In 1814 he was appointed as Military Secretary to the Prince of Orange and as such had much correspondence with Sir Henry Clinton. Just before the Waterloo campaign Colborne resumed his command of the 52nd Foot and led it at Waterloo. He was very glad to see the return of the Duke of Wellington, pronouncing the Prince of Orange 'not being fit to command an army'.[3] He was appointed a Knight Commander of the Order of the Bath and Knight of the Austrian Order of Maria Theresa and became an aide-de-camp to King George IV.

He went on to become Governor of Upper Canada and then Commander-in-Chief of all the armed forces in British North America, personally leading the offensive at the Battle of Saint-Eustache in Lower Canada and defeating the rebel force in December 1837. Later he was to become Governor General of all Canada and on his return to Britain was made Lord Seaton of Seaton in Devon. After that he was High Commissioner of the Ionian Islands, and then Commander-in-Chief, Ireland, before standing down in 1860 as a Field Marshal. He died at Valetta House in Torquay on 17 April 1863.

71st (Glasgow Highland) Light Infantry, 1st Battalion

Although the 71st Regiment of Foot can trace its formation back to 1758, this battalion was disbanded in 1768. Again in 1775 two battalions were raised as the 71st Foot when troops were urgently required to fight in the American War of Independence but disbanded by 1786. The true inauguration of the regiment was in 1777 as the 73rd Foot which served in Africa and India before being re-designated the 71st in 1786. The single battalion regiment continued to serve in India and Ceylon until 1798, when the few remaining soldiers were transferred to the 74th Foot and the regiment was sent home to recruit. It arrived back in Scotland in 1802. A 2nd Battalion was raised in 1804 but never ventured out of Britain before being disbanded in 1815.

The 1st Battalion served at the Cape of Good Hope and Buenos Aires before it was sent to the Peninsula and fought there throughout the campaign. It fought at the battles of Rolica, Vimiero, Corunna, Walcheren, Fuentes d'Onoro, Almeida, Salamanca, Vitoria, the Pyrenees, the Nive and Orthes.

During the peace that followed Napoleon's first abdication the battalion went to Ireland and remained at Limerick until ordered in January 1815 to join the troops collecting at the Cove of Cork to sail to America. Just like the 52nd, they were detained there by foul weather until instructed to join the army in Belgium. The battalion disembarked at Ostend on 22 April and proceeded via Ghent to Leuze, where it was assimilated into the 2nd Division. This was another large and very experienced battalion.

Brevet Colonel Thomas Reynell (1777–1848)

Colonel Thomas Reynell joined the army as an Ensign in the 38th Foot in 1793. He served in Holland and then the West Indies, including the capture of Trinidad. Changing roles, he served in Grenada and St Domingo as Assistant Adjutant General. Having fortunately survived three years in the West Indies, the grave of countless British soldiers, he transferred to the 40th Foot and served in Holland again and in Egypt. He then served in India from 1804–08.

Returning to Europe he was appointed Military Secretary to Sir John Cradock during his short period of command in Portugal and subsequently followed him to his command in Gibraltar. In 1809 he joined the 71st Foot in England and the following year went with six companies of the regiment to Portugal. He was Military Secretary to the Duke of Wellington and soon after was appointed Assistant Adjutant General to the 4th Division commanded by Sir Lowry Cole. In 1811 he accompanied Sir John Cradock to the Cape of Good Hope and upon succeeding to the command of the 71st Foot he joined the regiment again in England in 1814.

He was wounded at Waterloo but stayed with his regiment during the subsequent march to Paris. He was made a Companion of the Order of the Bath, Knight of the Austrian Order of Maria Theresa, and of the Russian Order of St Michael. He later returned to India, and commanded the 1st Infantry Division at the siege of Bhurtpore 1825–1826.

He succeeded to the baronetcy (6th Baronet) when his older brother died in 1829, and in 1831 married the widowed Lady Elizabeth Pack, with whose husband he had served in the Peninsula and at Waterloo.

95th Foot (Rifles)

An Experimental Rifle Corps was formed in 1800 of light infantrymen dressed in green as a form of camouflage and issued the highly accurate but slow loading Baker Rifle instead of muskets. In 1803 this corps became the 1st Battalion 95th Foot, followed by a 2nd Battalion in 1805 and a 3rd in 1809. Elements of all three battalions were at Waterloo but only the 2nd and 3rd Battalions were in the 2nd Division and form part of our study.

2nd Battalion

The 2nd Battalion served abroad in numerous campaigns from 1807, seeing action at the Cape of Good Hope, Montevideo, Rolica, Vimiero, Corunna, Walcheren, Cadiz and Barossa. One company of the 2nd Battalion had been sent to Holland with General Graham's force the previous year and had remained in Belgium during the ensuing peace. Five further companies of hand-picked men marched from Hythe Barracks on 25 March 1815 and arrived at Leuze on 1 April. This major detachment consisted of twenty-one officers and 550 men under the command of Colonel Hamlet Wade, and it marched via Ostend, Bruges, Courtrai and Tournai. The company that had already been in Belgium joined them at Leuze on 18 April and on 29 April Lieutenant Colonel Norcott took the command, with Wade returning to England. These men were sufficiently experienced campaigners.

Brevet Lieutenant Colonel Amos Godsil Robert Norcott (1777–1838)

Amos Norcott joined the army as an Ensign in the 33rd Foot in 1793. He served in Flanders in 1794; at the capture of the Cape of Good Hope in 1796 and then in Manila and India, being present at the siege of Seringapatam. He served in South America in 1807 and became a prisoner of war at the disastrous campaign to take Buenos Aires. Being exchanged, he served in the Peninsula War with 1/95th in the Portuguese campaign up until the Battle of Corunna. He then served at Walcheren and again in the Peninsula with 2/95th from1810 to 1814. He was involved in the siege of Cadiz, and at the battles of Barossa, Seville, the Nive, Orthes and Tarbes, being severely wounded at the latter.

He commanded 2/95th in the Peninsula from October 1813 to March 1814, and at Waterloo, where he was badly wounded. He was awarded the Order 2nd Class of St Anne, and of Maximilien Joseph of Bavaria. He was also made a Companion of the Bath and Knight Commander of the Royal Hanoverian Guelphic Order. He became a Brevet Colonel in 1819 and subsequently a Major General in 1830. He died at Cork in 1838.

3rd Battalion

The 3rd Battalion saw more limited service, having only been formed in 1809, but the men were still sufficiently experienced campaigners. The battalion had fought at the siege of Cadiz and the Battle of Barossa before the main body returned home in 1811. Two companies had then served at Stralsund in 1813 and in the campaign in Holland in 1814, remaining in Belgium during the peace. The rest of the battalion embarked for America and was unfortunate enough to suffer heavily in the disastrous defeat at New Orleans. The two companies already stationed in Belgium were the only ones which fought at the Battle of Waterloo.

Brevet Lieutenant Colonel John Ross (?–1835)

Major Ross served in Hanover in 1805 and at the siege of Copenhagen in 1807. He then went out to the Peninsula with 1/95th, being present from the original landings until the Battle of Corunna. He became a Major in the 95th Foot in 1809; and was again in the Peninsula with 3/95th from 1810 to 1811. He served at the battles and sieges of Corunna, Cadiz, Barossa, San Millan, Vitoria, the Pyrenees, Tarbes and Toulouse. He commanded 3/95th in the Peninsula from 1812 to 1814 and at Waterloo.

He subsequently became a Lieutenant Colonel in the Cape Corps in 1824 and a Major General in 1830. He died in April 1835.

1st Brigade of the King's German Legion Commanded by Brevet Colonel George Charles Augustus du Plat (1770–1815)

In British Army lists he is identified as Charles du Plat. He entered the Hanoverian Army as a Captain in the 1st Infantry Regiment. With the subsequent invasion of Hanover he joined the British service in the King's German Legion in 1803 with the temporary rank of Captain. He became a Major in the 4th Line Battalion in 1804 and a Lieutenant Colonel in 1807, then a Brevet Colonel in 1813. He had served in Hanover in 1805, the Baltic in 1807 and Sicily from 1808–12. He then served with his regiment on the east coast of Spain 1812–14. He died of wounds received at the Battle of Waterloo.

The King's German Legion

The King's German Legion was formed within months of the dissolution of the Army of Hanover after the Electorate was occupied by French forces in 1803. This force of ex-Hanoverian soldiers in British pay rapidly expanded to the size of a small army and it saw significant service throughout Europe. Its term of service actually expired six months after the Peace Treaty of Paris, but the corps volunteered to serve for another six months, an offer the British government were more than happy to accept. In March 1815, they were therefore still available for service during the Waterloo campaign.

1st Line Battalion KGL

The 1st Battalion had served in the Mediterranean in 1806–07 and in the Baltic in 1807 before serving throughout the Peninsular War. The battalion saw service at the battles of Talavera, Bussaco, Fuentes d'Onoro, Ciudad Rodrigo, Salamanca, Vitoria, San Sebastian, Nivelle and the Nive. This battalion sailed to England from France in July 1814 and was almost immediately ordered to Belgium, where it arrived in the September.[4] This was therefore a very experienced unit.

Major Friedrich Wilhelm von Robertson (1766-1849)

Major Robertson joined the King's German Legion as a Captain on 25 October 1803. He saw service in Hanover, the Mediterranean, Baltic and in the Peninsula from 1808–14. Robertson fought at the crossing of the Douro, and battles of Talavera, Bussaco, Fuentes d'Onoro, Ciudad Rodrigo, Salamanca, Burgos, Vitoria, San Sebastian (where he was wounded with the storming party), Bidassoa, Nivelle, the Nive, and Bayonne. He was promoted to Major in January 1811. He then served in the Netherlands in 1814 and subsequently in the Waterloo campaign. He was severely wounded at Waterloo but survived and was last recorded at Hamburg. He received the Order of the Bath and the Hanoverian Guelphic Order.

2nd Line Battalion KGL

The 2nd Battalion was another very experienced battalion seeing much service alongside the 1st Battalion, serving in the Mediterranean 1806 – 7 and the Baltic in 1807, before serving throughout the Peninsular War. The battalion was present at the battles of Talavera, Bussaco, Fuentes d'Onoro, Ciudad Rodrigo, Salamanca, Vitoria, San Sebastian, Nivelle and Nive. This battalion had returned to England in July 1814 and was then sent to Belgium in September 1814.

Major Georg Muller

George Muller held the temporary rank of Captain in the 2nd Line Battalion in November 1803 and became a Major in 1813. He served in

Hanover in 1805 and in the Mediterranean, before serving in the Peninsula from 1808 to May 1812 and again in 1813–14. He fought at the crossing of the Douro, the battles of Talavera, Bussaco, Fuentes d'Onoro (where he was severely wounded) and then fought in north Germany and at Waterloo. He was made a Knight of the Hanoverian Guelphic Order and a Companion of the Bath. He retired on half pay but became a Major General in the Hanoverian army and was Commandant at Celle.

3rd Line Battalion KGL

The 3rd Battalion had served in the Baltic in 1807 and then spent the remainder of the war in the Mediterranean, garrisoning various islands. It was an experienced unit but it had not seen any significant action during its long period of dull garrisoning service in Sicily and Malta. The 3rd Battalion returned from the Mediterranean and sailed directly to Holland in October 1814.

Lieutenant Colonel Friedrich von Wissell (?–1820)

Friedrich von Wissell joined the King's German Legion on 24 May 1806. He served in the Baltic, the Mediterranean from 1808 to 1812, the Peninsula and the South of France throughout 1813-14, and the Netherlands during the Waterloo campaign. He was invested with the Order of the Bath and the Hanoverian Guelphic Order. He died at Wiesbaden on 16 December 1820 whilst commanding the 2nd Battalion of the Hanoverian Guards.

4th Line Battalion KGL

The 4th Battalion had seen service in the Baltic in 1807 and the Mediterranean from 1808 to 1812, but it then saw service on the east coast of Spain in 1813–14. It therefore had seen two years of service in a relatively active theatre of war. This battalion had also returned to England in July 1814 but was soon ordered to Belgium in September 1814.

Major Friedrich Reh (?–1829)

Friedrich Reh joined the King's German Legion on 19 October 1803. He served in the Baltic, the Peninsular, in the years 1808–11, followed by a short interlude in the Mediterranean before returning to the Peninsula between 1812 and 1814. He then served in the Netherlands and Waterloo campaign. He became a member of the Order of the Bath and the Hanoverian Guelphic Order. He was placed on half pay on 25 July 1815 and died at Osterode on 24 July 1829.

3rd Hanoverian Brigade

The Hanoverian army was greatly expanded in January 1814 when thirty landwehr (militia) battalions were formed, based on specific provinces of Hanover. From that February the Hanoverian corps were regarded as separate from the British army and carried their own insignia on their flags. On 4 February 1815, these various battalions were formed into regiments, each consisting of one field (regular) battalion and three landwehr battalions. However, during the Waterloo campaign the battalions seem to have operated as separate units.[5]

Brevet Colonel Hugh Halkett, 7th Line KGL (1783–1863)

Hugh Halkett was born on 30 August 1783 in Musselburgh, Midlothian, Scotland.

His military career began in April 1794 when he joined his father's battalion of the Scots Brigade as an Ensign before he was eleven years old. He became a Lieutenant in 1795 and went to India in 1798, where he served until 1801. In 1803 he was nominated senior Captain of the Light Brigade under his brother, Colin Halkett. This unit became the 2nd Light Battalion of the King's German Legion. In 1805 he became a Major before he was twenty-two years old.

He served with the battalion on the Isle of Rugen at the sieges of Stralsund and Copenhagen in Denmark in 1807. His prompt action on outpost duty in seizing a Danish redoubt without waiting for orders won the approval of General Sir David Baird. In 1808 he went with the battalion to Sweden and then to Portugal, where he took part in the retreat to Corunna and then in the siege of Flushing on Walcheren Island. He married Emily Charlotte Bland Burges on 25 May 1810. In the winter of 1811–12, Sir Hugh returned to England for health reasons, his liver disease was acting up again as it had ten years earlier in India.

He returned to the Peninsula in July 1812 and commanded his battalion at the Battle of Albuera, where he had two horses wounded under him. After the battle, when he was taking his coat and jacket off, five bullets fell out.

In September 1812 he was promoted to Lieutenant Colonel. He commanded his battalion again the following year at the siege of the forts of Salamanca and at the Battle of Salamanca. He was also in the retreat from Burgos where the Light Brigade, which included the 1st and 2nd Light Battalions of the German Legion, formed the rear guard of the army.

In September 1813 Sir Hugh was promoted to Lieutenant Colonel of the 7th Line Battalion of the Legion, then in garrison in Sicily. Before the command could be assumed he was sent to northern Germany to help organize the new Hanoverian army that was to later serve with distinction in the Battle of Waterloo.

In command of a brigade of these troops in Count Wallmoden's army, Hugh distinguished himself at the Battle of Ghorde, Germany, in September 1813, and in the unsuccessful fight with the Danes at Schestedt, also in Germany, in the following December. On this latter occasion, when a Danish cavalry regiment was attacking, Sir Hugh, on horseback, dashed upon the standard bearer, seized the standard and escaped by clearing a hedge with a double ditch, over which many of his pursuers could not follow his remarkable display of horsemanship. He held command at the sieges of Gluckstadt and Harburg in Germany in 1814. Sir Hugh was promoted to Colonel on 17 March 1814.

He was severely wounded at Waterloo, where a grenade splintered and hit him in the forehead, putting out one of his eyes.

In 1815, when a Lieutenant Colonel in the British service, he received the Order of the Bath along with many other honours, including the Knight of the Swedish Order of the Sword, Grand Cross of the Royal Hanoverian Guelphic Order, the Russian Grand Cross of St Anne 1st Class, the Prussian Black Eagle 1st Class, the Grand Cross of Henry the Lion of Brunswick and the Grand Cross of Leopold of Austria. After the Congress of Vienna he went into the service of the state of Hannover. In 1818, at the age of thirty-five, he was promoted to Major General and was subsequently given command of the Regiment of Celle. In 1834 he rose to the rank of Lieutenant General and was given command of the 2nd Infantry Division of the Hanoverian army. In 1843 he was named Corps Commander. In 1846 he became Inspector General and in 1848 he was promoted to General of the Army and also functioned as the Commandant of the Army Corps in the war against Denmark that same year.

In June 1862 he became Baron von Halkett when he received a perpetual barony in the Kingdom of Hanover. The title also applied to his wife as well as his legitimate offspring, both male and female.

Landwehr Battalion Bremervorde

This unit was one of those formed in January 1814, forming one of the three landwehr battalions which, along with the Bremen Field Battalion, formed the Bremen Regiment. This battalion proceeded to the Netherlands during the summer of 1814[5] as part of the 'Subsidiary Corps' consisting of eight field battalions and fifteen landwehr battalions along with two hussar regiments, which was sent to protect it. Although it was a raw militia unit, Henry Clinton was approving of 'its appearance in the military air & steadiness of the battalion under arms' and 'the company officers are very attentive to their duty & all were able to account for every man belonging to them.'[6]

Lieutenant Colonel Friedrich von der Schulenburg

Little is known of this officer beyond what is recorded by Henry Clinton, who states that he had formerly served in the Prussian Garde du Corps and that the battalion had an advantage over the others in the previous military experience in the Prussian army of their Lieutenant Colonel.[7] He was dead before November 1824.[8]

Landwehr Battalion 2nd Duke of York's (Osnabrück)

The Osnabrück Landwehr Battalion was another formed in January 1814 and later assigned as one of the three militia battalions attached to the Osnabrück Field Battalion to form the Osnabrück Regiment. This battalion was also sent to the Netherlands as part of the 'Subsidiary Corps'. Henry Clinton states that 'This is one of those corps which continues embodied contrary to the terms under which they have been raised[9]... This is though young, a good & healthy new body of men.'[10]

Major Baron Louis Gudririg Graf von Munster

A very inexperienced officer who, according to Henry Clinton, had never previously served in the army, but partly made up for this by great zeal. He was awarded the Hanoverian Guelphic Order and Hanoverian Waterloo Medal; he was also promoted Lieutenant Colonel dated 18 June 1815. He was dead before January 1825.[11]

Landwehr Battalion 3rd Duke of York's (Quakenbrück)

The Quakenbrück Battalion was a sister unit to the Osnabrück Landwehr Battalion, forming the second of the militia battalions of the Osnabrück Regiment. This also formed part of the 'Subsidiary Corps' sent to the Netherlands in the summer of 1814. Henry Clinton indicates that this was a young battalion but well commanded by Major Bussche despite his inexperience.

Major Clamor Wilhelm von dem Bussche-Hunefeld.

I have failed to discover any history of this officer. He appears to have had no previous military background.

Landwehr Battalion Salzgitter

This landwehr battalion formed one of the three militia battalions which were attached to the Grubenhagen Field Battalion to form the Grubenhagen Regiment. This battalion only arrived in Belgium on 1 October 1814, replacing the Lauenburg Field Battalion in the 2nd Division.[12] Henry Clinton states that 'It is composed of very young men like most of the militia regiments but the battalion marched in good order.' However, he also stated later that it had 'arrived the latest in this country & is probably of the whole army the most backward in point of military instruction. The men are young, many even too young to bear fatigue and undersized.'[13]

Major Friedrich von Hammerstein

I have failed to discover any history of this officer. He appears to have had no previous military background. He was awarded the Hanoverian Guelphic Order and the Hanoverian Waterloo Medal. He was promoted to Lieutenant Colonel on 1 March 1816.

Divisional Artillery
Lieutenant Colonel Charles Gold (1769?–1842).

Charles Gold joined the Royal Artillery as a Gentleman Cadet on 1 April 1783[14] and served in India against Tippoo Sultan in 1792–93, and was at the capture of Ceylon. He rose to the rank of Lieutenant Colonel on 17 December 1813. Gold appears to have spent much of his career at home. He commanded No. 1 Company of the 5th Battalion Royal Artillery in 1802 but transferred to No. 7 Company of the 7th Battalion later that year, which he commanded until 1809. He was then sent to Walcheren with a reinforcement of two companies of artillery but only arrived in time to see the re-embarkation of the army. He commanded the artillery attached to the 2nd Division at Waterloo and was second-in-command to the Royal Artillery at Waterloo, for which service he was made a Companion of the Order of the Bath. He later served in the Army of Occupation in France, and at Gibraltar. He became a Colonel in 1825 but ill-health caused him to sell his commission in 1827 and he died at Leamington Priors in 1842.

No.4 Company 9th Battalion Royal Artillery

This company of the Royal Artillery had only been formed in 1806 and had served at home except for the Walcheren expedition and the Holland campaign of 1814.

Captain Samuel Bolton (1783–1815)

Samuel Bolton had become a Gentleman Cadet on 29 May 1798 and 2nd Lieutenant on 9 October 1799. He served at Copenhagen in 1807 and transferred to 'F' Troop Royal Horse Artillery in 1813 with which he fought at the battles of Vitoria, San Sebastian, the Bidassoa, Nivelle, the Nive and at Bayonne. He was given command of his own foot artillery company in 1814 (No. 2 Company 9th Battalion) but rather than join it, he was given command of Captain Charles Alm's company which was already in Holland as part of General Graham's force. He was killed close to the end of the Battle of Waterloo.

1st Horse Battery, KGL

The battery seems to have only served at home except in the Baltic in 1807 and in Holland in 1814.

Brevet Major Augustus Sympher (?–1830)

Sympher joined the King's German Legion Artillery on 17 November 1804. He served in the Baltic in 1807, Holland in 1813 and was slightly wounded at Waterloo and became a member of the Order of the Bath and of the Hanoverian Guelphic Order. He died at Hanover on 11 December 1830 as a Lieutenant Colonel in the Hanoverian Artillery.[15]

Chapter 5

Preparations for War

Henry Clinton was delighted by his new appointment and was very happy to serve under Lord Hill instead of the Prince of Orange, as can be seen by his reaction to the announcement in a candid letter to his brother:

> I told you this morning [in a previous letter] that the army was formed in brigades & divisions upon a new plan, & one by which the most is made. I will sketch the order of battle by which if you will be able to make it out you will see I have du Plat & his brigade, unfortunately several of these fine fellows [KGL] have been discharged, indeed there was a time when our government had left the matter open and to them it was a case of doubt from day to day, whether the German Legion existed or not, I advised Colborne to write to Bunbury just before I went to Paris knowing that it could not be a matter of indifference, either they would, or might want this corps or they did & might not. In one case it was very desirable to keep it of which we had then the option & this they knew, in the other case it was idly putting the public to the useless burthen of feeding & paying £800 a thousand soldiers. Some of the members of the government have shown a most culpable supineness.[1]

Clinton then immediately proceeded on a round of inspections to view his newly acquired units.

The British Brigade

Clinton inspected the 2nd Battalion 95th Regiment at St Amand near Ath on 5 April, just before the official announcement of his new position. It consisted of 2 Field Officers, 5 Captains, 13 Subalterns, 31 Sergeants, 14 Drummers and 405 Rank and File. The original smaller contingent had been bolstered by a sizeable hand-picked reinforcement from England, but it had apparently been rushed to Belgium and was both very poorly provided with equipment and ill disciplined:

> This body of men being the selection of 5 companies from the whole battalion, was ordered suddenly to embark at Dover where it had been stationed, it came out in a state totally unprovided for the field, not a camp kettle or billhook & from the appearance of the battalion it is to be supposed no pains have been taken with its discipline. Lt Colonel Wade,[2] the commanding officer seems as ignorant of all that an officer should know & inactive as any volunteer officer. The packs were ill put together & ill put on & even at this time some of the packs are filled out with frames. The caps are too small & the shade hangs over the eyes so that to see, the men must bring their heads back. General Adam in whose brigade this battalion is placed may make something of them.

A week later, Henry Clinton inspected the 1st Battalion 52nd Foot, which he judged to be past its best and far too arrogant to accept advice on how to improve. It must, however, be stated in their defence that the two battalions of the regiment had only been amalgamated seven days previously, with all personnel those deemed fit for active service transferred into the 1st Battalion and all those declared unfit transferred to the 2nd Battalion, which had then marched for England. The battalion had therefore little time to assimilate such a comprehensive change of manpower. It consisted of 1 Field Officer, 9 Captains, 30 Subalterns, 50 Sergeants, 21 Drummers and 904 Rank and File:

> Lt Colonel [Blank] the only field officer present does not seem quite equal to the command of this strong battalion, the men are generally a fine and serviceable body, but altogether this regiment lately the pattern of the English army has now more the appearance of the remains of a good system than the present possession of it. Though there are 9 captains there was hardly an officer who would account for any deficiency, but they are so used to be applauded that anything like inquiry excites only surprise or even displeasure. The arms however, are not in the order in which they certainly ought to be, the ammunition is in most part loose in the boxes with which the pouches that lately now are furnished. This regiment has not been provided with camp kettles or bill hooks. The caps are put out of shape as I have observed in many of the English regiments, they are however complete in shoes & linen and the excellent manner of packing & putting on the knapsacks is well attended to. The commanding officer excused the awkward manner in which this regiment moved by saying they had been for 5 months on board ship. There are no less

than 22 extra drummers & musicians, a fault which I recommended to General Adam to have corrected.[3]

Sir John Colborne was due to leave the service of the Prince of Orange and was destined to return to the 1st Battalion 52nd Foot. He therefore wrote to Clinton, appealing for the battalion to be cantoned more closely together to allow it to exercise as a unit, as it was undoubtedly rusty from months cooped up in transport ships:

> My dear Sir,
>
> I find the quarters of the 52nd Regiment are so scattered that it will be inappropriate to take advantage of the next three weeks leisure before the advance of the army, to get the battalion into that order which is so necessary at the commencement of a campaign. I must mention to you that since the battalion disembarked at Plymouth from the south of France it has had no time for drill nor can it have yet recovered from the effects of the peninsular service & at Chatham the duty was so severe, little could be done during the winter months and certainly after being three months on board transports and the manner in which they were marched off from Ostend, some time should be given to the commanding officer to make it the best and the most effective battalion in this army. I shall be much obliged to you if you can give the 52nd some village or town, where the companies are more together, and that the commanding officer can work hard whilst we remain in cantonments.[4]

However, Clinton replied with somewhat of a challenge, stating that it was not necessary to bring the regiment together if the company officers were up to the standard that they were in Spain:

> My dear General,
>
> ... with respect to the quarters of the 52nd Regiment it has been a great inconvenience to put them into such scattered quarters and I have most readily adopted every suggestion of General Adam for getting them more together. I hope at this time they are so disposed of that the companies in themselves are sufficiently collected to be under the eyes of their commanders, and with a battalion of your strength unless a town be given to it that is the most that can be expected. Indeed from what I have seen of the 52nd Regiment provided the company commanders are what they were a few years back; really competent to the instruction of their men and zealous in the performance of their duty, what the regiment most wants at this time it may as well remain disposed of as it is at present. If it collected together in a town however when you come and shall have made

> yourself thoroughly acquainted with the state, if you should think anything further can be done for the advantage of such a battalion I shall be glad to afford you every facility in my power.[5]

On 23 April, Henry Clinton wrote to Lord Hill regarding the imminently expected arrival of the 71st Regiment and the plan for its cantonments:

> If the whole of the 71st Regiment should be arrived at Ghent, it was to march this day & to arrive on the 25th in the neighbourhood of Ath, I should wish if you have no objection, to let the 71st go to Lessines & to be together therefore a few days, where I will inspect them & make my report to you. Colonel Colborne will be able to take the command of the 52nd about the end of this week & then I think the 52nd would benefit from being sent to Lessines, the 71st will in that case occupy the present quarters of the 52nd.[6]

On 26 April the 71st Regiment arrived at Frasnes to join the 2nd Division. On the following day, the 71st marched to Leuze, the 52nd to Lessines and the 2nd Battalion 95th to Frasnes. Henry Clinton was not slow to inspect the newly arrived 71st Regiment of Foot, which consisted of 3 Field Officers, 9 Captains, 26 Subalterns, 51 Sergeants, 15 Drummers and 666 Rank and File. He was impressed with their equipment, but less with their movements and particularly their extreme youth:

> A young and rather undersized body of men, but apparently in good order, the packs well put on and appointments clean & well kept, being what is called a light infantry battalion, the arms are brown & advantage has been taken of that circumstance to let them be last to clean as they ought to be kept. The pouches are of different patterns, many having wooden boxes to keep the cartridges separately. The clothing fits so ill that the commanding officer informed me more than 500 suits required to be altered. Though light infantry they move very ill in double quick time and are not expert, Colonel Reynell seems to be a zealous officer, but very little in the habit of commanding troops which is much against him & them. This regiment is complete in its field equipment with the exception of some felling axes.[7]

It was clear to Clinton that even the more experienced units in his division were not beyond the need for significant improvements to be implemented and for joint field exercises to be practised:

> In the course of the coming week, I propose if we can manage it, leading the division out together with the exception of the 52nd. The

> 71st & indeed the 2nd battalion of the 95th require a great deal of good practise, both made the same fault in closing their intervals, the change of front of the 95th was not at all what I should have expected from that battalion & the diminution of front was as faulty as so simple an operation can be.[8]

The reports from his brigadiers were disparaging of their own troops, ability to manoeuvre. This, though, was partly because there was a shortage of ground upon which they could practise:

> I had the 71st & two 95th yesterday on the Attre road as far as the hill beyond Villers Saint Amand & practised them a little in reducing & increasing their front. The former has not a good system, or rather the principles of the drill are not well understood. Colonel Reynell is very anxious & very willing to do well & all the most essential things he

will I hope very soon have put on a right footing. I will in a day or two show you the instruction I have proposed & as far as our ground here permits shall superintend its execution till it is accurately done. But you must be aware we are not fortunately situated for this purpose. The high road is the parade & it is only by doing at every parade one or two things perfectly correctly that faults are corrected. The pasturage is too far to go too often & the men are not in a state for drill when they arrive. They ought to execute well what they know (which with cause you will perhaps say is not much) but they can hardly be taught anything.[9]

However, his determination to improve their manoeuvring in brigades was quite evident:

I came here yesterday to superintend the exercise one of the brigades of the 2nd Division and propose remaining here till each of the brigades will have had 3 days of exercise in brigade if we should remain quiet so long.[10]

The persistent wet weather, however, induced General Adam to suggest, whether or not:

in the present state of the roads it might not be advantageous to postpone our movement for a few days until they get into better order.

Although it is certainly most desirable that my brigade should be brought together & it will derive much benefit from some days' exercise, yet the advantages will be greater if this can be accomplished with less inconvenience than at present.

Just now the men will move to the exercising ground in a most uncomfortable state over the crossroads & as they do not appreciate the necessity of the thing as you & I do think, minds will not be given to their business & they will not exercise as well as they would under other circumstances. The same observation applies to the officers in a certain degree, if they are put to less inconvenience, all will work with alacrity & good will. Another motive which induces me to take the liberty of making this suggestion, is that the horses will suffer materially in the present state of the roads. Probably the 52nd will destroy a pair for means, which would be avoided if the roads were in better order & the weather this evening promises so fairly two or three days will it is to be hoped, make a great change.

You will I am sure excuse my taking this liberty I have done, I am only induced to do so in order that any advantage may be derived from the very useful practise you propose to give us, for I am not only persuaded we shall profit by it but are concerned it is absolutely necessary that the brigade should move together, it is the only mode of remedying the defects which exist, which equally with you I am conscious of & most anxious to have an opportunity to correct.[11]

Henry Clinton replied curtly the following day, clearly unimpressed with the attitude of the 52nd:

> The state of the roads certainly is against any unnecessary marching, & if the 52nd cannot arrive at the general position for it near the exercising ground, but at the expense in shoes you apprehend, I think its march had better be postponed, ... I lament that there should be such a want of good feeling as that you describe, though I am well aware of its existence, but the inconvenience in the present instance of giving way to it would in my opinion be greater than any imaginative good to be gained by bending to it.[12]

General Adam's Brigade did exercise again on 12 June but apparently performed quite poorly and Clinton made some further remarks on the 71st Regiment, the six companies of the 2/95th and two companies of the 3/95th:

> These battalions having the name of light infantry and strong in officers, are slower & move more incorrectly than any troops that I have had anything to do with. The filing, wheeling & marching in line of the soldiers are defective from the want of proper instruction and from great apparent inattention. The officers very generally speaking are awkward & unable to command. It has been a great disadvantage to this battalion to have Colonel Reynell succeed to its command at the moment of embarking for service. Though a well informed & sensible man, with a great deal of zeal, having been long upon the Staff & never accustomed to command soldiers. If he is capable of detecting faults, he knows not how to correct them & it has been his misfortune to succeed to the command of a battalion which though in a very low state of discipline, from having acquired an high reputation in the late war, is animated with a firmness that it has nothing to learn & is not susceptible of amendment & this produces a feeling very unfavourable to the respect they owe their commanding officer, as all they do is wrong. The tardiness with which they get into motion & then move would be no additional mischief if it did not so much interfere with their getting right in spite of every aid. They seldom deploy in a straight line, or march in one, in no circumstances preserve their distances, give incorrect words of command & show no desire to improve.
>
> The 95th under Colonel Norcott have already made some improvement, their formations however are very faulty, they are

> loose, slow & incorrect & here [I] observed wrong words of command are introduced.[13]

However, Lord Hill had inspected the 71st Foot and he apparently found them in good shape, although it is unclear whether he required them to manoeuvre in his presence:

> Yesterday we reviewed the 71st Regiment near Leuze. It was in good order, and about 700 strong. After the review Lord Hill was repeatedly cheered by the men, who had served under him in Spain, and appeared much pleased with this mark of their gratitude and good opinion.[14]

The British Brigade was quite strong in numbers, the regiments being some of the largest with the army in the Netherlands. Their manoeuvring abilities as regiments was at a reasonable standard by June 1815. However, it is apparent that their ability to conduct brigade manoeuvres was still limited.

The King's German Legion Brigade

Inspections of the King's German Legion troops began immediately after Henry Clinton's appointment. On 17 April at Ath, Clinton inspected the brigade of Colonel du Plat in its entirety.[15]

The 1st Line Battalion KGL consisted of 3 Field Officers, 5 Captains, 26 Subalterns, 37 Sergeants, 10 Drummers but only 380 Rank and File. Clinton judged that they lacked direction and that their equipment needed improvement:

> A serviceable body of men, the colonel (Bodecker) is almost worn out, and not able to pay that attention to a battalion which it requires to have it in high order, the failings in this battalion are, a looseness in the files, neglect of the packs which require to be painted & better put up, a lack of practise in double quick time & the caps which are put on as it suits the fancy of the soldiers. The pioneers have no tools & should therefore fall in the ranks.

The 2nd Line Battalion KGL was in much better condition, consisting of 1 Field Officer, 3 Captains, 26 Subalterns, 41 Sergeants, 12 Drummers but still only mustered 415 Rank and File:

> A better body of men and in apparently better orders, the same neglect of the knapsacks is however observable and the Major Muller does not appear to be much acquainted with his business on the field of exercise. The same fault in the drawing up of the men.

The 3rd Line Battalion KGL was also in a satisfactory condition owing to the excellent work of the officers and was, in addition, a little stronger in numbers. In fact it interesting to note that Clinton believed it to be the best regiment in the army at that time. It consisted of 3 Field Officers, 10 Captains, 25 Subalterns, 42 Sergeants, 13 Drummers and 506 Rank and File:

> This regiment is composed of a very fine body of men, the officers seem to attend more to their duty & to perform it with better effect than in any regiment in the army, it is certainly in very good order. The arms, pouches, ammunition, every appointment is evidently the object of the officers' constant attention. The whole of this brigade is in a fitter state to take the field than any other in the army, the soldiers are provided with the light camp kettle & the bill hooks & the surgeon paymaster, quartermaster & adjutant with horses for the carriage of their occupation[al] necessary articles. This battalion is commanded by Lt Colonel Wissell. The state of health of this battalion is remarkable in 567 men there are only 17 sick.

Finally, the 4th Line Battalion KGL proved to be in a good condition, though this was actually a deterioration in its condition since the previous autumn. It apparently consisted of 1 Field Officer, 9 Captains, 24 Subalterns, 42 Sergeants, 8 Drummers and only 405 Rank and File:

> This battalion though compared with many others would be pronounced to be in good order is still very short of the state of the 3rd, nor is it to be compared to what it was in last autumn when under the orders of its excellent commander Colonel du Plat, Major [Blank] its present commander is worn out & not at all equal to the active duties of a battalion commander. This battalion is also without pioneers' tools. The accoutrements are good but not to be compared to those of the 3rd Battalion. I remarked the same fault of looseness in the files.

A visit a few weeks later to see the KGL Brigade at exercise led to a lengthy diatribe regarding the poorly executed manoeuvres of the brigade when brought together:

> I had occasion to point out to the commanders of your battalions this morning the inconvenience arising from their being unaccustomed to move in brigade or much larger bodies than single battalions. As it does not belong to them to put larger bodies together, nor have any of us very frequently the opportunity of such practice, they should make it a rule always to move their battalions upon fixed points representing the flanks of neighbouring battalions, and always correct

their lines upon such points. There are also other small defects, which as they interfere very materially with accuracy in movement I request you will draw the attention of your commanding officers to these corrections. There is I think a fault in the forming up of the men, no man should ever fall in without touching his neighbour, the touch of the elbow is the only guide a soldier has when in the ranks and this he must never lose without however projecting his arm from his side to retain it, from the want of due attention to this rule, the wheels are loosely made and after wheeling into line there is always disorderliness from the men not knowing to which flank to touch. When in line the troops must be taught invariably to touch to the centre, in wheeling and in marching in column to the post flank, if the platoon officer should have lost his distance it should appear, and is on no account to be attempted to be concealed by a loosening of the files. Great exertion is requisite upon the part of commanders of battalions to repeat or to give the words of command, in consequence of the command of the exercising officer, instantaneously and in a manner to be heard by their battalions, and they are not upon any account to give a 2nd word of command, until that which must precede it has been heard and executed, it happened today, in both battalions that the words Halt, wheel into line, quick march were given before the word Halt had been obeyed. It is in vain to expect a ready obedience to the column of march without some preparation, for it would be useless to attempt and absurd to expect the soldiers under such circumstances to be listening or attentive to their commander and it is for this obvious reason that in the instruction for marching, it is directed that previously to attempting to execute any move, or change form, then orders soldiers should be called to attention and if the orders therein prescribed are attended to after a few minutes the column should be properly closed and ready to wheel into line. The pace called double quick time may be most usefully employed on some very important occasions provided the troops are regularly and properly trained to its practise, but at present they do not distinguish this pace from an irregular run in which there is not equality of time in the several companies, nor any attempt to preserve the wheeling distance between divisions, this pace must be practised at the company drills before the battalion parades, but not until the officers and non-commissioned officers who must instruct the soldiers are acquainted with the length of the step and the time which will be regulated by a drummer until the troops shall have acquired a considerable degree of precision in this time. I advise you not attempting to execute any movement in a more accelerated pace than the quick time excepting in the formation of the square four deep.[16]

A fortnight later, however, Henry still found fault with the battalions and their manoeuvres, largely caused, it seems, by the lack of knowledge of the officers:

> The first step to be taken in order to give any instructions to soldiers is to qualify those who are to instruct them. I found the 4th Battalion of the German Legion upon the parade and the commanding officer told us he was proceeding to make them practise the formation of the rallying square. He then desired the officer of one of the companies to form the square, but so far from that officer having the assistance of the non-commissioned officers to instruct the soldiers, it appeared to me that Major Reh himself had a very imperfect idea of the mode of assuming this defensive shape & none whatever of showing it to those under his orders. Until the officers are perfectly acquainted with what is required of soldiers, it is in vain to employ them as instructors. I was sorry to see a whole regiment brought out to so little purpose, the company parades afford the only proper opportunity for company drills, the time wasted on the parade is highly prejudicial to discipline & to the best interests of the service.[17]

On 1 June Clinton observed du Plat's Brigade once again at exercise but found that the regimental officers still had little understanding of the manoeuvres: 'I saw Colonel du Plat's Brigade at exercise & practised the change of front in 2 lines, none of these officers are capable of moving with accuracy or expedition their battalions'.[18]

On 2 June the entire division again marched to the neighbourhood of Beloeil and on the following days they manoeuvred together on the pasturage of Quevecamp. There was still much to improve and on the 8th du Plat's Brigade again failed to impress:

> I left Ath early this morning & superintended the exercise of Colonel du Plat's Brigade on that pasturage from ten till two, these battalions are very backward & very awkward in said exercise.[19]
>
> ... Three of the commanding officers out of 4 are so near sighted as not to be able to determine whether their battalions are properly deployed, they are besides slow and incorrect in all their movements as well in circulating the word of command. In marching in column these officers rarely preserve their distance or march upon the true alignment. In marching in line, the first principle of touching to the centre & keeping the head straight are not understood, the commanding officers do not sufficiently attend to ascertaining the true perpendicular, or having ascertained it to ensure the advanced sergeants continuing to march upon it. The deployments are full of

> faults, in charging with bayonets they got into a run without any order & allowed themselves to be thrown into confusion.[20]

The following day he saw the battalion exercise once again:

> The deployment was rather better performed this day, the chief failing was in the incorrect dressing of the heads of the battalion columns in this line. The march in line was defective from the bad direction of the directing battalion, the correcting of the line by the Colour delayed from some of the commanding officers not knowing at which point to place themselves. The retreat to Soignies not well performed from the distance from the named battalion for direction not being duly observed. The halted battalions omit to form themselves by throwing back the outward flanks of their flank division the 8th of the circle. When the four deep on the centre formed column, the commanding officer omitted to name to which flank the divisions were to dress, which exposed them to the inconvenience of dressing to two points & the subsequent opening of their files. In marching in column very little attention is paid to the preservation of distances.[21]

It is clear that although the KGL Brigade was composed of good troops – even though there were not enough of them – their ability to manoeuvre as a brigade with precision was certainly still seriously wanting.

The Hanoverian Brigade

The Hanoverian battalions were also inspected immediately after the formation of the 2nd Division by Henry Clinton. First up was the 2nd Duke of York's or Osnabrück Militia Battalion, which now consisted of 1 Field Officer, 4 Captains, 13 Subalterns, 19 Sergeants, 8 Drummers and 531 Rank and File. However, little improvement was apparently evident since its last inspection:

> I could observe very little improvement in this battalion from the time I saw it at Oudenarde at least 7 months ago, although this battalion has been under the eye of Colonel Halkett who commands the brigade. The fault I found with these troops last year, with respect to the want of care of ammunition, putting up of knapsacks &c were attended to & have been perfectly corrected, but anything which depended upon the commander of the brigade has been entirely neglected, this battalion is no more expert in its movements than it was when I saw it last. These battalions have an ammunition wagon drawn by 6 horses, which carried 24,000 rounds, they have one wagon for the officers'

> baggage & they are to have one other for the same use, they have also a cart for the surgeon and put in requisition a cart for the carriage of their large iron kettles. The commander of this battalion is Major Count Munster who has never previously served. One great defect in the composition of these corps is in the scarcity of officers, they have only 1 field officer in the battalion, and 1 captain to companies of 150 men & their complement of sergeants is only 5 per company.[22]

The 3rd Battalion of the Duke of York's or Quakenbrück Battalion consisted of 1 Field Officer, 3 Captains, 15 Subalterns, 17 Sergeants, 7 Drummers and 530 Rank and File. This battalion was far advanced in regard to its abilities, but still required to improve its ability to coordinate its movements with other units:

> This is a very fine body of men & commanded by an officer who has been taught in the Prussian school, this battalion is in a much more advanced state than any [other] in Colonel Halkett's Brigade. Great attention has been paid to correct the faults which I found in these young troops when I saw them in the Autumn, though this is one of the battalions which I had last then inspected. But they are quite ignorant of the principles of moving in any larger body than a single battalion even to the extent of not knowing the distance at which one battalion should be from another.[23]

The Bremervorde Militia Battalion, also stationed at Tournai, consisted of 1 Field Officer, 4 Captains, 13 Subalterns, 17 Sergeants, 8 Drummers and 568 Rank and File. Clinton was in this instance very pleased with its vast improvement:

> This battalion is greatly improved in its appearance in the military air & steadiness of the battalion under arms, in the state of its ammunition, manner of packing & putting on their knapsacks, the company officers are very attentive to their duty & all were able to account for every man belonging to them. I saw in this regiment a few arms out of order, the commanding officer Count Schulenburg pays great attention to his duty.[24]

Clinton remained concerned, however, with the lack of improvement in the Hanoverian Brigade with regard to its movements as a combined unit. He therefore enlisted the help of the very experienced General Hinuber, the commandant of Tournai, to drive through training at a brigade level:

> My dear General,
>
> … I found Colonel Halkett's brigade well regulated in all its

> movements, particularly the battalion of Lauenberg, considering the so called materials of which the Hanoverian army in general is composed, there is no excuse if opportunities for practise have been wanting. The officers might at least have been more acquainted before with the principles of confined movements, that it should not be quite a novelty to them to find themselves required to conform to the movement of another body. As this failing must be seriously felt in the field, I shall be very much obliged to you if while Colonel Halkett's Brigade continues under your immediate command, you would occasionally see the different battalions or parts of them representing battalions move together, let them march together in line and enter an alignment at several points in it by wheeling to the other flank. The best practise for giving an inexperienced officer is to go through all these movements without the men, imagining that they are conducting platoons of a certain strength. I wish them also to be accustomed to move in double quick time, but before they attempt to execute any movement at that rate, they must acquire the habit of marching correctly in the double quick time, that is to say to take 150 paces of 36 inches in a minute, they should be taught this first by single men, then three or four together in one party and they must be accustomed to this pace without swinging the arms, otherwise the files become loosened and the accelerated fixed pace becomes a race and confusion will ensue. I trust to your zeal for all that relates to the good of the services to excuse the trouble which I have taken the liberty of giving you.[25]

On the same day General Hinuber wrote to Henry Clinton regarding the Hanoverian Brigade which he had recently exercised. Despite their inexperience he gave his qualified approval:

> the day before yesterday when I had the whole four battalions out as strong as they could number and went through many movements with them, which were executed much beyond my expectation. As not even two battalions have been moved in brigade before, they want the instruction required for those occasions. Between you and me, after the brigadier, the commanding officers and adjutants are a little better informed, the brigade will do very well.[26]

The Hanoverian troops still lacked some very basic skills. A letter from General Hinuber explained that the Hanoverian troop regulations even lacked a manoeuvre for forming square from line:

> We have in our regulations a method laid down to form them four deep from column, but not from line; I should therefore be much

> obliged to you to inform me which you think is the best mode for forming squares four deep from line & which is the method which you follow yourself and the troops in your division.[27]

On 1 May Colonel Halkett's Brigade marched out of Tournai, where it had been relieved by four battalions of Dutch militia.[28] The Salzgitter battalion had marched from Hanover in the spring and only joined the 2nd Division just before 6 May, when Henry Clinton inspected them immediately at Houtaing. He wrote a detailed statement on their present state. It consisted of 1 Field Officer, 3 Captains, 9 Subalterns, 15 Sergeants, 6 Drummers and 499 Rank and File. Henry was not impressed:

> This battalion of militia which has just joined the 2nd Division in the room of the Lauenberg Field Battalion is that which of the original Hanoverian army arrived the latest in this country & is probably of the whole army the most backward in point of military instruction. The men are young, many even too young to bear fatigue and undersized. As a battalion they are too loosely drawn up, unsteady under arms, their accoutrements are not generally in good repair, their ammunition not sufficiently looked after, their caps ill put on, themselves ill set up & their back tin kettles improperly carried. The commanding officer Major Hammerstein seems very little acquainted with his business & like the rest of the Hanoverian army, there are too few officers. The movements of this battalion are slow, unsteady & incorrect, the difference between the Hanoverian system and that followed in the British army remains a great inconvenience in moving together. This battalion is not yet provided with light camp kettles or entrenching tools & that the soldiers left their blankets in Antwerp.[29]

He then produced a further lengthy report on all of their faults:

> **Looseness of the files**
> The first object which necessarily attracts notice is the looseness of the files, there were in general considerable intervals between each file, it is not possible to march in line or to perform an ordinary wheel without great unsteadiness until the fault shall have been corrected. The files must always touch lightly by the elbow without pushing the arm at all from the side, in line the touch is always to the centre, in column and in wheeling to the pivot and inward flank.
>
> **State of ammunition**
> The ammunition requires to be more frequently exercised than appears to be the case, a great proportion of it must be fresh packed.

Accoutrements

Several of the packs stand in need of those little repairs, which the soldiers themselves, if they were made sensible that they would always be required to keep their appointments in order could easily apply. It is an easy matter to keep things in a serviceable state, but frequently in the course of service, impossible to restore them if once through a slight degree of neglect suffered to become out of repair.

Haversacks and tins

The bread and nothing else must be carried in the haversacks, and the soldiers must be taught to carry this with their bread and their tin with their soup meat in the most commodious manner, which must be uniform through the brigade. The packs are calculated to contain the regulated quantity of necessaries, what beyond those the soldiers may have in their possession must be left with the heavy baggage of the regiment. The sending away the greatcoats and blankets will afford us opportunities of getting rid of everything beyond the necessaries.

Posture

Many of the men have a very defective posture, they must be taught to stand upright and not let their heads fall upon their neck.

Manner of putting on the caps

The appearance of this battalion is materially hurt by the movement of putting on the caps, the caps must be put on the head perfectly straight, sufficiently forward that the shade may be of use to the eyes, and not so forward as to prevent the soldiers from seeing in a horizontal line without throwing back his head.

Field movements, march in line

In its field movements the battalion requires a great deal of practise, the march in line would have been very good if the field had been properly abased at first, but the men must not be allowed to turn the head in dressing and still less during the march in line, their only guide is the touch of the elbow.

Wheeling

The wheels were loose and irregular, the soldiers do not appear to have been taught in wheeling to touch to the pivot, and look to the outward flank.

Deployment

The deployment was very slow, if the commanding officers wish to make use of a flank man to assist the company officer to dress upon the point de vue and the whole of the operation must be performed with more expedition, there should be a very short pause between the words Halt front to the filing divisions and that of march to form on the line.

Changing the front of the battalion
In changing the front of the battalion, by what is termed the echelon march of companies or divisions, the officer conducting the division must be upon the inward or advanced flank of his division, viz, that which is nearest to the new line, he must be careful whether the change of the line be to the front, or to the rear, to bring his division exactly parallel to the alignment before he enters it.

Length of time, of step
It is necessary that the same length of time of step be established, plummets therefore of the several lengths must be provided to ascertain that the ordinary quick and wheeling time are the same as those prescribed by regulation.[30]

Unfortunately, although Henry clearly rated General Hinuber's abilities very highly, Huniber was soon writing to inform Clinton that he had resigned his post. The reason for this was that he had been offered only a lesser rank, commanding a KGL Brigade, as the division he then commanded was to be given to General Charles Colville:

With regard to myself, I have resigned my Staff situation as I thought that the command which was offered to me (viz. A brigade of the Legion) was below my acceptance. I only wait for the answer to my resignation to leave Tournai. Believe me always, with great truth and regard dear general, your very faithful humble servant Hinuber.[31]

Henry also wrote to Colonel Halkett to ensure that these faults would be hastily remedied, but acknowledged that the zeal of the Hanoverians would almost certainly remedy these faults quickly. He also demanded that guards were mounted to train the troops in this vital role and that the due respect was given to their officers:

I enclose with this some remarks which I have made upon the inspection of the Salzgitter Battalion, it is of material importance that the deficiencies which they point out should as early as possible be remedied. I really think that with the good will which I have always observed in the whole of the Hanoverian troops, officers as well as soldiers, a very great degree of perfection, in all that is to be expected of soldiers unaccustomed to field duties, is easily to be obtained, and

> without the degree of perfection, no troops can be considered as fairly qualified for field duties.
>
> I understand from Count Munster the other day that his battalion did not furnish any officer's guard in the quarters, no battalion should ever be without at least one officer's guard, I request that you will direct that this may be observed generally, there should also be a guard at the entrance by the principal road, to each of the battalion's cantonments. The non-commissioned officer commanding which should have the address of the commanding officer of the battalion of the commander of the brigade, and of the major of brigade in writing, and be able to direct any person to either of these officers. One object in requiring the mounting of these guards, after those of police and the facilitating any communication with the brigades, is to accustom the soldiers to the punctual discharge of the duty of sentries, to which object I request you will direct the most pointed attention of your officers. In young troops it is necessary to notice every feeling and I have observed such infrequently amongst the Hanoverians a want of respect to officers when not on duty, they allow officers to pass their quarters without noticing them, they must be taught at all times to pay marked respect to officers of all nations. I am sensible thus all which is required cannot be expected at once, but if you make the officers and soldiers sensible thus you look for improvement in these particulars, you will by so doing have done much toward obtaining it.[32]

Clinton continued to exercise his troops daily to raise their standards:[33]

> I am working to get my division in order, the Hanoverian Brigade makes great improvements in a little time this will be a fine army and we shall want these to replace the Saxons whose services we have been very awkwardly deprived of.[34]

The Hanoverian battalions were strong in both their quality of men and actual numbers. They had also been brought up to a good standard by this constant exercising, but were clearly less experienced and manoeuvrable than the other brigades of the division.

Chapter 6

War Clouds Gather

Alongside the training of the troops for the forthcoming campaign, Henry Clinton also had to consider many other aspects of equipment and organisation to provide for his troops on campaign.

Immediately upon his appointment to the 2nd Division, Henry Clinton turned his attention to the urgent need for a commissary for the division and wrote to Mr Drummond the Commissary General, asking for one to be assigned forthwith:

> Dear Sir,
>
> As the army has been formed afresh in brigades and divisions I hope you will be able soon to attach an officer of your department to each of these brigades as well as one to have a general superintendence to be attached to the 2nd Division to the command of which I have been appointed ... I conclude Mr Hood will be required to move ... in that case, to whom am I for the moment, to look for the performance of business and duties? The first objects are to furnish conveyance for a few weakly men at the rate of one wagon per battalion, transport for our reserve ammunition, and this at the rate of 50 rounds a man would require 16 wagons without counting the Hanoverian Brigade, for which I do not know what provision is to be made or what assistance to be afforded by our commissariat. If these wagons are not covered, they must be provided with covers and painted to preserve the ammunition in wet weather. I conclude the commissary attached to the division will have authority to do all this. The next thing is to have 3 days' biscuit with the necessary transport so that as we shall have always 3 days' food in advance, we shall at any hour be ready to undertake a move of 6 days. I hope you will be able to send zealous and intelligent men to us. H. Clinton.[1]

It was not, however, until the first week of May that Commissary Tupper Carey was appointed to provide for his division:

> On the 6th [May] I arrived at Brussels, the headquarters of the Duke of Wellington, and reported myself to my chief, Commissary General Dunmore, in whose office I found an official letter appointing me to the 2nd Division of infantry, at Ath, under Sir Henry Clinton. On the 8th I started from Brussels, travelling on my own horses, and next day arrived at Ath, and immediately reported myself. The place was enlivened by our troops quartered there and in its neighbourhood, but the inhabitants were, I thought, indifferent towards us, and the general opinion entertained of them was that they preferred belonging to France than to the union which had been formed for them with Holland.[2]

The supply of victuals to his division was of the utmost concern to Henry Clinton. One day on passing through the Hanoverian troops, he was made aware that the men were not receiving their full ration and he demanded that Colonel Halkett sort it out immediately:

> In passing through the quarters of the Osnabrück Regiment this morning, some of the soldiers represented that they had not received any ration of meat yesterday & they had in consequence made demands upon the inhabitants. I request you will call upon the commissary attached to the brigade under your command to explain the reason why the whole of the brigade was not regularly rationed yesterday & that you will direct him to see that the persons who furnished rations yesterday are forthwith repaid in kind [the] men's money at the contract price. We cannot take too great pains to prevent the troops from believing they have any claims upon the inhabitants as leading to mischief of the worst kind. I trust attention is constantly paid to a practise enforced by the Duke of Wellington in Portugal & repeated by Lord Lynedoch, of causing officers frequently to visit the quarters of the men to ascertain that no cause of complaint exists. The commanders of battalions you know are required to report the daily execution of this order to the commander of the brigade. I have great reason to approve of the zeal manifested by Count Munster for the maintenance of a good understanding between his soldiers & the country people.
>
> I shall be obliged to you to desire that the Salzgitter Battalion may be formed in marching order for my inspection tomorrow morning at 11 o'clock. I hope your Major of Brigade will be able to find some fallow field in which they may move without doing much injury. H. Clinton.[3]

Clinton was also forced to continue his barrage of demands towards the beleaguered Sir Hudson Lowe, this time on the proliferation of wagons required for all of the baggage and equipment of each battalion:

> I inspected yesterday the First Brigade attached to the 2nd Division, each battalion is provided with a wagon and 6 horses for their reserve ammunition, 2 wagons (the 2nd has been lately directed to be added) with 4 horses for the officers' baggage and a cart for the surgeon's chest and medicines. They have always had too a wagon furnished by the commissary to carry their camp kettles. Besides these I believe most of the commanders of battalions have been allowed carriages. I wish to know, on how far the General Orders are intended to effect these corps. The wagons for the officers' baggage are furnished by the public, if they were to be allowed bat and forage money, they might I have no doubt in a very short time equip themselves. The eight wagon horses would go far in carrying the baggage of the officers of a battalion, the wagons would be useful to the commissary. Is the surgeon to provide a horse instead of a cart? Does the order allowing a sum of money to quartermasters for the purchase of a horse for carrying the entrenching tools apply to the Hanoverian forces[?] With regard to the camp kettles, in the course of a few days every man will be provided with a small tin kettle. Therefore there would be no inefficiency of the heavy kettles, for which transport is required, were they to be left in store, even though it should not be found practicable to supply them with the smaller kind. The commanding officers represented that in the late marches these men who are generally very young had suffered much from the additional weight of the blanket, they have both greatcoats and blankets complete.
>
> Will packs be granted to the officers of the Hanoverians in the same proportion as to the rest of the troops?[4]

There was also eventually some good news regarding the supply of equipment to the Hanoverian brigade, with all of their shortfalls being made good:

> I have the honour to inform you that a supply of every article demanded for the use of the Hanoverian troops to equip them for field service, according to a return sent to me by Lt. General Sir C. Alten, has been directed to be forwarded to Ath, and delivered over for distribution to Colonel Berger, Chief of the Staff of the Hanoverian forces ... to be borne on account against the Hanoverian government in the same manner as the other stores.[5]

With regard to equipment, the large camp kettles were returned to stores and the men continued to use their personal ones.[6] General Adam also mentions that in his brigade the blankets had been fitted up to be able to be used as tents.[7] Clinton confirms that this was also the case in the Bremervorde Battalion.[8] However, it was made clear that the Hanoverian officers were not to be provided with tents, leaving them at a severe disadvantage on campaign compared to the British officers.[9]

As previously mentioned Henry Clinton had established a chain of beacons from the French frontier:

> I rode by Bury to the Chateau de Roncour to see Colonel Arentschildt who commands the advanced troops upon this side. I desired him to have beacons prepared for conveying by signals the quickest intelligence of the advance of the enemy to Tournai & Leuze.[10]

Two days later he wrote to Sir Hudson Lowe informing him of his plan:

> I have given directions for preparing beacons for a communication of this sort as far as this place and I will request General Cooke to have eminent points fixed upon for the placing of beacons between this place and the high ground upon this side of Hal, from whence the upper part of Brussels and the steeples of St. Gudule and the town house are distinctly visible.[11]

The scope of the chain of beacons is further explained in a letter to his brother:

> I have established a communication by beacons between the frontier, between Leuze & Conde, the most dangerous part of our frontier in its present state and Tournai on one side & Ath on the other, so that I should be apprised excepting in foggy weather of any hostile move, at Ath, in a very few minutes.[12]

These beacons were, however, prone to cause false alarms:

> If this should be the case, and indeed upon your own account it is desirable that the officers in charge of the beacons should be rather better qualified than they appear to have been for the performance of their duty, the same mistake, if mistake it could be, by which the false alarm was occasioned at Tournai, happened the other night at Beaumont.[13]

Apart from marches, regular drills and eating, there was very little else for the troops to do and boredom easily set in. The routine of a regimental officer during this period of 'phoney war' was therefore far from onerous and was well described by Lieutenant John McDonald of the 23rd Fusiliers:

> I am billeted in a house, about the size of Boradale, with an uncommon nice family of father, mother & five children. I feel myself quite at home. I will give you a journal of a day, we rise every morning at five to exercise the men for the campaign, at eight come home and breakfast, after breakfast take a book from a very good little library in the house and stroll into the garden, here we romp among the groves & banks till you choose to sit and eat fruit, of which there is the greatest abundance, the same as in England, about two, lounge out, pay your visits & return at four to dress for dinner at the mess, at seven we generally ride out in the country for an hour or two, from nine to eleven always with the family, who are never alone, sometimes in one house sometimes in another. When the same wise and, important occupations you have often seen 'Ansa Rhue'[14] & which I suppose are common to all nations, takes up the whole of your mental & bodily faculties, thus I have described our every days work, don't you sympathise with what we unfortunate soldiers have to suffer for our country, but then again we have grand races every Tuesday, and seldom a day without some review of eight or ten thousand men, which varies the scene & keeps you from [boredom?].[15]

Henry Clinton wrote to his brother, talking about his division and stating his delight in two of his brigade commanders. On the other hand he declared that he was a lot less happy with the efforts of Colonel Halkett to improve the Hanoverians:

> Since I last wrote to you I have been very busily employed in striving to get my division in some order, I have two excellent men in Adam & du Plat at the head of two of my brigades, the Hanoverians are not so well commanded, by Colonel Halkett, a zealous man would have perfected them, but under him they have made no progress in the last 7 months, however as a centre brigade they will do I hope well, their being clothed in red is something ... We shall not make a very grand appearance on Thursday for I have here only Adam's & du Plat's Brigades and a brigade of artillery, indeed the Duke of Wellington will not find at any point a very formidable force assembled.[16]

On Wednesday 19 April at 04.00 hours Henry Clinton received notice that the Duke of Wellington would inspect his troops near Ath at 17.00 hours that afternoon. The Duke rode along the ranks of Colonel du Plat's and General Adam's brigades, the artillery of the 2nd Division, the 1st Light Division KGL and two troops of horse artillery. The inspection was over by about 19.00 hours. In Ath he was received by the garrison (the brigade of Colonel du Plat), being under arms, the artillery firing a salute of nineteen guns: [17]

> On 19 April was my first opportunity to see the Duke of Wellington and Lord Hill, who reviewed our brigade on the road from Ath to Mons. The stern facial expression of the Iron Duke and the kind look of Lord Hill left me with a deep impression; I would have immediately recognised both generals again under any circumstances.
>
> The division as such performed its exercises under the command of Sir Henry Clinton himself … Particular attention was given to the line formation four deep and the rapid change into squares, both from line as well as from a column, formed by two battalions and by one, also at the company level; it was even required that nine men, each form up in orderly groups that are capable of resisting cavalry charges.
>
> Apart from going through the various forms of deployment, some training was also undertaken in building little tents, with the soldiers' woollen blankets, some pegs, and two muskets, which were to house six men. But as far as I can remember, very little use was made of this kind of covering in the ensuing campaign, and only whenever the regular tents were not available, something that occurred on occasion during the first days of marching in France. [18]

The Duke of Wellington and Lord Hill were very pleased with most of the troops they inspected:

> This is the first place we have arrived at on a tour which Lord Hill is about to make round the cantonments of his corps in order to see in what state of improvement they are. The Duke of Wellington and his lordship reviewed today the 2nd Division under the orders of Sir Henry Clinton. They were all in excellent order except the artillery, which the great man found fault with. All the wigs dined together in the evening, and the Duke was exceedingly communicative.[19]

Henry Clinton also informed Colonel Sir George Wood that Captain Napier was fearful of losing his command of the artillery of the division because of the Duke's poor view of the care taken of the artillery horses:

> Captain Napier commanding the brigade of artillery attached to the 2nd Division has been informed that he is likely to be superseded in the command of his brigade. It is true that when the Duke of Wellington was at Ath to see the 2nd Division about a month ago, he did remark upon the indifferent condition of Captain Napier's horses, I inspected his brigade on the following day and many of the horses were out of condition & others not at all fit for the service, the latter have for the most part been since changed.

At the desire of Captain Napier I inspected his brigade yesterday and although there are some few horses not of the proper sort for artillery service, I had the satisfaction of observing a very material improvement in the condition of the whole. The guns are all perfectly well served & the whole of his appointments are in a state of order which marks a great deal of attention in the commanding officer, it is but justice to Captain Napier to make this report to you.[20]

It would seem that the Duke had his way, as Captain Bolton was drafted into the battery to take command at Waterloo. During dinner Henry Clinton learnt from the Duke that the idea of augmenting the KGL battalions by allowing volunteers to join from the Hanoverian brigades had been vetoed. Therefore the legion battalions would be reduced to six companies from ten and the spare KGL officers would be transferred instead to the Hanoverian battalions to bolster them:

he has not been able to effect what appeared the most advantageous manner of augmenting our disposable force, that is, by allowing a proportion of the Hanoverians to volunteer into the legion & filling their places from their depot, by which we should have had 8 battalions of 1,000 men each of excellent troops, properly officered, but he will reduce the battalions of the legion to 6 companies leaving the officers of the other 4 companies to be added to the Hanoverians & so greatly improve the quality of those battalions.[21]

The official order to reduce the KGL battalions to six companies each soon arrived:

General Orders 25 April Brussels

1. In consequence of instructions from His Royal Highness the Commander in Chief, the 1st, 2nd, 3rd, 4th, 5th and 8th line battalions, and the 1st and 2nd light battalions, King's German Legion, are forthwith to be formed into six companies of each battalion, and the rank and file are to be distributed among these companies.
2. This arrangement is, therefore, to be carried into execution without loss of time, and the transfer of the men's accounts from the companies in which they have been serving to those in which they will serve hereafter, is to be made from the 25th instant inclusive.
3. The officers and serjeants of the companies, from which the drummers and rank and file will have been transferred under this order, are to continue in the strength of the several battalions to which they belong, and are to receive their pay and other allowances as usual, but they are to be disposable for service with other corps.

4. Lists of the names are to be transmitted forthwith to Lieut. Gen. Charles Baron Alten, who will receive directions from the Commander of the Forces regarding the service on which they are to be employed.
5. The Commander of the Forces expects that the Commanding officers of the several battalions of the legion will carry this order into execution in the spirit in which it is intended to be carried into execution; and that they will take care that, among these officers and serjeants to be allotted for service out of the legion, there is not only the due proportion of the numbers, but likewise the fair proportion of the experience and ability, of each rank.

By a General Order dated 9 May the following King's German Legion officers were transferred to serve with the Hanoverian Brigade of Colonel Halkett:

Landwehr Battalion Bremervorde
Captain von der Decken 2nd Line Battalion, KGL
Lieutenant Wahrendorff 1st Light Battalion, KGL
Lieutenant Doring 2nd Light Battalion, KGL
Ensign von Suckow 7th Line Battalion, KGL
Ensign Cropp 2nd Line Battalion, KGL
Ensign Luning 2nd Line Battalion, KGL

Landwehr Battalion Osnabrück
Captain Dreves 3rd Line Battalion, KGL
Lieutenant Appuhn 3rd Line Battalion, KGL
Lieutenant von During 1st Line Battalion, KGL
Lieutenant von Weyhe 1st Line Battalion, KGL
Ensign Knop 2nd Light Battalion, KGL
Ensign Neuschafer 7th Line Battalion, KGL

Landwehr Battalion Quakenbrück
Captain Hulsemann 1st Light Battalion, KGL
Lieutenant Poten 8th Line Battalion, KGL
Lieutenant Schadtler 1st Light Battalion, KGL
Lieutenant Hurtzig 2nd Light Battalion, KGL
Ensign Friedrichs 2nd Light Battalion, KGL
Ensign Meyer 2nd Light Battalion, KGL

Landwehr Battalion Salzgitter
Captain Rudorff 1st Light Battalion, KGL
Lieutenant Hotzen 8th Line Battalion, KGL
Lieutenant von Both 1st Light Battalion, KGL
Lieutenant Winckler 5th Line Battalion, KGL

Ensign Rubenz 1st Light Battalion, KGL
Ensign von Welling 1st Light Battalion, KGL[22]

At the same time the rifle companies of each of the KGL line battalions were ordered to be grouped together as a separate battalion:

> an order was issued that the light companies [rifle companies] of an infantry brigade were to form a battalion, commanded by a staff officer or captain, on all occasions that the brigade was deployed, whether in line or in column, on the march or before the enemy. In our case, the rifle companies of 1st, 2nd, 3rd, and 4th Line Battalions were combined into a battalion, to be under the command of Captain Heise of the 4th Line Battalion, most senior of the four company commanders.[23]

It was also important that the division clearly knew what its orders were if fighting suddenly broke out. Henry Clinton received a secret memorandum, written by Lord Hill, directing the operations of the 2nd Division if attacked:

> 1. Should this country be attacked, the line of attack will be either between the Lys & Scheldt rivers or between the Scheldt & Sambre or by both these lines.
> 2. In the former case, that is of an attack between the Lys & the Scheldt, the cavalry posts of observation between Menin & Furnes are to retire upon Ostend, those between Menin & Tournai on Tournai & then to join their regiments.
> 3. The 2nd Division will assemble at its headquarters & be in readiness to move at a moment's notice.
> 4. In case the attack should be between the Scheldt & the Sambre, the 2nd Division will collect at its headquarters & fall gradually back on Enghien with Colonel Arentschildt's & the Hanoverian cavalry. Colonel Arentschildt will receive his orders from Lt. General Sir Henry Clinton.
> 5. The garrisons of Menin & Tournai will stand fast but that of Ath will retire with the 2nd Division unless the works should be sufficiently advanced to render the place tenable against a coup de main.
> 6. In case the attack should be made by both the supposed lines the 2nd Division to observe the instructions contained in the above memorandum 4–5.[24]

Halkett's Brigade had been moved out of Tournai to a position too far from the assembly post of the division at Ath and the replacement of the Lauenberg battalion by that of Salzgitter was still to be actioned:

> Colonel Halkett's Brigade marched on the 1st from Tournai and occupied, according to the instructions I had received, some villages on the road from Leuze to Rocroi, as however Ath is to be the point near to which the 2nd Division is to be collected in certain circumstances, I consider that this brigade would be too distant, I propose therefore moving it tomorrow to some villages between the roads of Lessines and Tournai, the most distant of which will not be more than a league or 4 miles from Ath. The Militia Battalion of Salzgitter has not yet joined Colonel Halkett's Brigade to which it has been annexed instead of the Lauenburg Battalion which is still with him. I have written to General Alten to request him to order the Salzgitter Battalion to join Colonel Halkett and I will then send the Lauenberg Battalion to Count Kielmansegge.[25] ... The farthest will not be more than 4 miles from Ath so that in an hour & a half the 2nd Division may be assembled.[26]

On 9 May the 2nd Division was ordered to expand its area of cantonments towards Lens, which would be vacated by Alten's troops when they marched to Soignies. This was because rumours of the approach of Napoleon's forces to the border had put everyone on alert. Charles Broke sent orders to Henry Clinton that:

> Lord Hill is to request you will occupy Lens in the morning, if Sir Charles Alten should march upon Soignies & Braine le Comte. You are still however to retain your cantonments in Ath.
>
> These movements are made by the Duke in consequence of certain information which he has received of a body of the enemy's force having been collected at Valenciennes & Maubeuge & from which he is induced to suppose an attack to be indicated.[27]

In reply to Broke, Clinton confirmed that:

> A battalion of the legion has been ordered to march towards Lens & will proceed to return according to what may have been done by Sir Charles Alten. One of the Hanoverian Battalions will in this case replace that of the German legion in Ath, the other three of Colonel Halkett's Brigade will be in Rebaix and Bouvignies The other will cross the Dender and occupy the village of Isieres and Lanquesaint.[28]

In advance of the division there was an observation outpost at Bury consisting of: '100 men of the 95th Regiment with two pieces of cannon furnished by the horse artillery at Leuze. Under the present intention I will not withdraw this post without further orders from Lord Hill'.[29]

On 26 May the 2nd Division was marched to villages within a short distance of Quevaucamps for the purpose of exercising on the pasturage common as a complete unit. This was the only ground capable of holding them all without serious injury to the farmers' crops for which they would be liable. Henry took his quarters at the Chateau of Beloeil, but the exercise merely confirmed that the division was barely capable of manoeuvring as a single unit:

> I attempted to execute some movements with the 2nd Division, the simple move of entering an alignment by wheeling up to it, though previously practised in battalions was very ill executed & the march in line, by General Adam's Brigade & that of the German Legion as bad. After exercise the troops encamped under their blankets and in the afternoon marched back to their quarters.[30]

He elaborated further on this major divisional exercise to his brother:

> Yesterday evening at six o'clock I began to manoeuvre my division generally in two lines, but finished by forming a line of 11 battalions & a detachment, as soon as the exercise was over I made the whole encamp by brigade and after dining and reposing, the troops returned to their quarters, it is to be regretted that we have not ground at hand which enable us to make frequent practices of this sort, the troops want the practise of moving in large bodies, that this could be of great service to them.[31]

On 14 May Colonel Sir Henry Dawkins joined the 2nd Division as Assistant Quartermaster General. But the Duke of Wellington wrote to Baron Alten to make it clear that the cost of providing for Hanoverian troops was out of all proportion to those from other nations. He therefore began a renegotiation of the subsidy to bring it into line with the other nations:

> Great Britain pays to Hanover, for the service of 15,000 men in this country, at the rate of nearly 40l per man per annum; whereas she is subsidising all Europe at the rate of 11l [Guineas] per man per annum. The Hanoverian troops are landwehr, half officered in proportion to their numbers, and we have lately been obliged to give them officers in the British service to do duty with their corps; the troops of all other nations are fully officered, and are troops of the line.
>
> I do not complain; I am perfectly satisfied with the Hanoverian troops, who I am convinced will do their duty; ... In fact, including their provisions, the Hanoverian troops now cost the British

> government between five and six times as much as any other troops in the world.[32]

A few days later, the Duke made it clear that the subsidy would be substantially reduced. This was to be a serious blow to the Hanoverian government, but they did not reduce their troop levels: 'I am authorised to grant to Hanover a subsidy for 26,400 men, at the rate of £11 2s per man per annum from the 25th of May.'[33]

There were, however, regular changes of cantonments for the troops as the army moved into position for the expected start of operations in July. The quarters of General Adam's Brigade were changed on 1 June as follows:

> the 71st will take up their new quarters. This brigade will then be dispersed of as follows.

52nd Regiment	Ellignies-Sainte-Anne
71st	Blicquy,
	Chapelle-a-Oie
	Bury – 1 Company
2nd Battalion 95th	Tourpes – 4 Companies
	Aubechies – 2 Companies
3rd Battalion 95th	Tourpes

> I shall have the 71st as much as possible collected on the side of the villages nearest the pasturage for part of the commune of Blicquy as tends to the high road near Leuze.[34]

It was reported that the enemy intended to attack on 15 June but these rumours were constantly appearing and this was just the latest.[35] However, something made Henry Clinton more cautious than usual that night, as he wrote to countermand the orders given to the Hanoverian Brigade which was about to march to the neighbourhood of Beloeil. He also made full preparations for war, sending his wife to Brussels and also arranging for the sick to be transported there out of the way:

> From intelligence which has reached me I wish your brigade not to move from its present quarters until further orders, but give a caution to your commanding officers to be ready to march upon the shortest notice. I have desired Mr Maling[36] to have all those of our sick who must be sent to the general hospital to be collected in Ath tomorrow, from where they will proceed on the following day to Brussels, under charge of an officer from the division and a sergeant from each brigade.[37]

Still nothing actually occurred, no orders arrived and Henry Clinton reverted to ordering minor changes to the cantonments of his troops:

> I find that the villages of Blicquy & Capelle a Oie afford as much corn for troops, as Willaupuis, Thumaide and Ramegnies, I wish you therefore to make this change in your quarters, so that you may have no part of your brigade more distant from the chaussee of Ath & Leuze than the 52nd Regiment at Ellignies-Sainte-Anne, you will however have as a picket a company at the crossroads at the barrier of Bury to be relieved as often as you shall think proper. I do not think it shows much attention to the interest of the publick [sic], to condemn as spoiled, the whole of 3 days' food, because the regiment having that quantity in possession had been exposed to a few showers of rain, none of them heavy. I believe if this was at the cost of individuals,

> with no better means [of] restoring it, than those which may be resorted to by almost every soldier of the 52nd though within present quarters, a very small portion would have been found unfit for food. … I do not think this change of quarters need at all interfere with the exercise of your brigade tomorrow, indeed the day should be favourable but at any rate I should wish the change to take place.[38]

But as the day closed on 15 June Henry Clinton made a prescient comment in his diary before retiring to bed:

> Considering the proximity of Bonaparte at the head of so large a force, it appears that our army is a good [deal] scattered. Bonaparte might either fall upon our army before it is collected, or engage the Prussians before the Duke of Wellington could march to their support.[39]

Chapter 7

War Breaks Out, 15–16 June

At dawn on 15 June Napoleon's army had begun crossing the border on its march initially towards Charleroi. The fact that the Duke remained unaware of Napoleon's attack until later that day remains evident by a mundane letter he despatched to Henry Clinton at 13.00 hours in the afternoon of the 15th, which he penned before the news of the invasion could possibly have arrived at Brussels:

> My dear Clinton,
>
> Some of the general officers would wish very much to have the divisions numbered over again and to have their old numbers, which appears to be a very natural wish; and I would be very much obliged to you if you would let me know as soon as you can if you participate in it. They would then stand thus.

Present Numbers	New Numbers	General Officer
1	1	General Cooke
2	6	Sir Henry Clinton
3	5	Charles Baron Alten
4	2	Sir Charles Colville
5	3	Sir Thomas Picton
6	4	Sir Lowry Cole

> Ever Yours Sincerely,
>
> Wellington.

The letter from the Duke suggesting a change of divisional numbers is perhaps quite famous now, but it is possibly more astounding that Henry Clinton felt able to sit down at Ath early in the morning of 16 June and reply to the Duke – and he was not amused!

I have this morning only had the honour to receive your Grace's letter of yesterday's date communicating to me the wishes of some of the generals respecting the renumbering of the divisions of this army; and desiring to know if I participated in their wishes, I thank Your Grace for the consideration which this letter evinces, and I will state my own feeling upon the subject of it. If the whole of the divisions had been formed at the same time, and commanded by those generals who had served with the army formerly under Your Grace's command, the replacing those generals as they had formerly stood, would have been a very natural arrangement, and one to which I certainly should have felt no sort of objection; circumstanced as this army is, the case appears to me very different, there is an imaginary advantage belonging to seniority, and I cannot participate in wishing for a measure, the effect of which would be to deprive the division which Your Grace has appointed me to command, of that advantage.[1]

Unbeknown to Clinton, Napoleon's threatened attack had actually commenced, but news of his advance through Charleroi had only reached Brussels around 16.00 hours on the 15th. It was much later before the Duke of Wellington was convinced that this attack was not a feint and ordered his troops to concentrate at Nivelles.[2] Only at 22.00 hours did the Duke issue his 'after' orders which included the direction to Lord Hill that: 'The 2nd and 4th divisions of infantry to move from Ath and Grammont, ... and to continue their movements upon Enghien'.[3]

It appears that Lord Hill did not attend the Duchess of Richmond's famous Ball[4] and, likewise, Henry Clinton had chosen to remain at Ath with his division. It was not until 05.30 hours on the morning of 16 June, however, that Henry Clinton was aware of events and, given the time it took despatch riders to travel, it was a couple more hours before all of his brigades had been informed:

Sir,

In consequence of instructions from headquarters I am directed by Lord Hill to request you will collect the 2nd Division immediately upon the receipt of this order at Ath and adjacent, and be in readiness to move at a moment's notice.[5]

Henry Clinton recorded in his diary that day:

This morning at ½ past 5 I received orders to collect my division near Ath & immediately afterwards, to march to Enghien. As the army had not been ordered to move into nearer quarters I concluded the Duke

> of Wellington had such good intelligence of the enemy's plans, that he felt no uneasiness from the movement of the enemy which certainly seemed to indicate the intention to attack.[6]

Also, in a letter to Lord Lynedoch, he added:

> It was not until the 16th at 9½ in the morning that I received orders to march to Enghien. My division being so quartered that they could not collect at Ath under 3 or 4 hours and as it happened, had not passed that place till 3 in the afternoon.[7]

The KGL Brigade was ordered to assemble around 08.00 hours but its composite battalions were scattered in various cantonments. The 1st Battalion was, however, quickly assembled at Ath:

> At half past eight o'clock[8] in the morning, the battalion was ordered to break camp immediately. It arrived one hour later at the designated assembly point [Ath]. General Clinton gave the orders to continue our march without waiting for this day's provisions, which were already en route.[9]

The 3rd and 4th Battalions, which had marched out on exercise, were unable to assemble at Ath until much later:

> The battalion had just returned from its exercises on this morning when it received an order to march off at once and to join the brigade[10] on the highway from Ath to Enghien, near the village of Meslin l'Eveque. We therefore left Lens at 11 o'clock, marched through the villages of Cambron[11] and Gibecq and met the brigade at the assigned destination in the afternoon, where we already found General Clinton's Division fully assembled.[12]

This is confirmed by Lieutenant Dehnel, 3rd Line KGL:

> On the morning of 16 June we were engaged near Lens in field exercises, when an orderly came galloping up and interrupted the exercises. After reading the order that had just been received, Colonel du Plat convened the officer corps and told us that the brigade would immediately march off to Enghien. Only the officers' batmen and other indispensable men would be allowed to stay behind and, under the supervision of the regimental quartermaster, collect all effects left behind in the quarters and transport them to the brigade as fast as possible. The brigade went off on its march without delay; there was none of that good hot coffee with extras, although most of us had not

Positions Prior to Invasion

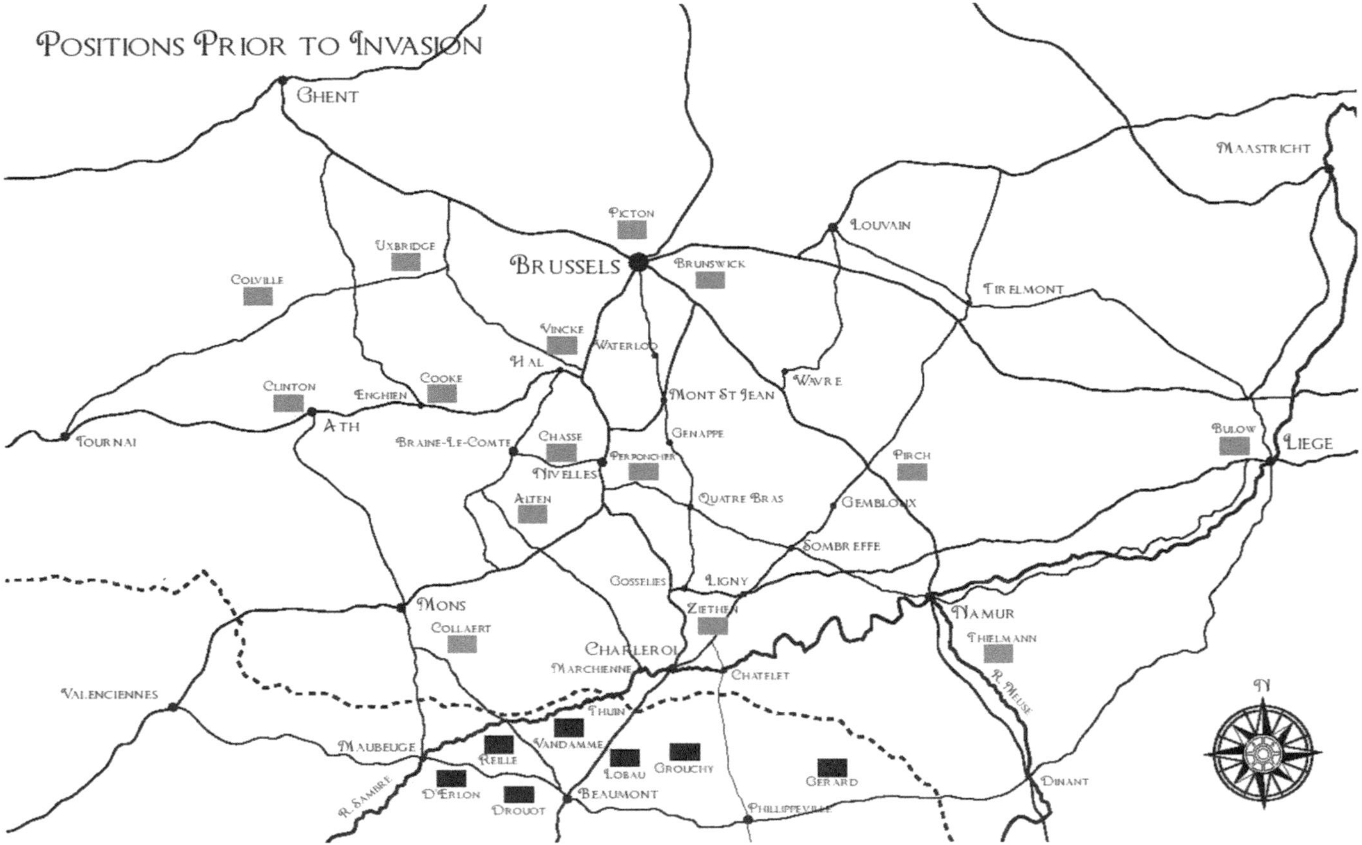

eaten anything in the expectation of a certain return to quarters. But as a precaution and according to regulations there was a small store in each haversack of bread, biscuits, and a drink, which served us very well indeed.[13]

The Hanoverians were also soon assembled:

the brigade was cantoned near Ath, and the Bremervorde Battalion in the village of Isières.[14] On 16 June at 8 o'clock in the morning, we received the order to break camp. By 10 o'clock we were already marching and, after the brigade's other battalions had joined us, we marched without interruption. [15]

A further order was despatched early on the morning of 16 June to Lord Hill from the Duke of Wellington to: 'request that you will move the 2nd division of infantry upon Braine le Comte immediately ... His Grace is going to Waterloo'.[16]

This order to continue the march on as far as Braine le Comte was received by Clinton around 14.00 hours immediately on his arrival at Enghien with the head of his troops. The British brigade, however, stood nearer the border, with 2nd/95th at Mons receiving the order to assemble much later and consequently being the very last to arrive at Ath:

on the fifteenth our regiment were on outpost duty on the French frontier near Mons and were just getting into play with some French lancers when we were ordered to retire and with the whole of the division in that part of the country to march immediately to the Duke of Wellington's headquarters, this was a distance of about fifty one miles! We started about four o'clock in the afternoon, trudged on the whole night and arrived the next evening at the place of assembly for the British and Belgian armies.[17]

It would appear that Henry Clinton could not wait for their arrival and had ordered the remainder of the division to march previously, ordering the British Brigade to follow on behind and to catch up as it could:

With 2 brigades & 2 batteries I arrived at Enghien about 2 and there found orders to march to Braine le Comte, but here we fell in with a column of cavalry moving by the same narrow road, so that the head of my column did not reach Braine le Comte till 9.[18]

The weather was warm and sunny, making the march a very uncomfortable one, requiring frequent halts to refresh the men. Here they encountered the cavalry which was also moving by this road and they were delayed by the congestion:

> we arrived at Enghien at 5 o'clock, from where our march took us over some very poor country roads to Braine le Comte. On our way, some distant rumbling could be heard for quite a while, as if from an approaching thunderstorm. But since at the time the skies were still clear and without clouds, I could not concur with the opinion of a thunderstorm coming up. In my opinion those were not weather phenomena that announced themselves; I believed it to be the thunder of battle. The further we moved in the direction assigned to us, the stronger the rumble of the thundering noise, in which one could distinguish single muffled blows of greater intensity.[19]

A further command, received whilst still on the march to Braine le Comte (presumably passed verbally as no written orders have ever emerged) instructed the division to continue its march to Nivelles. It was, however, not until 21.00 hours that the leading elements of Clinton's troops arrived at Braine and another rest was found very necessary. Here a very welcome rum ration was issued: 'Being dark General Clinton ordered us to lay down on the road side for two hours, so we halted & every man got [a] half pint [of] real rum to keep his spirits up'.[20] Not all the troops of other divisions were so lucky to gain a tot of rum and looked on jealously:

> we proceeded on our march, in about an hour we passed the 52nd Regiment who were serving their men out with one ration of spirits. We marched by them in gloomy silence cursing our quartermaster for not having provided us with the same dose. But the object was [be]fore us and with us every eye was bent forward in the direction that we supposed the enemy layed [*sic*].[21]

A couple of hours of rest was given to allow the congestion to ease and to refresh the men:

> Once past Enghien, we left the highway and then followed a country road in poor condition. Towards evening, we heard the sounds of a cannonade coming from not too far away. A rumour was also spreading that the French had attacked our advance posts, which was gaining credibility from the fact that there was a major converging of troops of all kinds on this road. These hurried on in forced marches and thus made the road nearly impassable. At 8 o'clock we halted at a small village, about half an hour from Braine le Comte, and were led to a small field of clover, where the brigade had hardly space

enough for its closely crowded columns to rest up. Here we remained until half past ten o'clock.[22]

Henry Clinton had ridden ahead to Braine le Comte and had found time to apprise his wife of what had occurred that day. The obvious rush and confusion of the march did not augur well and he advised Susan to move from Brussels further to the rear:

> My dearest Susy,
>
> It is a pity that we did not march from Ath one day sooner, all this severe fatigue might have been avoided. We did not get clear of Ath till about one o'clock, I arrived at Enghien at 3 & then received an order to march to this place, it has not been possible for my division to reach Braine le Comte & yet 1½ hours ago, I received an order to march on to Nivelles, 3 leagues further. I know not what has passed today, but it seems that the enemy has taken us rather by surprise. I advise you by all means & without going into the reason, to go tomorrow to Antwerp.[23]

At 23.00 hours the tired troops were ordered to resume the march. A night march with no moon is extremely trying and when heavy rainclouds arrived to drench the men and turn the roads into quagmires, it became a tedious and exhausting slog. The troops eventually started arriving at Nivelles around 05.00 hours and when each brigade subsequently arrived and halted in a nearby field, all but those appointed as sentries soon collapsed from exhaustion and slept heavily:

> We then broke camp and marched through Braine le Comte in extremely bad weather, with rain coming down in sheets. Not very far away from this town, we came to a large forest (Foret de Soignies[24]), where the roads were hardly passable for man or beast because of the bad weather and heavy travel of artillery and cavalry units and the many wagons that had bogged down and got stuck.[25]

The British troops finally began to arrive at Braine le Comte around midnight to find the division had marched on, but they also halted to get a short rest and to feed. Ensign Leeke of the 52nd records:

> We reached Braine-le-Comte at midnight, on the 16th, and remained there till a little after two on the morning of the 17th, in the midst of torrents of rain. It was with some difficulty I got my horse under cover. I found there were some persons in a large barn, and, on making some attempt to open the large door, was told in a strong Scotch accent 'There's no room here, we are all full here;' however, by

> kicking up a great row and on insisting on having the door opened, I at last succeeded, and found within only two men of the 71st Highlanders. The lower room of an adjacent auberge I found crowded with men of the brigade waiting for their turn to purchase something to eat; I was directed to a room upstairs, where I found some bread and cheese on the table, and two 71st officers lying their full length on two beds fast asleep. After eating some bread and cheese I took the liberty of lying down by the side of one of them, although they were perfect strangers to me, judging that, according to the laws of war, the one half of the bed fairly belonged to me.[26]

Commissary Tupper Carey had been forced to remain at Ath to ensure that the supplies would follow the division, but having ridden at speed, he soon caught up with the division on the march:

> I did not leave Ath before the middle of the day, having to make various arrangements for sending supplies after the troops. But as I rode fast and the march was a very long one, I overtook the division on the road. As it was only during the night that we reached Nivelles, we were too late to assist in the affair of Quatre Bras.[27]

Chapter 8

The Retreat, 17 June

Whilst the 2nd Division had been marching inexorably towards Nivelles on 16 June, two major battles had been fought. Having invaded Belgium on 15 June, Napoleon had driven the light Prussian forces back, whilst he had despatched Marshal Ney with the left wing of the army along the direct road to Brussels. In the early evening Ney's advance patrols discovered troops of the Netherlands army defending a major crossroads known as Quatre Bras and here he halted whilst his main force arrived so that he was ready to attack them in the morning.

Napoleon with the main army had driven the Prussian forces back on his right towards Sombreffe. He had therefore succeeded in his first objective, which was to drive the allied armies apart; now he had to defeat one of these armies emphatically whilst preventing the other from providing support.

The following morning, Napoleon found the Prussians forming up for battle along a ridge line behind the Ligny brook and heavily fortifying the villages dotted along the line of the stream.

Meanwhile Ney was urging his troops to close up so that he could attack Wellington's troops at Quatre Bras, but this took all of the morning to complete. Unbeknown to Ney, Wellington had few troops in position at the crossroads that morning and an immediate attack would have almost certainly succeeded. But by the time he finally formed his forces up and advanced, Wellington's reserves were arriving from Brussels. The battle became a slogging match with neither side giving ground without a severe contest. Initially the battle went well for the French and the cavalry attacks made through the head-high crops caused a number of British battalions to be surprised and roughly handled. However, as the afternoon wore on, further reinforcements arrived, enabling the Duke to take the initiative and drive the French back. By the end of the day the forces faced each other near where they had stood the previous morning and both sides had each suffered around 5,000 casualties. It was a drawn battle and everyone expected the contest to continue on the 17th.

Meanwhile Napoleon ferociously attacked the larger but less experienced Prussian army at Ligny. The contest here lasted all day, with the villages along the stream being turned into charnel houses as the troops fought hand-to-hand in a desperate attempt to win control of the bridges. Having forced Marshal Blücher to use all of his reserves, Napoleon sent forward his Imperial Guard, supported by the heavy cavalry. As night fell, they smashed through the exhausted Prussian defences at the village of Ligny and drove deep into the Prussian centre, effectively splitting Blücher's army in two. The Prussians were forced to retreat having lost about 12,000 men and possibly another 10,000 who deserted in the night, whereas the French lost around 6,000 men. It was a great victory for Napoleon, but there was no immediate pursuit.

Orders had been despatched by Wellington after the Battle of Quatre Bras for the rest of the army to concentrate at the crossroads, in preparation for an expected resumption of the battle the next day. The 2nd Division was ordered to move at daybreak to Quatre Bras.[1] Clinton appears to have received the order at Nivelles:

> The night was very rainy & the road heavy and bad, so that it was choked with baggage & it was not before 8 that my division could be collected there & then we received orders to march to the village called Les 4 Bras.[2]

Having collected his division at Nivelles, he immediately marched for Quatre Bras. However, having passed through Nivelles and marched for an hour or more towards the crossroads, he suddenly received new orders to halt at Nivelles.[3] The German troops confirm that the orders to return to Nivelles arrived after they were well on their way to Quatre Bras:

> In the morning at 7 o'clock, we passed through Nivelles, on the way to support the troops positioned at Quatre Bras. After [marching] two hours past this location there was a halt; upon receipt of an order, we set off on our march back.[4]

The road was encumbered by a great number of wounded, supply wagons, and civilians fleeing the fighting:

> On the far side [of Nivelles], we encountered a large number of wounded of the army, and only now did we learn with certainty that on this road, at Quatre Bras, a superior French force had yesterday attacked our advance posts. ... After we had passed through town,

> we encountered the Prince of Orange who rode on with us, and we therefore firmly believed that now we would see some fighting. After we had marched for 1 hour, we halted and rested on this road. We remained here until the afternoon when we suddenly received the order to march back to Nivelles.[5]

During the morning of the 17th, Wellington eventually learnt that the Prussians had been defeated at the Battle of Ligny and had retreated, but in good order, to Wavre. This compelled Wellington to retire with his army to a position he had picked out a year before, just south of the village of Waterloo. Here the two allied armies would again be close enough to support each other:

> As soon as the Duke of Wellington was apprised of this move [the Prussians to Wavre] he ordered the 2nd Division from Nivelles & the army at les Quatre Bras to fall back on Waterloo and all the troops arriving from the right that had not reached Nivelles, to remain at Braine le Comte till further orders.[6]

An opportunity had been taken to allow the men to cook, but the arrival of immediate orders to march meant that all had to be thrown away:

> Since the men had not had anything to eat all of yesterday nor today, General Clinton agreed to let the men cook their meat at a suitable location. The men had hardly put down their things in order to go for water, when a new order arrived to hurry towards Waterloo at the greatest speed.[7]

The division was required to cover the retreat of the mass of baggage at Nivelles and they could not march from the town until around 14.00 hours, after the last of the baggage had safely passed through the town: 'Having a good deal of baggage to protect I was not able to get out of Nivelles till near 2 o'clock, soon after which we heard that the French had entered it'.[8]

The 2nd Division was to retire from Nivelles along the highroad to Mont St Jean, where the road converged with the *chaussée* from Quatre Bras to Brussels. The men were exhausted, hungry and, to make things worse, the heavens opened:

> This day being the 17th we commenced our march pretty cheerfully considering that we had no rations since we started the previous morning. We begun to feel the wolf biting, formed hard marching and little sleeping is none so pleasant without nourishment. By the evening

> of the 17th we were greatly fatigued from the extreme inclemency of this day's weather and from marching nearly 8 French leagues since 6 o'clock in the morning in the greatest rain that ever I saw, the heavens seemed to have opened their sluices and the celestial floodgates bursted open, so showered the 17th on us. I need not mention that all we had about us was completed soaked; by the same our blankets which was on the back of our knapsacks were completely drenched.[9]

The division retired without major incident and the regiments stopped to cook and rest during the march:

> About midway between Nivelles and Hougoumont, the 52nd halted for rather more than two hours, 200 yards to the left of the road. I heard Sir John Colborne ... asking if any of the officers could lend him the cape of a boat-cloak, as he wished to lied down for a couple of hours, and try and get some sleep; I had a very large boat-cloak with a cape and hood to it, I unhooked the cape and handed them to him. He wore them over his uniform the whole of the Battle of Waterloo.[20]

During the afternoon it began to rain heavily and the men were forced to march on in sodden clothing sticking to the skin:

> We set off again at ten o'clock the next morning on the 17th June & marched 9 leagues about 4 o'clock in the afternoon & then we was in front of the enemy, but the rain fell on so hard that the oldest soldier there never saw the like in their life, I really thought that heaven and earth was coming together. There was a few shots fired on both sides that night but the guns would not go off, we was on one long high hill and the French on another facing us·.[21]

They passed large numbers of soldiers and civilians lining the sides of the road, taking a rest:

> Each side of the road was now lined with soldiers of different regiments, and with some women and drummer boys, who had fallen out from fatigue. From this time until some time after we had reached ... Hougoumont, no less than five mounted officers were sent, one after the other, to bring up stragglers belonging to the 52nd.[22]

General Hill was, however, wary of French cavalry attacks and ordered his troops to be ready to fight:

> A few hours later, General Hill met the column and gave the order to immediately attack the enemy with the bayonet should he arrive

> before us at Waterloo, and to do our utmost to drive him back. Should this not be possible, we were to retire upon Halle [sic]. Towards 4 o'clock in the afternoon, we saw a column to our right. The light companies were told off to reconnoitre; they determined that these were Nassau troops. At 5 o'clock we arrived at the position; at 6 o'clock there commenced a heavy cannonade and small arms fire, accompanied by a heavy thunderstorm which lasted until dark. At our campsite the soil was so softened by the heavy rains that it gave way under one's feet.[23]

Eventually at around 17.00 hours the division arrived at a point where the Nivelles road joined the main Genappe – Brussels road. Here they met up with the rest of the Anglo-Netherlands army and were ordered to encamp in a field near the tiny hamlet of Merbe Braine for the night:

> As we had come up to within about half an hour from the large village of Waterloo, a halt was called, and the army took up positions at this location. The French also advanced, and we heard some skirmishing going on in the evening. During the remainder of the day, there was some reconnoitring for the general, and issuing of dispositions for the troops. Very heavy rains set in, in the evening and continued through the night; the bivouac was most uncomfortable as a result, the more so since we had not had anything to eat or drink since the morning of the 16th. Things remained quiet otherwise.[24]

It is clear that Wellington was not sure at first that Napoleon was following him with the bulk of his force:

> The enemy only followed our retreat without any attempt at pursuit. The Duke of Wellington believed the enemy to have retired on his side & thinks if Blücher had remained upon his position Bonaparte would not have received the attack.[25]

The Hanoverians soon arrived as well:

> [we] marched off from there at half past one o'clock in the morning of the 17th passed Nivelles on the Brussels road to the area of Braine l'Alleud. It here set up bivouac with the other battalions of the brigade in a location circumscribed by the acute angle of the Nivelles to Brussels highway in front, the village of Braine l'Alleud to the right rear, and the village of Merbe directly in the rear. Merbe Braine was occupied by a detachment of Brunswick lancers; two battalions of line infantry and the artillery of that corps had occupied the ridge, with the village to their right. To the left of our position were some

> battalions of the King's German Legion; no troops could be seen to our right.[26]

Nevertheless, not all of the supplies on the road could be escorted by the 2nd Division and some of the supply wagons were captured by marauding French cavalry.

> I was taken prisoner on the 17 June near Nivelles with the loss of nine wagons loaded with provisions for the regiment I am attached to. I am happy to inform you that no blame is attributed to me whatever. I received a letter from the officer commanding the 1st Royals about twelve o'clock on Thursday [Friday] evening the 16th to proceed to Nivelles without loss of time, which orders I readily complied with and when within ten miles of the town I was given to understand that the British army was retiring, supposed[ly] upon Waterloo. Scarce had the British troops left Nivelles but the enemy was in the town. I found it impossible to retreat with the wagons as the advance of the enemy was [so] rapid, the commissariat lost on that day I believe lost nearly one hundred carts & wagons.[27] I am pleased to have it in my power to inform you that I made my escape the same evening and reached Brussels early in the morning and was at Waterloo before one o'clock on the 18th.[28]

A few of the division who fell behind on the march were made prisoner by the French cavalry.[29] The trying and confusing day was summed up by Ensign Barnett of the 71st Foot:

> We sat by the fire till the Assembly sounded (a fine evening) & then marched about 10 miles. The greatest confusion on the road, artillery wagons etc, they halted us in a hayfield & we began to make soup supposing we were to stay all night, but about 1 o'clock they marched us 10 miles further, by which time we heard a very heavy firing, it rained torrents, we took up a position on a hill, 52nd, 71st & [2nd & 3rd Battalions] 95th Regiments, we made straw hats & got something cooked (our baggage was sent to Brussels) we had not seen it since we left Leuze. About the dusk of the evening they (the enemy) attacked us & we were obliged to move 2 miles further, when we took up another position. By this time it was 10 o'clock, fatigued to death & too late to build huts or light fires.[30]

Chapter 9

A Night to Forget

Having arrived near Merbe Braine, the division was ordered to halt and prepare food. Few, however, had any provisions to prepare, as the store wagons were nowhere to be seen. The incessant heavy rain also made it impossible to light fires to cook by or even to warm the men a little. The few fires attempted simply smoked away, providing little warmth or comfort. There were no tents and little shelter available. Most of the men simply had to lie in the mud, covered by their blanket, and attempt to gain a few fitful moments of rest whilst trying to ignore their hunger pangs, the cold and the unpleasantness of lying in a sea of mud, whilst a veritable river ran beneath and around them. Because of the proximity of the French, sentries were posted by each battalion, as usual, to avoid surprise. All, however, remained quiet.[1]

It was a different story behind the front line, where there were scenes of chaos and abject fear. Commissary Tupper Carey went on to Waterloo to seek out supplies without much success:

> We reached Hougoumont and continued a short distance onwards, then halted on the left of the chaussee, on which we had been marching where the division remained as a support in the rear of the right of our position. From the length of march we had made, and from the bad state of some of the crossroads, the baggage, tents and provisions had not come up, so that we were without any of the little comforts they afforded. Owing to the active operations which immediately followed they only made their appearance some days after, very much diminished, a large proportion having been lost in the panics of the 17th and 18th …
>
> During the 17th the troops were arriving from all directions to take their respective places in the position, and it appeared to me, having witnessed the movements of our army in the Peninsula previous to a battle, that the concentration of our troops in this

instance was attended with confusion. Fortunately the consequences were not bad, owing to the slow advance of the enemy, which enabled us to complete during the day all the necessary arrangements for the expected fight on the following morning. During these movements we had thunder storms and heavy rain, which drenched us all. Finding my division was likely to be stationary, I left them, and went into the village of Waterloo, where the headquarters had been established, that I might, if possible, obtain supplies or at least ascertain what was to be done to get them. I found nothing but bustle and confusion in the village, which was encumbered with troops &c. I therefore determined to ride on at once to Brussels, as there only I hoped to effect my object, and at the same time to get a fresh horse, expecting to find my groom, who was on it and had orders to look out for me. It was late in the afternoon and the road was thronged with wagons loaded with supplies of bread and forage, corn, baggage, animals and other conveyances belonging to the army. I had hardly proceeded a mile when suddenly a panic seemed to have seized everyone at the cry of the enemy being at hand. It seemed ridiculous to me, who had just arrived from the front, where all was quiet, except the occasional booming of guns at long distance; but when a cry of the sort occurs among a set of men without anyone to control them, the disorder which ensues is hardly to be conceived. It gathers strength and to stem it is impossible. Never did I witness a scene of such confusion and folly. To add to its bad effects, it was raining hard, and we were in the Forest of Soignes. The servants got rid of their baggage, let it drop on the ground, then jumping on their animals, galloped off to the rear. Others dispersed in various directions in the wood. The peasantry, carrying provisions in the country wagons, cut the traces of the harness and ran away with the horses, abandoning the wagons. As the tumult progressed down the road with approaching darkness, the apprehension of danger became so general, with the followers of the army as well as with officers and detachments of troops on their way to join their regiments, that the whole went towards Brussels like a sudden rush of water increasing as it went. With other mounted officers I endeavoured to get ahead of the current (seeing the impossibility of checking it) by galloping in the forest away from the road, but we were brought up so often by enclosures and other hindrances that we were obliged to return to it, and follow the stream.[2] Thus we were obliged to creep on by degrees as the tide flowed, until two o'clock in the morning, when we at last got into Brussels. The rain was coming down in torrents the whole night, but, fortunately for myself, I had a cloak strapped on the pommel of my saddle, which helped to keep me, when on, free from

> a good portion of wet. Many there were, however, round about me who had not that advantage, being in their uniforms. One poor man in particular (a brother officer), who was next to me, was in full dress, with his gold epaulettes and white duck pantaloons, which from their brightness appeared to have been put on for the first time. Help him I could not.[3]

It is now that we can introduce another group to our study – from Colonel Hugh Mitchell's Brigade of the 4th Division. This consisted of the 3rd Battalion of the 14th Foot, 1st Battalion 23rd Fusiliers and the 51st Foot. This brigade was attached officially to Sir Charles Colville's 4th Division but Colonel Mitchell happened to be at dinner with Lord Hill at Grammont when the order to march was received. Knowing that Sir Charles Colville was based at Oudenarde and therefore could not receive the news for many hours[4] and realising that he thus could not receive orders from his superior to march until very late in the day, Colonel Mitchell appealed directly to Lord Hill for permission to march immediately. This was granted and on arrival at Nivelles the brigade was temporarily attached to the 2nd Division and as such would serve throughout the Battle of Waterloo.

> Colonel Mitchell commanded the brigade to which my father's regiment was attached at Waterloo. It may appear strange that it was the only brigade of Sir C Colville's Division actually present at the battle. The brigade was stationed in the neighbourhood of Grammont, where Lord Hill was then quartered; and when his lordship received the order to advance, Colonel Mitchell was dining with him. He solicited and obtained permission to advance forthwith, without waiting for orders in the usual way from head quarters; had he waited, he could not possibly have been present.[5]

They too suffered similarly that night, but a few were lucky enough to receive a warm welcome on their arrival, as Ensign the Honourable George Kepple 14th Foot remembered: 'Prior to taking up our position for the night, the regiment files past a large tubful of gin. Every officer and man was in turn, presented with a little tin-pot full'.[6]

Henry Leeke of the 52nd had tried to sleep but failed dismally=:

> Our servants made a bed of straw [stripped from the roof of a newly thatched cottage] on the wet ploughed field, and all four of us ... lay down and being covered with our boat-cloaks, tried to go to sleep; it was very hot and there was heavy rain, and the straw conducted the rain into the inside of my stock, so that I was soon glad to get up.[7]

The rain was incessant:

> Wearied with two days of incessant marching, I threw myself on the slope of the hill on which I had been standing. It was like lying in a mountain torrent, I nevertheless slept soundly till two in the morning, when I was awoke by my soldier servant, Bill Moles. Rising from the bivouac, I followed him into a small cottage, where fragments of chairs, tables, window-frames, and doors, were heaped into the chimney place. Around the fire made of the fuel thus supplied, were three men seated on chairs and drying their clothes. Not a word was spoken, but room was made for me.[8]

Few would forget the horrors of that night, although some were fortunate enough to get hold of a few supplies, as Henry Dehnel of the 3rd Line Battalion KGL recalled:

> Without any kind of breakfast but what our haversacks had held [when] we had marched off in the morning of the 16th, and since that time no foodstuffs had been delivered. But since then we had been moving almost all the time, and had been thoroughly soaked several times. These intermittent showers were only moderate precursors of what kind of discomfort was yet to come; because now we were struck by a truly violent storm. The rain came down in sheets so that the few camp fires could hardly be kept burning. Added to that was my empty stomach's reminder of the empty haversack. In this miserable situation the appearance of my stalwart batman Geige[9] was most agreeable: he arrived with a few full bottles in his right hand, and in his left hand and under the arm some meat and a large piece of bread. I was greatly delighted in beholding this truly revitalizing sight, and his own pleasure shone all over his face from being able to be of such great help to us.
>
> Without a moment's hesitation did we, (Sode, Rönne, and myself), intend to begin our delicious meal when I thought of our captain. This man, a truly disagreeable superior, had done almost anything to make himself unpopular, both with the men who had not forgotten the humane Captain Lueder, and with the officers; von Rönne in particular had had to put up with many a fit of his bad temper; but one readily forgets all discord in the camaraderie of a warrior's life. I then hurried over to where the captain was lying at the camp fire, touched him on his shoulder, and invited him to have a share of our delectables. He angrily turned himself over on his other side and forbade any further disturbance in his customary rough manner, with the ominous words; 'I don't want either wine or anything else; tomorrow everything will be over anyway!' Upon my repeated

encouraging words there was no response except sullen grunts, I let him lie there and thoroughly treated myself and my two dear comrades with what Geige had brought. Sode mentioned also that Captain Diedel[10] had been particularly gloomy all day. When Rönne expressed being glad that the first of the day's activities had begun, Diedel had told him, 'that he would soon have to forsake his gladness'. After having finished our meal, every one of us still had a piece of bread and some wine that was carefully stored away. Then we laid down on our wet bedding, with our feet towards the fire, and slept passably well into the new day, in spite of the pouring rain, and of the troublesome thoughts that may occupy one's mind on the eve of a battle, that was generally expected to happen, and with the occasional thunderclaps.

On the following morning, the 18th, we got up from our completely softened muddy place of rest, near which not a trace of the high undulating corn existed anymore which we had found on our arrival.[11]

Private John Smith of the 71st was a little more succinct:

betwixt the 17th and 18th was one of the dreadfullest nights of rain ever I was aware, the water running out of the shoes on my feet.[12]

The bugle call before dawn was a blessed relief for most, although moving about in saturated clothing without much prospect of drying them or obtaining any food did not enamour the men.

The Hanoverians were also woken before dawn. The Salzgitter Battalion, which had arrived with the brigade between Waterloo and Braine l'Alleud at 6 o'clock on the previous evening, and there had set up its bivouac, received the order from you, my dear colonel, to stand ready in front of the bivouac at 4 o'clock in the morning.[13]

However, as the sun rose slowly the rains finally eased, allowing fires to be lit with some prospect of receiving some warmth from them and drying clothes out:

There was a large wood behind us & Wellington told us all to get wood & make large fires and dry ourselves and get our guns fit by daylight as the enemy could not hurt us, so we made large fires & they was about 4 miles in length & when the French saw it they done the same & it was one of the [most] beautiful sights I ever saw.[14]

Standing in reserve, the division was better able to take advantage of the fires and with a blind eye turned by their senior officers. They could seek out food from unofficial sources, although some reported this as done with official sanction:

> At day break on 18th we saw nothing of the enemy, it continued (as it had done all night) to rain tremendously! Our wounded were in a desperate situation, and those who were not wounded were like so many half drowned and half starved rats. At about seven o'clock however to our great satisfaction the skirmishers were called in, and as a reward for our nocturnal labours, we had leave from General Adam who commanded our (Light) Brigade to plunder three farm houses which were near us![15] The idea of a fire was a most consoling one! Chairs, tables, sofas, cradles, churns, barrels and all manner of combustibles were soon cracking in the flames, our fellows then proceeded to the slaughter of all the living stock the yard contained, and in less that an hour we had as delicious a breakfast of beef, pork, veal, duck, chicken, potatoes and other delicacies as I ever made an attack upon.[16]

The marauding was to become widespread throughout Wellington's army owing to the complete breakdown of the commissary supply chain during the hasty marches:

> we moved forward at a considerable pace up to our knees in mud and it continued to rain with the utmost fury all the time until we arrived near another town outside of which we camped and began to pitched [sic] our blankets up to shelter us from the rain, for we had no tents up. We had marched with such rapidity as to outstrip all the baggage and stores. We had now orders to send parties of men for rations in the town that was quite convenient to us. I was one of the party, when we arrived in town all we could see was the points of bayonets and [famished?] soldiers and all busy employed in getting rations not by a regular distribution out but by marauding. It was utterly impossible to get anything for love or money, for those [famished?] soldiers had stripped the town of every kind of provisions. By much to do we got about half a ration of spirits, not one ounce of bread could be obtained in all the place, so we returned to our camp with this half ration of spirits per man. This was poor comfort after 2 days hard marching and not as much as a mouthful of anything except water. When the men got this liquor, some of them it made quite drunk, for not having anything on the stomach, you would wonder to see a man apparently strong after taking about 3 table spoonful of spirits dropping down quite drunk. ... we moved to the ground appointed for us, where we laid upon our arms that night. The rain continued with the same unabated fury during the whole of the night, towards the morning the weather got a little lighter and as the day dawned it had nearly ceased. Raising then we were ordered to light fires and clean our arms & our appointments, by this time

hunger began to be felt pretty generally. Myself and my comrade took 2 wooden [cudgels?] each and our haversacks and went to seek for something to eat; when we got about a couple of fields beneath of the camp we saw a pig and calf closely pursued by 4 or 5 German soldiers, some with knives and others with their bayonets. When we thought to become partakers of this banquet we thought that those Germans would share with their allies, but I do not know if we did not go away if they would not make us share the fate of the 2 beasts. We passed on to [a] little village when we saw a wagon of flour disposed in large casks and others of these Germans were busy filling their vessels and we pushed up among the rest and commenced storing our little haversacks. You must know that our coats must be drenched with the previous days and nights rain. In the struggle to get at the casks of flour in the scuffle I tumbled into the flour cask, the flour stuck to the wet coat [&] I was as wet if not as white as a miller. When I had filled the haversacks we were yet at a loss what to mix our dough in, on a dresser in a large farm house we saw the very thing we wanted, a fine large milk pan, we brought it with us. By this time we had succeeded very well, but our canteens were yet empty and wherever that to fill them we did not know where to get anything to put in them, water there was none in the camp, so we were nearly despairing of getting anything not only to drink but to wet the flour although there were a draw well in the yard, but it was said that the French had poisoned the water. In our way back to camp we saw a little to our left a very large gentleman's house, we immediately made for this house, we immediately commenced our search more for something to eat than for money, but to our great mortification the house had undergone a complete ransacking and plundered of every portable article and what they could not be carried away, they smashed in pieces, so that our hopes to get something to eat was blasted. It certainly was a great pity to see the damage done to this superb mansion which was of the most exquisite taste in its architecture together with its outhouses and extensive and well laid out gardens, which formed at once a little paradise on earth. Even the fine statues that decorated the front of this house were with the turrets and obelisks as well as the beautiful fountains and cascades that had been the admiration of ages were demolished by the soldiery. By looking with wonder at this great work of art we had almost forgot our necessity we were now bent upon getting, something to put in our canteens. At last we thought that there must be a cellar of wine and spirit vault belonging to this house which upon examination we found the house was well furnished with all sorts of viands & spirits. When we came to the vault door we were agreeably surprised to see the cellar filled with the choicest beverage but like everything else,

> this place had undergone the severe discipline of the German soldiers, a most disagreeable proof of which was there to be seen to bear testimony of the unguarded and gluttonous propensity of 2 German soldiers who after drinking so excessively as to render themselves totally insensible and laying themselves down and there slept while the wine and liquors out of about 40 or 50 pipes was flowing on them where it appears that after they had drunk all they could drink & no more they neglected to turn the key of the vessel. When we entered we approached the men we found them dead, without any mark of violence. This had an effect on me, up to this time I had not been fond of tippling and up to this day I have not been drunk or if I have the faculties of my understanding never for a moment left me. Be this as it may I do not think that the sight of those drowned men was the effect of my temperance, neither do I think that it was out of any religious principles, for this great vice which [is] almost universal among English soldiers & sailors. I must not run away with my story for now my comrade and myself commenced filling our canteens with wine & brandy, this done we thought a little money would not be amiss, so we went and examined all the apartments without finding anything. We then shouldered our cargo and as we were passing through the courtyard we saw the first living thing we saw about the house, this was a large hound dog who seemed to have been the faithful guardian of this noble mansion, tied up by a chair and lying on a heap of straw. We to prevent starvation to the poor animal loosed him from his chain; while I was loosening the staple which was very fast I lifted the little cot up off the ground which was sunk about a foot in the earth when to my agreeable astonishment I saw 2 leather bags full of silver in dollars, each contained about 130 pieces. Thus happily supplied with money and good provision we lost no time to proceed to our camp where we saw our remaining 4 messmates half starved. They began to open to their eyes at the sight of such a fine cargo of flour, brandy and here we commenced to mix our flour not with water but wine and brandy.

His success, however, caused him great uneasiness when he returned to his battalion:

> When we had mixed our flour we made cakes of it and laid it on the cinders and before they were scarcely browned, when the old saying was verified that hunger breaks through stone walls, for there was no less than half the regiment looking as if they would rob me of what I had so much trouble in getting. The officers seemed as anxious to partake of our casks, some of them thought it rather strange that gentlemen like them should stoop to ask a common soldier for

State of the 2nd Division of Infantry under the Command of Lt. General Sir Henry Clinton GCB Headquarters, Beloeil, 18 June 1815

		Regiments 52nd Regimant	71st Regiment	2nd Battalion 95th Regiment	3rd Battalion 95th Regiment	***Total***
Officers	Colonels					
	Lt Colonels	1	1			*2*
	Majors	1	2	2	1	*6*
	Captains	10	9	6	2	*27*
	Subalterns	41	32	20	7	*100*
	Staff	6	6	6	2	*20*
Sergeants	Present	64	61	37	11	*173*
	Present Sick	1		1		*2*
	Absent Sick	1				*1*
	Command	3	1	3	1	*8*
	Total	64	62	41	12	*184*
Trumpeters &	Present	22	21	17	6	*66*
Drummers	Present Sick					
	Absent Sick					
	Command					
	Total	22	21	17	6	*66*
Rank & File	Present	998	774	567	175	*2514*
	Present Sick	20	28	13	4	*65*
	Absent Sick	13	5			*18*
	Command	7	2	5	9	*23*
	Prisoners of War					
	Total	1038	809	585	188	*2620*
Horses	Present	82	71	43	29	*225*
	Sick					
	Command					
	Total	82	71	43	29	*225*
Alterations	Men Joined		1			*1*
	Men Dead					
	Men Deserted		2			*2*
	Men Discharged	1				*1*
	Men Given					
	Men Discharged					*2*
	Men Promoted	2				
	Men Reduced					
Horses	Joined	1				*1*

1st Line Battalion KGL	2nd Line Battalion KGL	3rd Line Battalion KGL	4th Line Battalion KGL	Detachments 6th & 7th	***Total***	Battalion Bremervorde	2nd Battalion Duke of York (Osnabrück)	3rd Battalion Duke of York (Quakenbrück)	Battalion Salzgitter	***Total***	**Strength of Division**
		1			*1*	1				*1*	**4**
2	1	2	2		*7*		1	1	1	*3*	**16**
6	7	4	5		*22*	5	4	4	4	*17*	**66**
16	17	19	19		*71*	19	18	18	16	*71*	**242**
5	5	6	6	1	*23*	4	3	4	3	*14*	**57**
26	29	34	25	2	*116*	22	28	22	26	*98*	**387**
4	4		4		*12*	2		4	2	*8*	**22**
2	1				*3*						**4**
3	2	5	4	7	*21*	5	2	4	1	*21*	**41**
35	36	39	33	9	*152*	29	30	30	29	*118*	**454**
10	11	13	8		*42*	8	8	7	8	*31*	**139**
1	2				*3*						**3**
1	1				*2*						**2**
			1		*1*						**1**
12	14	13	9		*48*	8	8	7	8	*31*	**145**
391	415	495	412	13	*1726*	589	558	511	572	*2230*	**6470**
48	49	30	15		*122*	17	22	42	28	*109*	**296**
6	18	5	2		*31*	1	8	19	3	*31*	**80**
25	15	21	33	19	*113*	13	11	7	10	*41*	**177**
5	18				*23*						**23**
455	515	551	462	32	*2015*	620	599	579	615	*2411*	**7046**
49	50	52	49	1	*201*	16	16	16	16	*64*	**490**
49	50	52	49	1	*201*	16	16	16	16	*64*	**490**
		1			*1*						**2**
	1				*1*						**1**
	3				*3*						**5**
							1		1	*2*	**3**
											2
	2	2			*4*			2		*2*	**7**

> something to eat. Others thought that the men would consider it an honour to give an officer anything he might want, but they found out that there was no use of looking on in silence or think that their presence was sufficient to terrify the soldiers out of their dear earned grogg.[17] At last they saw that if they intended to get any of the cake that they must lay aside that lofty distinction and submit to say 'comrades will you share with your officers in this time of need, and if a couple of dollars can be of service to you, here they are'. While the officers and soldiers were pressing very hard on us I was afraid that the crowd being so great and they were still increasing they would make a rush on me and deprive me of all. One of the officers offered 2 dollars for a small piece of the cakes, at this crisis I heard a rumour in among the crowd that in the case of hunger, everyone had a right to whatever was at hand. I immediately took this hint and took my cakes in my hands and at this time a circumstance occurred that saved me as well as my cakes, for it was not me having them in my hands that could save them for just as I cased them in my hands their fury was increased to such a point that they were on the point of rushing on me when the bugle sounded to arms and the colonel calling for the officers to fall the men in and march off immediately, so that was the very thing that saved my cakes. I gave one of the officers a small piece of the half toasted dough for which he gave me 2 large pieces of silver; he had not gone many yards before some of his comrade officers robbed him of the greatest part of it.[18]

Finally, the call to arms was heard, fires were rapidly doused and the battalions formed up because the French were preparing to attack:

> I was sent out with a party for wood & water, before I could find which, it was 12 o'clock.
>
> I came into the regiment & threw myself down on the ground at the first place I came to, without even a greatcoat & raining very hard, I fell asleep directly & never even woke till the Assembly blew & woke with my side in a puddle of water.
>
> I got up with my teeth chattering, but begged a smoke from a man in my company, out of an old dirty pipe, who had a little tobacco, this warmed me & made me once more fit for a march.
>
> They then took us on the memorable morning of the 18th into the hollow on the right of the whole line, close to Hougoumont.[19]

Chapter 10

Starting Positions

Wellington ordered his troops to form in line of battle along a low ridge just south of Mont St Jean farm, with his reserves placed in two further lines hidden from sight on the gently sloping ground behind the ridge. Napoleon began to organise his troops as they arrived, along a roughly parallel ridge some 1,000 metres to the south running very near a solitary tavern on the high road to Brussels named 'La Belle Alliance'. The deceptively shallow valley between these ridges would form the killing ground for this day, but as one neared the British ridge the gradient of the slope became more pronounced and required a greater effort to march up it.

The general layout of the Battle of Waterloo needs no major introduction here, but suffice to say that the allied forces (British/ Netherlands/Brunswick and Nassau) under the Duke of Wellington numbered some 63,000 men and stretched along the ridge from Hougoumont to a point just behind Papelotte on the extreme left. Three significant farm complexes – Hougoumont, La Haye Sainte and Papelotte – protected this line. Being hastily fortified and standing just in front of the ridge, they served to restrict and break up French attacks unless seized by the attackers. Napoleon stood before them with around 67,000 men blissfully unaware that Marshal Blücher's army of some 60,000 men was marching to join the battle and to attack the French right wing. But it would be many hours before this would come to fruition, radically altering the balance of power. For now, Wellington's inexperienced and heterogeneous army would need to stand alone against the most fearsome army in Europe.

Sir Henry Clinton commented favourably on Wellington's chosen position and revealed that the previous August Wellington had selected the position as one he might need at some point on the future:

> The position is a good one and had been noticed by the Duke of Wellington in the excursion he had made last August, I copied the

> remarks which he then briefly made. ... About half a mile in front of our position & to the left of the Nivelles road is a large solidly built farm with extensive buildings & around it enclosures & some open wood, called Hougoumont. It was of the first importance for us to hold this post, & in the morning of the 18th some preparations for defending it were made, such as loop holes &c. Two battalions of Brunswickers[1] were lodged in the enclosures & the building was occupied by the light companies of the Guard.[2]

Around 08.00 hours the 2nd Division formed up in columns along the road to Braine l'Alleud:

> We retired yesterday from Quatre Bras to this place without any serious loss, and took up a moderately strong position across the two high roads from Nivelles and Genappe to Brussels, about two miles from Waterloo where these roads unite. Our right flank rested on Braine l'Alleud, which was occupied by a Flemish battalion, and the ground between it and the Nivelles road was held by Mitchell's Brigade of the 4th Division. Close to the high road in front of our right was a small road and chateau called Hougoumont, which were at the foot of Mont St Jean, the height on which we were posted, and were occupied by a strong detachment from the Guards. Along the summit of Mont St Jean to the high road from Genappe was placed the greater part of our artillery supported by the infantry of the 2nd Division; the Guards, some Dutch and Belgian troops, the Brunswick Oels contingent, and the greater part of our light cavalry were in the rear of these and in reserve. The remainder of the 1st corps, supported by the heavy cavalry, extended on still farther to the left, and a little beyond the high road to Genappe; in this front and close to the road was the little farm of La Haye Sainte. Our infantry was concealed from the view of the enemy, being posted a little behind the summit of the ridge, and was formed in small squares of battalions, having only the artillery and a few small parties of cavalry visible. Our troops remained in this situation with but little variation during nearly the whole of this bloody day.[3]

The KGL Brigade formed up in battalion columns and moved up to the left of the Light Brigade, its left touching the Nivelles road in rear of the main ridge. The rifle company from each battalion of the KGL had been detached and formed into a four-company light battalion under Lieutenant Heise:[4]

> Between 6 and 7 o'clock on the morning of 18 June, the brigade advanced a short distance and took position on one of the ridges in

> front in the first line of the order of battle. The 2nd Battalion had the Brussels highway about half of a musket shot to its left; at the beginning there were no troops on the other side of the highway; to the right of the brigade stood an English brigade of Clinton's Division. After several changes in our position, the line advanced a little in the previous direction.[5]

The Hanoverian Brigade formed a reserve behind the other two brigades but still moved forward in their support:

> On the 18th, we moved closer to the just mentioned ridge. I believe we were part of the reserve of the right flank. Our brigade was posted in a line of columns. We occupied a terrain that rose gradually forward from us to a crest, on which the first line was positioned. To our rear were tilled cornfields, meadows and swampland, traversed by a country road which was bordered by a few lowly shrubs. By the way, there were one or two houses close to our rear, to which, later on, the battalion was to bring its wounded.[6]

Three companies of the British Light Brigade were deployed initially to defend Merbe Braine:

> Early on the 18th, Captain Diggle's company, No. 1 of the 52nd, was sent with two or three companies of the 95th into the inclosures of the village of Merbe Braine, facing Braine l'Alleud; they were withdrawn some time before the action commenced.[7]

In his desperation to feed his division, Commissary Tupper Carey took advantage of some Dutch wagons he had discovered full of biscuit, to supply his own troops:

> I started again for Waterloo, after having in vain inquired for my groom and second horse. I passed through the sad relics on the road of the preceding night's adventure, and arrived about eight o'clock on the ground occupied by the division, hoping that the baggage and provisions expected by roads different from that from Brussels would have made their appearance and put us at ease in regard to provisions and other comforts; but there were no tidings of them. Some meat and biscuits had been given to the men for these three days' march, 16th, 17th and 18th, but, with their usual improvidence it is very likely little remained for the last day's consumption. Spirits they had none, and they therefore fought the battle without any artificial stimulant to their courage …

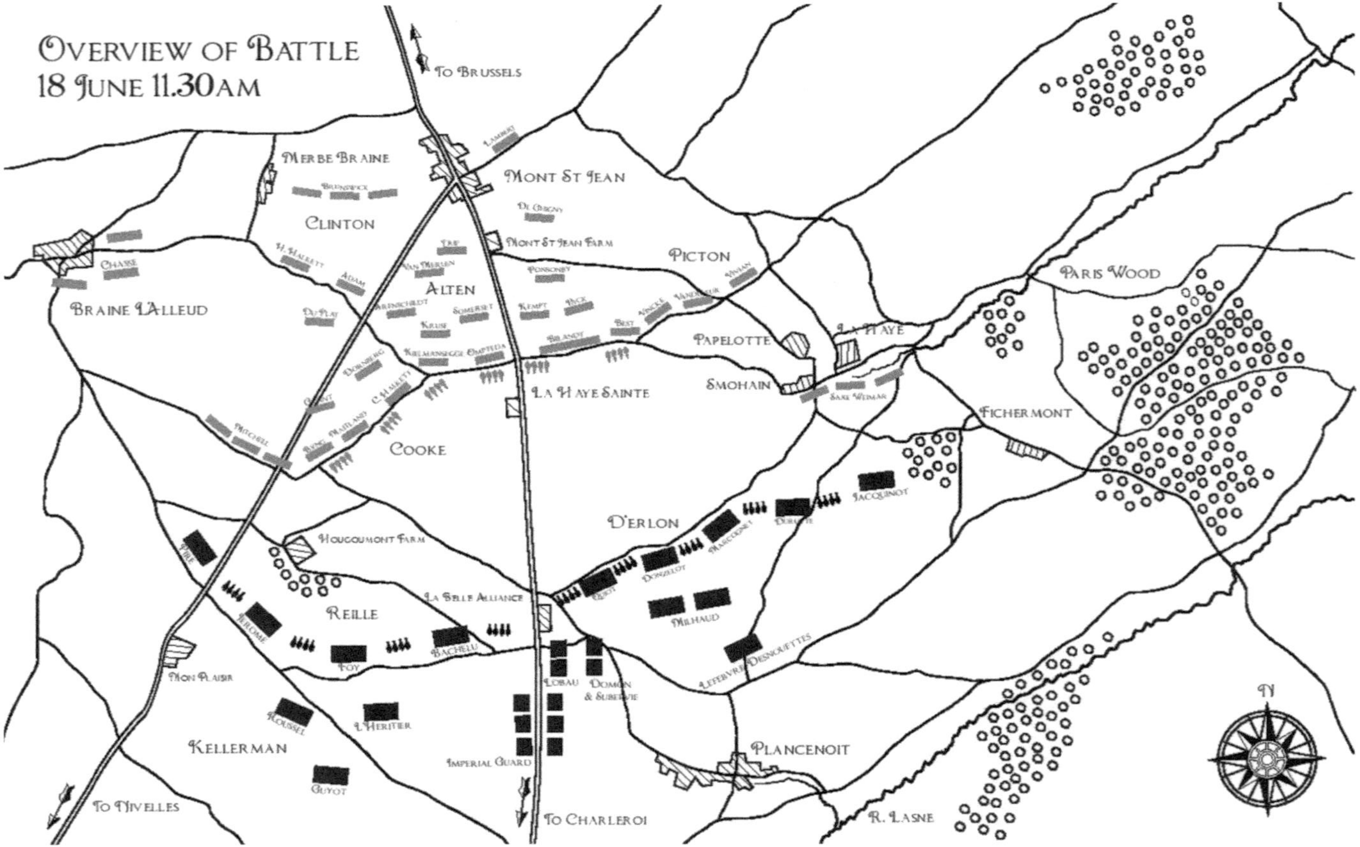
Overview of Battle
18 June 11.30am
To Brussels
Merbe Braine
Mont St Jean
Clinton
Mont St Jean Farm
Picton
Paris Wood
Braine L'Alleud
Alten
Papelotte
La Haye
La Haye Sainte
Smohain
Fichermont
Cooke
D'Erlon
Hougoumont Farm
La Belle Alliance
Reille
Milhaud
Lobau
Domon
& Subervie
Mon Plaisir
Kellerman
Imperial Guard
Plancenoit
To Nivelles
To Charleroi
R. Lasne
N
Chassé
Brunswick
H. Halkett
Adam
Du Plat
Kielmansegge
Ompteda
Kruse
Somerset
Kempt
Pack
Bijlandt
Best
Vincke
Vandeleur
Vivian
Ponsonby
De Ghigny
Lambert
Mitchell
Byng
Maitland
C. Halkett
Dörnberg
Saxe Weimar
Piré
Jérôme
Foy
Bachelu
Quiot
Donzelot
Marcognet
Durutte
Jacquinot
Lefebvre-Desnouettes
Roussel
L'Heritier
Guyot

While on the field an individual came up to me and inquired if I spoke French, and having answered in the affirmative, he told me he had in his charge, a little distance off, several wagon loads of biscuit for the Dutch troops, but as he could not find them, and as the drivers were afraid of remaining any longer where they were, and threatened to throw their loads on the side of the road and save their horses and wagons, he did not know what to do with them. I demurred for a moment as to what I should do, the temptation being great, but finding the man very urgent and knowing that no one would derive any benefit from the biscuit if left on the ground, I desired him to bring it up to the division. This was done without delay. The heads of the casks in which the article was contained were then knocked out in an instant and the contents soon found a vanishing point down the throats of those who needed it … Our troops were permitted to cook while all remained quiet, but as the onset was momentarily expected on the troops in our front, the chance of succeeding was very precarious. It so happened that those whose meat was preparing for soup had at last to throw the liquor away, for at about eleven o'clock the men were ordered to fall in and stand to their arms, and very shortly afterwards we heard the commencement of the skirmishing which was soon followed by the first attack on Hougoumont, a little before midday. The cannonade speedily became violent, but the balls did not reach us. The General,[8] seeing me still with the division, called me to him and told me that I was no longer required on the field, but requested me to endeavour to find them out when the action was over and if possible bring up supplies. I remained a little longer looking on, until the troops received orders to change ground, and I then joined other commissariat officers similarly situated as I was. We retired a short distance to the rear watching the progress of the action, but as it spread from right to left the whole position became enveloped in a dense smoke, and nothing could be perceived. We thought it therefore advisable to ride to the fork where the two chausses met leading to Brussels, to enable us more readily to learn what was passing, and, in case either of success or disaster, to be prepared to do our duty or to follow in the retreat.[9]

The biscuits were soon distributed:

My servant came to tell me some breakfast was going on amongst the officers of Captain McNair's company, the company to which I belonged. Our breakfast consisted of a biscuit each and some soup, which was in one of the servant's mess tins; I was, unintentionally on his part, done out of my drink of broth by one of the officers

> exclaiming, just as I put my lips to the tin, 'Come, Master Leeke, I think you have had your share of that.' This half-mouthful of broth and a biscuit were all I tasted that day.[10]

The soldiers now became quiet and serious, contemplating their fate and thinking of loved ones far away. It was time for commanders to remind them of their duty.

> Upon completion of this essential and most important business, Lieutenant Colonel von Wissel had the battalion form up, and with terse, simple yet heavy words, told us that we would have to face on this day some hot and heavy fighting, and urged us to perform [our duties] with courageous steadfastness and show patient endurance under the privations imposed on us by the circumstances. The battalion thanked its well respected commander with a spirited Hurrah!
>
> The Duke of Wellington and Lord Hill, as well as the Prince of Orange, rode up quite close to where we were, obviously engaged in determining the deployment of the individual troop bodies at this position chosen by the British commander-in-chief for the impending battle to cover the city of Brussels …
>
> The position of our brigade was to the west of the Nivelles highway and to the south of a road that leads from the area of the right centre of the line to Braine l'Alleud. The four rifle companies were posted on the left flank. These had been combined into a provisional battalion under the command of Captain Heise in accordance with regulations issued earlier, for that day as well as all the later concentrations of the brigade of the campaign. The brigade, by left rearward wheeling of the companies, had formed an open, right-marched-off column, with its front to the southwest. Afterwards, the arms were piled and the men were allowed to rest.
>
> The ridge on which the first line of the army was posted, about 650 to 700 paces from our location, to our regret, kept us from being able to see from our position the deployment of the French army in line, often described as unusual for a Napoleonic battle. It was later said to have been a most impressive and grand spectacle for our troops in the first line. But then we, and with us the entire second line, formed in accordance with the Duke of Wellington's instructions, were hidden from observation by the enemy. Our view to the west was more open; however, only the extreme left wing of the French army was stationed in that direction, of which a small part could be seen to the side of the advance post of Hougoumont that was occupied by our troops. Towards the east, we could view the space between the first and second line for a considerable distance.

> Shortly after the brigade had piled arms, a continuing loud shouting could be heard coming from the direction where the enemy must have been standing. The distance from where the shouts originated was too great for us to distinctly understand anything, but we could only assume that those were the Vive l'Empereur! shouts of the French army, whereby it used to salute its great and much adored leader. A period of quiet then set in, during which the commander of our division, Sir Henry Clinton, on horseback with his aides-de-camp halted some 50 paces before the centre of our brigade. His person stood out not only because of his tall figure and stiff military posture, but also by the unusual manner in which he wore his cocked hat. He always put it on sideways[11] and different from other English officers who wore their hat, ornamented with a drooping white and red feather, so that its extended tips served as peaks in front and back.[12]

As to the infantry of the 4th Brigade, they formed *en potence* to the front line, watching for any French movements to the west. Here the main danger appears to have been hordes of French lancers with artillery support, but they were of course also keeping a wary eye out for any infantry flanking manoeuvre towards Braine l'Alleud, which would turn Wellington's right.

The 51st placed three companies along a trackway as skirmishers, being supported by a squadron of the 15th Hussars: 'one squadron [15th Hussars] was detached to the right in rear of Hougoumont, having a subaltern's picket placed on the high road leading to Nivelles'.[13] The remaining companies and the 23rd and 14th Regiments continued in square formation or column for much of the day. They had little opportunity to fire in anger, but had to stand and suffer from the incessant cannonade throughout the day.

The two armies were now formed up and ready to commence battle. Private Jeremiah of the 23rd attempted to describe the scene rather melodramatically:

> Our orders was now to march to the front and occupy a position near the ever memorable Hougoumont. ... When we arrived on our destined ground a grand sight opened to our view, the whole British as well as Brunswick, Hanoverian, Dutch & Belgians were marching to occupy their respective positions, this must be one of the most cheerful and glorious sights that ever a British soldier saw, to see nearly 100,000 men moving with the regularity of a mass line, every regiment moved as steady as if on a parade in St James's Park, I shall never forget this grand sight. About 10 o'clock on Sunday the 18th day of June 1815 the whole of the allied forces under the command of

the Duke of Wellington were drawn up in order of battle in 3 lines extending something short of 2 miles, the sight was at this time truly grand and imposing, it would be folly in me to attempt to describe the glorious sight, awe brung at this moment when all was silent as the grave, not a word or whisper to be heard, all waiting for the signal from our noble commander.[14]

Chapter 11

Battle Commences

The battle commenced with each side sending out a cloud of skirmishers, and the rattle of sporadic musketry rang out across the low valley between the opposing sides. The Anglo-Netherlands infantry was ordered to lie on the ground to avoid as much as possible the heavy cannonade which was unleashed upon them by Napoleon's massed artillery:

> About this time the light infantry of all the front line were ordered to the advance and cover the front of the line, this done immediately there appeared coming over the opposite heights a line of tirailleurs or French riflemen, both lines were now descending and approaching each other from their respective hills and in the valleys between the 2 armies they met and commenced skirmishing. The French videttes were then approaching quite fast when the Marquis of Anglesey ordered our light cavalry to counteract the French videttes. This you may depend is a very handsome sight, while we were anxiously looking at those skirmishers as far as the eye could see each side. We could see coming over the opposite hill the tops of lances quivering in the air and the men and horses appeared and showed us a long line of Polish lancers supported by immense bodies of cuirassiers, horse grenadiers, light cavalry of all description. By this time our officers of the army thought that it would be a cavalry affair and that we infantry would be as mere spectators, but all was not done yet. All our cavalry were held in readiness but we were soon undeceived by seeing immense columns of infantry coming over the hills supported by a great force of artillery and cavalry. By this time the skirmishing was very hot and [the] French began to throw round shot at our columns and reinforce their skirmishers, our light infantry began to give way on all sides and the French kept pouring fresh troops into the plains. Hitherto our army were lying down on the

ground to avoid the shot & shell, the French seemed to be quite awake to the British being in square threw shot & shell into our columns so that our colonel ordered us to form line so as to reduce the chance of hitting us.[1]

The French made their first move, with an attack upon Hougoumont. This caused orders for additional cannon to be moved into position to protect this wing. Among others, Major Sympher's horse artillery troop and Bolton's Brigade were sent forward and placed on a height behind the main ridge to prevent a flank attack from around Hougoumont towards Merbe Braine. As the battle progressed the 2nd Division was ordered forward to protect these batteries:

This repast was just finished and our fellows had got themselves thoroughly dry when we were ordered to fall in and proceed as fast as possible with the 52nd and 71st Regiments (which comprised our brigade) to the front to protect three brigades of artillery which were ordered out to the edge of the hill on which the British and Belgic armies had taken up their position.[2]

The division moved into the second line, close behind a number of gun batteries which were deployed on a ridge line a few hundred yards in rear of the main ridge. It was placed there to protect the area around the chateau/farm complex of Hougoumont and the low-lying ground to the west. Hougoumont stood like a bastion protruding out from the right-hand end of Wellington's ridge. As such it had been turned into a miniature fortress, to be defended to the death, by elements of the Guards, some Brunswick sharpshooters and a battalion of Nassau infantry. If this post was lost, Wellington's line could be turned and simply rolled up. It was, however, largely hidden from the view of the French, being in a dip in the ground and shrouded by a significant wood and orchard that enclosed it on that side.

The KGL Brigade formed a line on the forward crest of this ridge to protect the front of the batteries, with the British Brigade deployed in the immediate rear of the cannon. Halkett's Brigade moved forward from Merbe Braine, but still formed the reserve of the division:

The battalion remained in this position with the brigade until about 11 o'clock at midday of the 18th. Around that time, a horse battery of the King's German Legion, commanded by the former major, now Lieutenant Colonel Sympher, had taken up position before us on the elevation on this side of the highway. It was joined on the same ridge and at some distance to the right by several guns of the Brunswick artillery. The brigade then advanced several hundred paces by

The 52nd in action, by Robbie McSweeney.

A painting of the 'crisis' of the Battle of Waterloo, at around 19.00 hours, as seen from the Anglo-Allied lines. (Anne S.K. Brown Military Collection, Brown University Library)

The Capture of a French Battery by the 52nd Regiment at Waterloo, by Ernest Crofts.

Colonel, later Field Marshal, John Colborne, 1st Baron Seaton, commanded the 52nd Regiment at Waterloo.

Major General, later General Sir Frederick Adam was in command of the British 3rd Brigade at Waterloo.

'The Capture of General Cambronne' by Richard Knotel.

Sir Charles (Carl August von) Alten, commander of the 3rd Division at Waterloo.

Lieutenant General Sir Henry Clinton, who led the 2nd Division.

General Rowland Hill, 1st Viscount Hill, the man Wellington called his 'right hand'.

Lieutenant Colonel Thomas Reynell led the 71st (Highland) Light Infantry at Waterloo.

A panoramic scene of the Battle of Waterloo, by painter and caricaturist William Heath.

General Sir William Clinton.

Sir Hudson Lowe, who became famous as the Governor of St Helena during the period of Napoleon's captivity.

Major General (later General) Sir John Ormsby Vandeleur commanded the British 4th Cavalry Brigade at Waterloo, consisting of the 11th, 12th and 16th Light Dragoons.

The memorial to Henry Clinton and his wife Susan in the Church of St Mary Magdalen, at Barkway in Hertfordshire.

This painting by William Henry Brooke, entitled 'Battle of Waterloo' carries the additional words: 'The Duke of Wellington now ordered the whole line to move forward – nothing could be more beautiful.'

> battalion columns and took up a new position to the left of the previous one, near the highway.[3]

These guns soon became a target for the French batteries to the west of Hougoumont, particularly one which had set up on the Nivelles road, and the division began to suffer casualties:

> Shortly after this the 3rd Brigade was ordered to advance … to the Nivelles road, on the edge of which it remained for some time exposed to a fire of artillery, by which a considerable number of men were disabled.[4]

The KGL Brigade suffered similarly:

> … both sides started a violent cannonade. Our division (the 2nd) was posted at the centre and more to the right flank. Although we were not going into action any time soon, we were, however, exposed to the gunfire all the time. It steadily closed in on us in the afternoon. Still, our battalion was extremely lucky, we had no significant losses, even though masses of balls and shells were flying in our direction.[5]

To reduce the effect of this fire the men were ordered to lie down again, here some actually fell asleep, while others lying close by were struck by ricocheting cannon balls and shells, never to rise again: Our brigade (General Adam's) was formed in columns of battalions in rear of our guns; here we were cruelly mauled with shot & shell.[6] Because of the undulating lay of the land, individual battalions found the fire more or less intense depending on their positioning. It was in some circumstances even allowable to duck under a cannon-ball!

> Most of our casualties at this time were occasioned by shell bursting over us, but we saw many cannon-shot ploughing up the ground near us … Serjeant Housley while standing in rear of the column, narrowly escaped having a round shot through him, by stooping just as he saw it in a line with him at some little distance; this was quite allowable when his comrades were lying down at their ease.[7]

The KGL units nearest to the Nivelles road would appear to have suffered the most:

> the enemy began the cannonade from the opposite ridge and, at the same time, had a battery of about 4 pieces cover the highway. Before the brigade, somewhat to its right and almost in front of the 2nd and 4th Line Battalions, some heavy musketry fire was developing in two

Hougoumont Farm

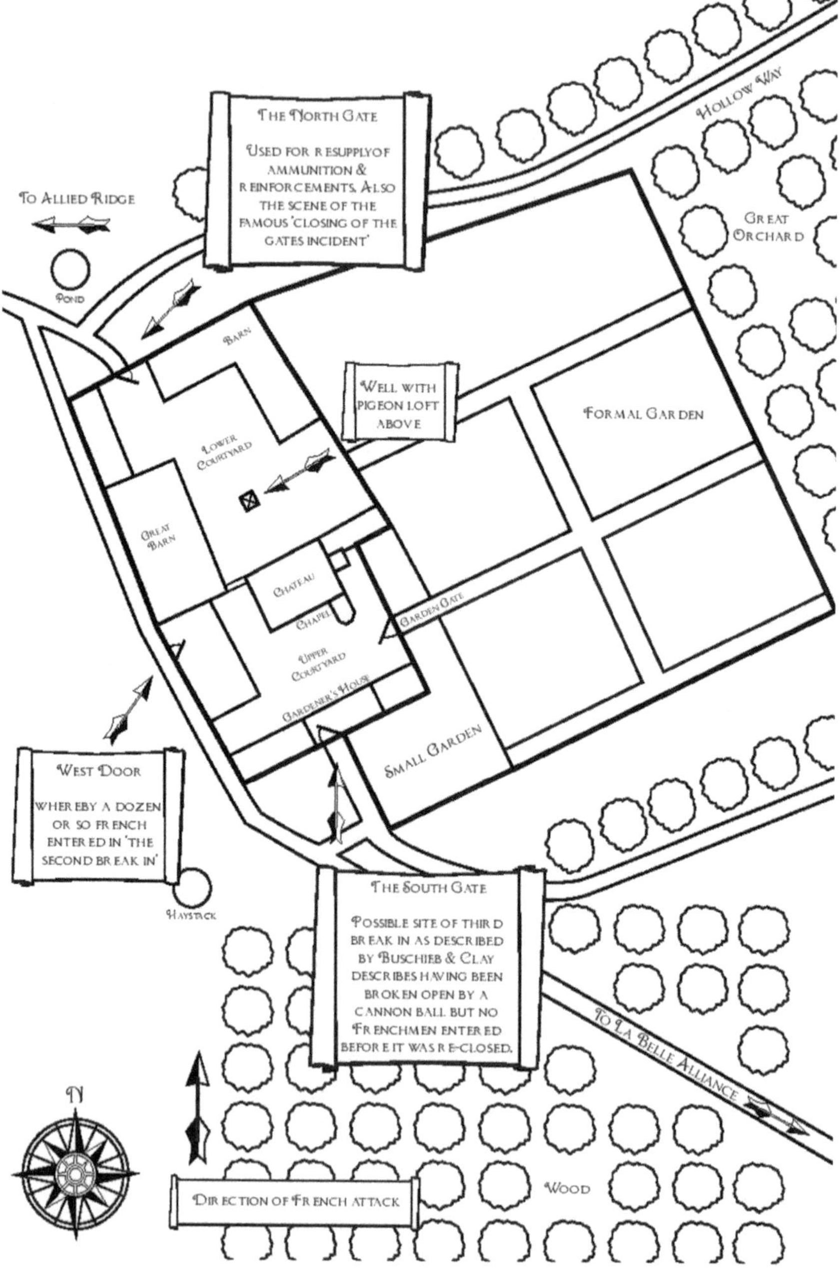

> small woods (or enclosures) in the lower terrain fronting us. The enemy's cannonade became noticeably more vigorous as more of our artillery went into action. It was primarily the left flank of Colonel du Plat's Brigade which suffered from the enemy battery drawn up on the highway.[8]

The 3rd Battalion KGL, nevertheless, did suffer similarly:

> The time might have been half past eleven when the quiet was interrupted by individual musket shots to our front at the outpost of Hougoumont which soon were followed by several cannon shots, that must have originated on the right centre of our side, judging by their sound, and then by a continuous rolling musketry and cannon fire. Very soon we had occasion to notice that the artillery fire did not only emanate from the British side, because solid shot now howled not only above and about us, and shells hissed through the intervals between the companies standing in open column order. Soon, balls and the shell splinters flying about us from exploding shells between and above us felled both officers and men. The wounded were taken to the hollow way near the rear of our position, where several surgeons put on temporary dressings.[9]

The British Light Brigade also suffered, being just behind the guns, as so graphically described by Private John Smith of the 71st:

> the grape shot, cannon shot and shell, heavy gunshot of all descriptions as thick as it could fall, I could not mention what it had the appearance of. Limbs, arms, heads was flying in all directions, nothing ever touched me in the smallest [way]. We covered the big guns first when we went into the field was halted in rear of them in close column and ordered to lay down which we did. To be engaged was a pleasure to that the shells [&] heavy shot of all kinds was pouring about us. There was a great many of us was killed, there a great deal of them fell asleep with the fatigue for all their neighbours being knocked to pieces beside them, it was a shocking thing to see it.[10]

Indeed, even the Hanoverian Brigade, positioned nearer to Merbe Braine and largely concealed in a dip in the ground, still took casualties from this heavy cannonade, more often presumably from shot that had ricocheted from the front line rather than aimed shot:

> We then immediately marched to the position adjoining the centre, where we formed the right wing. We formed in divisions at half

> distance and now received an order to let the men lie down and rest up. The position was favourably located in a slight depression but our men were within range of enemy fire right from the beginning of the battle. Unfortunately, my battalion suffered significant losses in this first position, in which the brigade remained for 3 hours until 2 o'clock in the afternoon.[11]

The 3/14th also suffered from the cannon fire:

> A bugler of the 51st, who had been out with skirmishers, and had mistaken our square for his own, exclaimed, 'Here I am again, safe enough'. The words were scarcely out of his mouth, when a round shot took off his head and spattered the whole battalion with his brains, the colours and the ensigns in charge of them coming in for an extra share. One of them, Charles Fraser, a fine gentleman in speech and manner, raised a laugh by drawling out 'How extremely disgusting!' A second shot carried off six of the men's bayonets, a third broke the breast bone of a lance Sergeant (Robinson), whose piteous cries were anything but encouraging to his youthful comrades. The soldier's belief that 'every bullet has its billet,' was strengthened by another shot striking Ensign Cooper, the shortest man in the regiment. These casualties were the affair of a second. We were now ordered to lie down.[12]

Occasionally these young troops, seeing action for the first time, required a steadying word from their commander:

> When they first went into action, my father of course watched his young soldiers with an anxious eye. At one time there was a report that some hussar regiment was driven back. 'They have driven back the —— Hussars'[13] said one young soldier to another.
>
> 'What of that?' replied his comrade; 'they must blow off the froth before they come to the porter.'[14]

Whilst the 2nd Division endured the unceasing cannonade, Napoleon turned his attention to Wellington's left. After a severe cannonade, he launched d'Erlon's corps totalling some 18,000 men against Wellington's troops just to the east of La Haye Sainte. This attack was valiantly countered by Picton's troops, but soon their commander was dead and the British line was in danger of being overrun. At this moment Lord Uxbridge led the British heavy cavalry in a mass attack that swept d'Erlon's troops back across the valley in full flight and leaving hundreds of dead and wounded and around two thousand prisoners. The British cavalry lost control and charged on at the guns beyond. Although some reached them, it was only to find themselves disordered and no match for the formed ranks of French lancers who sought to cut off their retreat. Turning to return to their own lines, many of the British cavalrymen were cut down or were wounded, meaning that the heavy cavalry was largely a spent force for the remainder of the day.

Chapter 12

Into the Cauldron

The division was left in reserve, frustrated by the continual cannonade without any ability to strike back, until approximately 16.00 hours, when it was ordered to move into the front line, indeed in advance of the existing front line. The first to move was the KGL Brigade, which marched in squares to a position immediately behind the sunken road, near the orchard of Hougoumont, in an effort to prevent this important post from falling, which to all appearances looked likely to occur. The combined battalion of rifle companies led the advance. They were to come under intense fire, as described by Lieutenant Henry Dehnel:

> It [the KGL Brigade] advanced beyond the Nivelles highway towards Hougoumont after having changed fronts in a left-marched-off column of companies, with the rifle battalion at its head. After we had marched for 300 to 400 paces and had passed a small elevation, it became necessary to close the column to ¼ distance to be able to rapidly form square in the customary four deep ranks because of the French cavalry being engaged with ours on this side of the main position. The stretch of way that we passed over was covered with the fallen; ... Our rifle battalion was ordered to move in the direction of three trees which stood some 300 paces away from the nearest hedge of the Hougoumont outpost. We had hardly arrived there and formed square when enemy cuirassiers charged us. Upon their approaching to within a few feet, our commander, Captain Heise, gave the order to fire which made them turn back with considerable loss. All the other battalions of our brigade had a similar experience; but soon afterwards we lost, apart from a good number of other officers, our brave and noble brigadier, Colonel du Plat, who had been severely wounded by an enemy bullet. Command of the brigade was taken over by Lieutenant Colonel von Wissel, who in his turn had been replaced by Major von Luttermann in the command of the 3rd Battalion.[1]

The four KGL battalions followed the light battalion into position behind Hougoumont, remaining in squares:

> We moved slightly to the left and crossed the highway from Waterloo to Nivelles. We passed over a ridge from which we could survey a plain (fields of wheat in front) and were surprised to see our cavalry overrun and pursued by French cuirassiers (who belonged to the Imperial Guard, as we learned later). At the same time, from what we could see, our infantry advanced in squares in order to support our cavalry. The squares of our brigade also quickly marched down the hillside. Our cavalry now reformed behind us. Although the French cuirassiers charged our squares, they were soon driven back by our vigorous musketry and two artillery batteries posted behind us on a ridge. During this period we suffered severely from the heavy skirmish fire of French tirailleurs who were located in a wood to our right. They could not be overcome by the light companies of our brigade, who had earlier been detached; the French certainly were several battalions strong. There were tirailleurs also in front of us who were covered by a square of French infantry slightly to our left.
>
> The cuirassiers reformed and made another attempt to break through our centre. They charged the squares of our brigade but were received with such murderous fire that they fell into disorder and took to flight. We shouted 'Hurrah!' and pursued them with levelled bayonets for some distance, which upset them so much that they never stopped. Soon thereafter, our brigadier, Colonel du Plat, was badly wounded; Lieutenant Colonel Wissell then assumed command of the brigade, and Major Luttermann that of the battalion.[2]

Here the German battalions were hidden from the French artillery by the thick woods, but they continued to suffer tremendously from skirmish fire from within the orchard. They were also constantly threatened by French cavalry, who hovered a little way off, looking for any opportunity to charge.

They were supported apparently in this advance by the 1st KGL Dragoon Regiment in pushing the French back into Hougoumont orchard. They were to lose a great number of men quite rapidly in this fighting, including their commander Colonel du Plat, who fell mortally wounded and was carried to the rear:

> The 1st and 2nd Line Battalions formed separate squares, the 3rd and 4th [3rd and 1st] Battalions were combined in a single square. After we had advanced in squares some 1,000 paces, enemy infantry (about 1,000 to 1,200 men in my opinion) appeared diagonally to our left on a wave like eminence. They were in line and 400 to 600 paces from

> us. The brigade manoeuvred its squares so that the 2nd Battalion became its right flank, and then halted. There was a brief exchange of musketry fire. Soon, however, Colonel du Plat gave the order to advance and attack the enemy with levelled bayonets, who did not expect this attack. As soon as we advanced, he retreated and took cover on our right flank in an old oak wood, which was surrounded by a fairly deep ditch and an earth mound. (I believe Colonel du Plat fell here during the advance, as I did not see him again afterwards). On our arrival on the elevation we observed a well spread out line of infantry 800 to 1,000 paces from us. In front of it stood a line of French cuirassiers, 600 to 800 men. They were attacked, I believe, by the 2nd [1st] Dragoon Regiment of the King's German Legion, but it was repulsed by the fire of the French infantry in the wood and driven back by the enemy cuirassiers as far as the rear of our squares. Since those were now held up by the fire from our squares, it was our dragoons' turn to pursue the fleeing enemy, and this was repeated 2 to 3 times.
>
> A part of the enemy's infantry, which had taken the previously mentioned oak wood [at Hougoumont], caused the brigade severe losses with his fire, as he was now on our right flank due to the advance of our line, and less than a musket shot away.[3]

But, being posted near the hedges of Hougoumont in squares, the battalions found themselves constantly plagued by skirmish fire from close range. With their own cavalrymen now clear of their firing line, the French skirmishers redoubled their destructive fire from the orchard. Casualties began to mount rapidly:

> Near the chateau at a place where the battlefield was marked by three trees we had to fight off several vigorous cavalry charges and then suffered considerable losses from a battery moved against us at a distance of about 400 paces, and also by skirmish fire from the hedge of Hougoumont.
>
> After Captain Holle of the 1st, and Captain Diedel of the 3rd Line Battalion had been killed, the commander of the rifle battalion, Captain Heise, was mortally wounded, and many men had fallen, the fourth captain, Beurmann of the 2nd Line Battalion, was struck by a ricochet on his head that rendered him unconscious for a short time.
>
> It was urgently necessary for us to extract ourselves from this critical situation.[4]

Eventually it became necessary to drive the French skirmishers off and the Light Battalion, the 2nd Battalion KGL and 3/95th were sent in to try and wrest the hedges from the French:

> In the meantime, the remnants of the [French] square had taken up position in a garden to our right and in a ditch in front of us [at Hougoumont], and were so close that their fire caused us to lose several officers and men. Their fire was mainly directed at the artillery placed in front of our squares, forcing their crews to leave their guns and to join us. The square of the 95th Regiment to our left therefore changed from square to skirmish order and drove off the enemy skirmishers. At the same time, the 2nd Line Battalion was ordered to drive the enemy out of the garden, which was then successfully done.[5]

These troops joined with the 3rd Guards who were already heavily involved in the contest for the orchard:

> We once more advanced, and resumed our station along the front hedge, from whence there was no further effort to dislodge us. But soon after Sir Henry Clinton having sent down some landwehr (with offers of further reinforcements, if necessary), I sent them with two of my own companies into the wood, where they kept up a heavy fire.[6]

Bolton's and Sympher's brigades of artillery had also moved onto the main ridge at this time, to bolster further the main artillery line. It seems that Wellington no longer feared a major attack round his right flank. Lieutenant Henry Dehnel describes the fighting in the woods:

> The various attacks of the enemy cavalry upon the squares of our brigade ended as they did earlier. Soon after these heroic horsemen had turned back towards some lower ground, pursued for a short stretch by the advancing battalions with shouts of Hurrah!, and the well-directed cannon fire of Sympher's and Bolton's brave batteries, our rifle battalion faced a most critical situation.
>
> Both the fire from an enemy battery that had moved up to our left, and the skirmish fire directed at us from the Hougoumont gardens [orchards] all of a sudden became extremely deadly. Captain Heise, our battalion commander, was mortally wounded, and killed on the very same spot were captains von Holle and Diedel, of whom the latter had been a great example for us with his brave and calm demeanour, and had now succumbed to the fate whose foreboding had caused his low spirits on the previous evening. The fourth captain of the battalion, Beuermann, received a glancing shot to his head, through which he lost consciousness for a considerable time and had to be laid down near Hougoumont a short time later. At the same time, grape shot blew down a corner of the now small square so that

from that moment on the battalion changed to more of a round formation than a square one, as the men were drawing together. Since the enemy musketry from the hedges of Hougoumont before us kept causing us losses, and remaining further in this position would completely annihilate our small group, I then, together with the fellow officers of my company von Sode and von Rönne, and with us all the other officers of the battalion, stepped before its front and led it against the nearest of our annoying enemies. The brave riflemen followed us at the double-quick, with firm determination, with an Hurrah! and levelled sword bayonets. The enemy did not wait for the clash of arms, however; they yielded and withdrew behind the next line of hedges.

Shortly thereafter, swarms of enemy tirailleurs pushed ahead past the hedges and toward the main position, but were energetically thrown back by General Adam's advanced brigade, upon the Duke of Wellington's personal instruction …

The arrival of our rifle battalion, much weakened as it was, and of the 2nd Line Battalion, provided both necessary as well as welcome and energetic assistance to the Guards fighting at Hougoumont. The attacks and advances of the French tirailleurs, until then of increasing vehemence, diminished at that moment, and there was a pause in the fighting, as sometimes happened in a battle. During that period, Corporal Brinkmann, of the rifle company now under my command after Diedel's death, made a French tirailleur officer his prisoner, who had not immediately followed his retiring men, by a quick jump over the hedge that we had occupied.

Our riflemen put up a great fight throughout; although wounded several did not go to the rear and kept on fighting. After Captain Beuermann joined us in observing the enemy tirailleurs – he had recovered from unconsciousness for some time and had taken over his command again – an English soldier approached us, whose left arm had been smashed by a cannon ball so that his lower arm seemed to hang on by just a strip of flesh or a tendon. His right arm he held in to his lower body. His bronzed face that may have seen many an enemy in all parts of the world was slightly contorted from his pain. He calmly asked us to cut off his injured arm, or have somebody do it, since it was inconveniencing him very much. To my question why he did not hold the arm with his right hand until he had had medical help, the badly wounded warrior held his hand off from his lower body for a brief moment, looking reproachfully at me, and now I saw that the hand had covered two holes from enemy bullets from which blood was flowing. Without any moaning nor repeating his wish, the unfortunate man took a few steps, then tumbled and, crying 'Oh dear Jane!' suddenly fell down and was dead …

> The impression made on me and those around me of the death of this British warrior was soon effaced when an officer galloped up with the information that the French right wing had already been attacked for some time by the Prussians …
>
> In the meantime, in our particular part of the battlefield, between the orchard hedges and the wood of Hougoumont, the Allied troops had become mixed up and interspersed due to the incessant attacks of the enemy tirailleurs and the open order of fighting, the moving up of reinforcements and the frequent alternating between advances and withdrawals.[7]

Fortunes fluctuated throughout the remainder of the battle, with neither side gaining absolute ascendancy of the orchard:

> The 2nd Battalion received an order from one of General Clinton's ADCs to take and occupy this wood, and, after the battalion had deployed from square, this was done without significant enemy resistance. That copse must have been one of the woods before us where the sound of vigorous musketry fire could be heard to come from at the beginning of the battle, because among the dead we found, apart from a number of Frenchmen (they wore blue with red), several men of the light infantry of the English Guards and some Brunswickers.[8] The other battalions of the brigade remained in squares.
>
> After about half an hour, the enemy had turned round the wood, which apparently had had its rear section unoccupied, and attacked us in our right flank with several hundred men, if my estimate is correct. This he combined with an assault in open order on our front. The wood was then abandoned. Since the other battalions had held their position, our battalion immediately reformed outside the wood, renewed its attack, and was fortunate enough to be able to take it and remain in its possession during the fighting later on. The battalion lost a number of soldiers and officers during the second attack. Captain Thiele was killed; Captain Claus von der Decken was badly wounded in his chest; Captain Purgold suffered a minor wound on his side; Captain von Wenckstern similarly on one of his ears.[9]

The Light Battalion fought tenaciously in the orchard but, with little visibility through the dense undergrowth, it was easy to be surprised:

> Lieutenant Dehnel, of the 3rd Line Battalion, took the initiative, with his sabre raised, he stepped in front of the square and shouted: 'Forward!'

With him in front were the remaining officers, Ensign Heise of the 1st, Lieutenants Dawson and Lowson of the 2nd, Lieutenant von Sode and Ensign von Rönne of the 3rd, and von Lasperg and my humble self of the 4th Line Battalion of the German Legion. We immediately advanced to the attack, followed by our brave riflemen, against the French tirailleurs behind the first of the hedges surrounding the orchard of Chateau Hougoumont, and with the bayonet drove them out and also out of a second one behind the first hedge.

Because the French received reinforcements we had to fall back to the first hedge, and then the fighting continued back and forth until we eventually retook the second hedge and held on to it. During this action I was on the extreme left flank of our skirmish line.

At the point where the second hedge adjoins in a right angle that hedge which encloses the Hougoumont orchard on its east side there was a narrow opening which led to the field between the opposing armies. I walked through this opening for a view of the lay of the land. But on stepping outside I at that very moment, faced a French officer on horseback who was riding along, and close to, the hedge.

Having hardly outgrown my boyhood at the time, I – to tell the truth – was caught unawares. Without further thought I grabbed the reins of the horse with all my might. If the strong enemy horseman had resisted, things would have turned bad for me. But I received help from the wing corporal of the company who had come through the opening directly behind me and ensured that the officer remained our captive.

After our prisoner had dismounted from his horse he gave me his well filled purse, his watch and other precious things, which I passed on to the corporal with the instruction to return half of the money to the officer. I was then thinking what to do with the captured enemy and the horse when Captain Beurmann of our rifle battalion, who just had somewhat recovered from his contusion, walked up to me and said: 'My dear little huntsman' [Schütz] – [which became] my nickname that was often jestingly used at that time by my officer comrades – 'that horse is indeed too large for you, just let me have the animal'.

My liking of the older brave officers and a heavy dose of bashfulness prompted me to say 'yes' immediately. Apart from a certain, albeit somewhat questionable and dampened victor's elation, nothing much remained to the 'little huntsman' of the extraordinary feat of capturing an enemy officer, on horseback besides, but the humble role of beholding how Captain Beurmann sent horse and prisoner back under escort and the corporal pocketed both purse and watch.[10]

Immediately after du Plat's Brigade advanced, so in turn had Adam's Light Brigade in four-deep line, an unusual formation, but one that gave greater solidity to the units in case of surprise cavalry charges:

> They kept us in rear of our artillery, doing nothing till 12 o'clock [more like 16.00 hours], several shots by this time had killed many of our men, we were then formed … & so advanced from the rear of the line, to the most advanced post, there was a wood on our right occupied by the Germans.[11]

Chapter 13

The Cavalry Charges

Adam's Brigade marched onto the forward slope to bolster the front line, not only to drive off some French infantry who were peppering the artillery with musket fire, but also to protect the allied cannon along the ridge line above them from the threatened mass cavalry attacks.

The 71st formed up with their right flank near the corner of the orchard of Hougoumont with the 3/95th in close support, the 2/95th on their left. Whilst in four deep line, the 52nd apparently formed a reserve, but on moving into squares with the approach of the French cavalry the 52nd formed in two squares of wings filling the gap between the 71st and 2/95th. General Adam explains:

> There was not space to form the 52nd in line with the 71st and 95th, and the 52nd consequently was a sort of reserve to the brigade.
>
> The enemy's infantry were very soon disposed of, and the brigade continued to advance to ... where the cavalry of the enemy, being prepared to attack, the brigade was formed in columns and then in squares. The interval between the 71st and 95th was larger than desirable, and when the cavalry were just reaching the 71st Sir John Colborne brought down the 52nd to fill up the space and [threw] in a most effective oblique fire on the cavalry, which were in the act of attacking the 71st Regiment.[1]

This seemingly suicidal position was found not to be so dangerous as the undulating ground masked them, to a great extent, from the direct fire of the French cannon. However, during the march over the ridge line and down the forward slope of the ridge they were certainly very vulnerable and suffered accordingly. Private John Lewis of the 2/95th describes the intense fire:

> My front rank man was wounded by a part of a shell through the foot & he dropt as we was advancing. I covered the next man I saw

> and had not walked twenty steps before a musket shot came sideways and took his nose clean off, & then I covered another man which was the third; just after that the man that stood next to me on my left hand had his left arm shot off by a nine pound shot just above his elbow & he turned round and caught hold of me with his right hand & the blood ran all over my trousers, we was advancing so he dropt directly. After this we was ordered to extend in front of all & our large guns was firing over our heads & the enemy's large guns & small arms was firing at the British lines in our rear & I declare to God with our guns & the French guns firing over our heads, my pen cannot explain anything like it. It was not 400 yards from the French lines to our British lines & we was about 150 yards in front of ours, so we was about 250 yards from the French & sometimes not one hundred yards so I leave you to judge if I haden [sic] a narrow escape for my life.[2]

The loss in the command structure of some units was severe. Captain Logan of the 2/95th suddenly found that he was the senior officer left standing: 'About five minutes after we went into action I succeeded to the command of the battalion in consequence from three field officers being severely wounded'.[3]

Having arrived in position, it was not long before they began to endure heavy cavalry attacks. Logan continues:

> We were now attacked in square by lancers & cuirassiers supported by 18 guns which played into our square at one hundred yards distance. We repulsed this attack but suffered cruelly, one shot knocked down nine men. We were attacked again four different times but my little battalion maintained their ground. The general finding we were so terribly exposed, sent me an order to fall back upon our guns.[4]

Many eyewitnesses mistakenly thought the cuirassiers, encased in their breast and back plates, were part of the cavalry of the Imperial Guard:

> we was extended in front, Boney's Imperial Horse Guards [cuirassiers] all clothed in armour made a charge at us, we saw them coming & we all closed in & formed a square just as they come within 10 yards of us & they found they could do no good with us, they fired with their carbines on us & come to the right about directly & at that moment the man on my right hand was shot through the body & the blood run out of his belly & back like a pig stuck in the throat, he drop

> on his side, I spoke to him, he just said 'Lewis I am done' & died directly.
>
> All this time we kept up a constant fire at the Imperial Guards [cuirassiers], they retreated but they often came to the right about & fired and as I was loading my rifle one of their shots came & struck my rifle not two inches above my left hand as I was ramming down the ball with my right hand & broke the stock & bent the barrel in such a manner that I could not get the ball down. Just at this time we extended again & my rifle was of no good to me, a nine pound shot came and cut the sergeant of our company right in two, he was not above three file from me so I threw down my rifle and went and took his rifle as it was not hurt. At this time we had lost both our colonels, major, and the two oldest captains & only a young captain to take command of us,[5] ... Seeing we had lost so many men & all our commanding officers my heart began to fail, & Boney's Guards [cuirassiers] then made another charge on us, but we made them retreat as before & while we was in square the second time the Duke of Wellington and all his Staff came up to us in the midst of all the fire & saw we had lost all our commanding officers. He himself gave the word of command, the words he said to our regiment was this, '95th unfix your swords, left face & extend yourselves once more, we shall soon have them over the other hill' & then he rode away on our right & how he escape being shot God only knows, for all this time the shots were flying like hail stones.[6]

The French cavalry, though, simply retired to reform, before attacking once again. Private John Smith of the 71st recalled:

> We went on cheering and charging them many times to the rear, the cavalry was the boldest we ever seed, charged us many times but we stood like a rock, they came close to us when they fell to the ground in fifties and sixties, horses and men tumbling in heaps that we could not get advanced over them.[7]

The KGL squares suffered similarly:

> From now on, the enemy moved his numerous cavalry into battle, and we were attacked seven times, always by fresh cavalry, cuirassiers, lancers and dragoons, but they were driven off each time and suffered losses.[8]

General Adam was conspicuous in command of his brigade, hopping from square to square between the cavalry charges. Private John Smith saw him:

> Ours is a light brigade, the 52nd, 71st, 95th commanded by one General Adams, a brave soldier as can be. When the French cavalry charged us, he always went in the centre of our regiment, gave us the greatest praise a regiment could get, he was wounded that day and a great many of our officers, several of them killed and about 300 of the men wounded and killed.[9]

During any lull in the cavalry charges, the battalions were immediately stung by further fusillades from the French skirmishers who were largely hidden in the undergrowth of the orchard. To add to the punishment the men were taking, every time the cavalry left them the cannonade resumed, particularly against the British Brigade. Ensign Leeke of the 52nd describes his experiences:

> I caught sight of the ball, which appeared to be in a direct line for me. I thought, shall I move? No! I gathered myself up, and stood firm, with the colour in my right hand, I do not exactly know the rapidity with which cannonballs fly, but I think that two seconds elapsed from the time that I saw this shot leave the gun until it struck the front face of the square. It did not strike the four men in rear of whom I was standing, but the four poor fellows on their right. It was fired at some elevation, and struck the front man about the knees, and coming to the ground under the feet of the rear man of the four, whom it most severely wounded, it rose again, passing within an inch or two of the colour pole without doing further injury.[10]

The 3/95th utilised the square of the 71st as a solid base for its own operations. As its commander Major Eeles recalled:

> During one of these charges of the enemy's cuirassiers on the right angle of the front face of the 71st square, I moved my company from the rear to the right, in line with the rear face of the square, and placing myself in front of it, kept every man from firing until the cuirassiers approached within thirty or forty yards of the square, when I fired a volley from my company which had the effect, added to the fire of the 71st, of bringing so many horses and men at the same moment to the ground, that it became quite impossible for the enemy to continue their charge. I certainly believe that half of the enemy were at the instant on the ground; some few men and horses were killed, more wounded, but by far the greater part were thrown down over the dying and wounded. These last after a short time began to get up and run back to their supports, some on horseback, but most of them dismounted.[11]

During the ensuing waves of mass French cavalry attacks the 2/95th, 71st, and the 52nd, which because of its strength was formed into two squares of each wing, and the KGL battalions, stood like breakwaters before the allied cannon on the ridge above, breaking up and dissipating the force of the masses of cavalry before they reached the ridge line. Ensign Jack Barnett of the 71st:

> It was a beautiful sight to see 10 or 12 fine regiments formed in hollow squares, the French cavalry galloping all round us, not able to penetrate.
>
> The Germans at this time gave way in the wood, consequently we were obliged to retreat in this manner, for 2 or 3 hundred yards, the Germans were again reinforced, we then advanced, 71st in line in the centre, 52nd in square on our left, 95th in square on our right, to charge, it seemed to be the last push, for the Duke was in the rear of our regiment & actually gave the word of command himself. Directly we began to advance, the cuirassiers made a desperate charge on us. Our men never fired a single shot, till they were nearly touching our bayonets, front rank kneeling, they then gave a volley. You heard a scream & saw them fall like leaves, horses with legs shot off limping about, the few who were not killed, faced about & our dragoons who were in rear of us, past by us & cut them down in all directions.[12]

This pivotal role in defeating the mass cavalry attacks has largely been overlooked by previous historians. This placement of eight squares across the front of the ridge severely inconvenienced the French cavalry attacks and significantly reduced their impact when they reached the main allied crest. This clever manoeuvre, which seriously disrupted the French cavalry attacks, was the Duke of Wellington's own idea and it worked magnificently. The serried waves of unbroken lines of French cavalry cresting the ridge in perfect formation, as depicted so magnificently at the rotunda at Waterloo, is pure fiction. The French cavalry arrived on the ridge line already disordered and half spent as an attacking force, which puts a very different appearance to this whole period of the battle. The role of the 2nd Division in this essential service has been completely forgotten and ignored, until now.

On the very right hand pivot of the line stood the square of the 23rd Fusiliers, who did not escape the onslaughts of the cavalry either. As Private Thomas Jeremiah so vividly recalled:

> At this time the French cavalry approached and galloped up to our very bayonets. One circumstance I shall ever remember, that was a French regiment of cavalry headed by a bold and intrepid officer, he rode up in front of his regiment and when within a few yards of our front

company. He exclaimed in English 'Come on you English cowards' this he said several times, this irritated our soldiers and our noble colonel was not one to put up with a language of this description and from a Frenchman who we were taught to despise as our natural enemy for many years. Our colonel seemed a little irritated by the bravado of this audacious soldier and immediately gave the word 'Fusiliers forward' this cheerful order was obeyed with alacrity, we moved in close column until we arrived at the summit of the hill from whence we could see the whole of the French army moving down in dark black masses. We were scarcely arrived in our position on the hill when the above mentioned officer came at the head of his brigade of cavalry of horse grenadiers. He made up to our very bayonets under a most tremendous fire of musketry; at the same charge they drove the 23rd Light Dragoons in some confusion on the 2nd line. The both 23rd's horse and foot were together all this day to bear witness of each other's valour. ... now the same dragoons headed by the same intrepid general came again at full charge, the French advanced with the utmost speed and corresponding fury and charged with horrible yells. They passed us after failing to break in[to] our square and was very nearly annihilating one of our regiments who were all composed of inexperienced soldiers. However, this 2nd charge was beaten off as well as the 1st and now we were to prepare for the 3rd which was not long coming. It appeared that as long as this brigade and its daring commander occupied the plains in our front that there would be no peace for us, so we were to a man anxious to lay their commander low in the dust, at this time the enemy's infantry were manoeuvring in great force in our front and we expected a serious attack on the whole of our right. An extensive line of infantry were advancing in quick time towards us when we began to form line, they gave us a volley and immediately wheeled into open columns and under cover of the smoke which their fire occasioned, they [cavalry] came at full gallop with dreadful yells and but for the maturity of our colonel and officers we should to a man [have] been cut to pieces before we could form square ... This 3rd and last charge for this desperate French fire eater for just as he had arrived in front of our square he was shot dead. I had the satisfaction to see him lie wounded on the ground within 2 yards of me, he had received 3 balls, I was one myself who fired at this hero, for a hero indeed [he] proved himself and had the whole of the French generals and bands being so determined on conquest and victory as [he] was, ... With this man's fall fell likewise the courage of his soldiers who though they charged they were less audacious from formerly, in short they only showed themselves twice more after the death of their brave commander. This brigade was relieved by a body of cuirassiers who annoyed us very much during the remainder of the day. Our light troops routed and desolation spread, as

> I said that the flank of the columns of attack reached our regiment whose iron ranks stood so firm as although they might kill us they could never rout us, at this trying moment our brave colonel told us to be steady and wait well for his word of command and which was strictly obeyed until they were within 30 or 40 paces of us when we opened a most destructive fire which staggered their advancing columns and while our brave and beloved colonel was reminding us of our former exploits on the peninsula he received his mortal wound just as he saw his commands obeyed. It required all the attention of our officers to restrain our men, for they were burning with revenge for the loss of their most beloved commander who had on so many actions led the regiment to victory and conquest in former campaigns.

It would appear that some squares nearly broke under these ferocious attacks. Private Jeremiah continues:

> The 14th Regiment was nearly annihilated by the desperate charge on our right wing,[13] however, this confusion was only momentary for they immediately rallied into a regular formation under a most murderous fire which made a considerable havoc among them but stimulated by the example of the Welch Fusiliers they resumed their position in the line from whence they were so nearly routed.[14]

The mortal wounding of Colonel Ellis had a profound effect on the regiment. As Lieutenant John McDonald states:

> We lost our gallant colonel [Ellis][15] in the action of the 18th, in him the service has lost one of its brightest ornaments and a most particular and worthy friend. We had repulsed two charges from the French cavalry and regiment being in square, when we observed a regiment of the Chasseurs of the Imperial Guard and making direct for us, our men remained steady as rocks and drove them back again with immense loss, but the poor colonel received a ball which finished his mortal career two days afterwards, he is universally regretted in the army. My Captain was also killed and the other a subaltern wounded (Mr. Griffiths) the field of action was the most horrid sight that can possibly be imagined, indeed there has been nothing more bloody in modern times. The hill we served on was attacked twelve different times during the day.[16]

The Hanoverian Brigade was also marched forward in support, but it remained just to the rear of the ridge line behind the cannon line:

> At about half past three o'clock, our cavalry posted on the left flank of the main line had been driven back, and our brigade was therefore

> forced to immediately form square. When soon thereafter our cavalry had reformed and taken up its former position, we stood again in line, the apparent danger having been averted.[17]

Here the brigade split into two wings. The Bremervorde and Quakenbrück battalions moving to the right to stand in the corner of the line behind Hougoumont, whilst the Osnabrück and Salzgitter formed squares on the ridge line to protect the cannon. This brigade operated as separate wings throughout the rest of the battle:

> At this time, the enemy seemed to have the intention to turn the left flank, and we therefore left the position we had held until now, formed into column and, with the entire brigade, made up a square in close column formation.
>
> The two battalions of the right wing (Bremervorde and Quakenbrück) were soon ordered to march off to the right, whereupon the Salzgitter and Osnabrück Battalions individually formed squares four ranks deep. Two howitzer shells fell into my square on that occasion and killed several ranks; but each time the ranks were calmly closed again.[18]

The 3rd Brunswick Light Battalion was also apparently stationed here to support the defenders of Hougoumont:

> At about 2 o'clock in the afternoon, a strong formation of enemy cuirassiers appeared some distance away and moved up from the area between Hougoumont and La Haye Sainte, whereupon the brigade formed square. The enemy cavalry retired, however, without carrying out an attack. Towards about 4 o'clock in the afternoon, the battalion advanced in column formation across the highway, with Hougoumont to its right, through the first depression formed by the terrain, and up to the opposite ridge, where it took position in the first line. (The brigade's other battalions apparently were assigned different destinations, because from then on the battalion was by itself).
>
> The Brunswick 3rd Light Battalion stood on the same plateau in square in front of the battalion at a distance of 60 paces. To the forward right, a very strong English battery had its position on the elevation; to the forward left were English infantry at a distance of several hundred paces.[19]

The 4th Brigade, temporarily attached to Clinton's Division, remained in its position protecting the right flank. The incessant cannonade continued, however, which now proved much more deadly to the men as they were forced to stand in squares to ward off any French cavalry which had successfully passed over the ridge:

> One young officer of the regiment had often been laughed at by his brother officers for his particularity as to dress and appearance; he had even been accused of effeminacy. Some of them said, 'I wonder how F___ [20] will get on in action!' He soon gave them an opportunity of deciding. On a sudden charge of the enemy's cavalry, a young bugler of the 51st, took refuge in the square of my father's regiment. The poor fellow was rejoicing in his safety, and just crying out 'I am all right now' when a cannon ball struck him on the head, and scattered his blood and brains on the colours borne by the dandy ensign, covering the face of the latter at the same time. When the smoke cleared away, the ensign's condition was discovered, his uniform being soiled, and he carefully wiping it.
>
> 'I should like' said he, very quietly 'to wash my face and hands after this!' Among the officers there was an Irish lieutenant,[21] an old Peninsular campaigner, who was coolly looking about him at the passers by far and near. ... a large body of French cuirassiers appeared in sight. It seemed doubtful which of the squares that were dotted about, they would honour with a visit. In the mean time, my father's anxiety for his 'boys' induced him to address them in the following style. ... 'Now my young tinkers' said he, 'stand firm! While you remain in your present position, old Harry himself can't touch you; but if *one* of you give way, *he* will have every mother's son of you, as sure as you are born!'
>
> After a slight pause, the cuirassiers made a sudden charge upon the regiment to the left of my father's;[22] and after several attempts to break the square, they sounded a retreat, and retired in the utmost confusion. The attacked regiment waited only till the enemy was entirely clear of the 14th, when they opened upon them with a murderous fire, while at the same moment several guns on the other side of my father's corps played upon them. For a minute or two, the smoke was so dense, that it was impossible to see a yard in advance; but when it cleared away, a scene of the greatest disorder presented itself. Numbers lay strewed about in all directions, dead, dying and wounded. Horses running here and there without their riders; and the riders, encumbered with their heavy armour, scampered away as they best could, without their horses ...
>
> Mr. Keppel was sitting on a drum, just in front of my father's mare, when she was shot; he was even stroking the poor thing's face at the time that the ball struck her down, broke the bit of the bridle, and knocked him head over heels, drum and all. The animal plunging

> in her agony, threw the square into great confusion, and her misery was speedily put an end to by the soldiers' bayonets.[23]

The brigade was now supported by the Dutch troops of Chasse's Division moving from Braine l'Alleud towards Merbe Braine:

> During the course of the continuing attacks and defensive manoeuvres, Wellington decided to reinforce his front line, which had been greatly weakened by the considerable losses it had suffered, by advancing the 2nd Division under Sir Henry Clinton, together with Sympher's and Bolton's batteries, and by replacing them with General Chassé's Netherlands Division, which until then had been posted near Braine l'Alleud. The time might have been about 5 o'clock when du Plat's [1st KGL] Brigade left its position, where we had rested for five long hours under a cross fire of artillery, as it were, but with remarkably low losses.[24]

However, the appearance of the Dutch in their dark blue uniforms initially caused some consternation in the British ranks. As Lieutenant Colonel Tidy recalled:

> At some distance on the extreme right, he espied a body of Belgian troops; their strange uniform leading him to suppose they were French, he exclaimed 'Och, murder thin! Thim's French safe enough!'[25]

Captain Mercer of the horse artillery also describes how they were initially mistaken for Frenchmen, but were happily identified correctly before they were actually fired upon:

> We saw two dense columns of infantry pushing forward at a quick pace towards us, crossing the fields, as if they had come from Merke Braine. Everyone both of the 14th and ourselves, pronounced them French, yet still we delayed opening fire on them. Shouting, yelling, and singing, on they came, right for us; … luckily, Colonel Gould recognised them as Belgians.[26]

One cavalry attack swept through the chequer board of squares and then tried to return to its own lines via the road to Nivelles, only to discover too late that the road where it ran through a cutting was blocked by an abatis made of farm implements and any other materials found close at hand. The French cuirassiers were trapped and the soldiers of the 51st Foot lining the banks of the cutting fired down upon them. Captain Digby Mackworth an aide-de-camp to Lord Hill, recalled the scene:

> The French cavalry frequently charged in masses under cover of a tremendous fire from 240 pieces of artillery. Four times were our guns in possession of their cavalry, and as often did the bayonets of our infantry rescue them. For upwards of an hour our little squares were surrounded by the elite of the French cavaliers; there they gallantly stood within 40 paces of us, unable to leap over the bristling line of bayonets, unwilling to retire, and determined never to surrender: hundreds of them were dropping in all directions from our murderous fire, yet as fast as they dropped others came up to supply their place; finding at last that it was in vain to attempt to break our determined ranks, they swept round our rear and, rushing into the Nivelles road, attempted to cut their way back to their own lines. But the whole road was lined with our infantry on both sides, and at the advanced part of it was an almost impassable barricade of felled trees. Here fell the remainder of these brave cuirassiers, of whom not one was taken without a wound.[27]

Others claim that every man was killed in this massacre, but the following version of events by Captain Horace Churchill seems more probable:

> They rode through us, passed our artillery, galloped through our intervals of infantry, went through some of our cavalry & then attempted to form in our rear. Nothing could ever be seen equal to the conduct of their troops. The whole of this first attack was made by cuirassiers, a most extraordinary circumstance happened now. Our artillery … after having been rode over & passed by the French cavalry, rose up to their guns, turned them & actually fired at the enemy when in our lines. Our artillery performed wonders of steadiness, notwithstanding this, our squares of infantry remained entrenched. Our artillery was re-manned & again began the tremendous cannonade.
>
> A second body of the enemy's cavalry then repeated the bold attack & did exactly the same. … The day seemed to turn on a straw, Lord Hill then (unusual) favoured one division of his corps[28], before in reserve. The enemy could make no impression; their cavalry charged our squares with greatest determination, they could not trick them. Our cavalry rode round but did not charge the enemy. There was one general row, the enemy were beat back, or rather retired in very good order to his position. We now thought it all over, it was about 4 o'clock. The enemy had made great efforts but our troops foiled him everywhere. We would not follow him, he had retired rather than been beat back.[29]

Eventually the French cavalry were worn down, their horses exhausted and their attacks progressively ceased to be as menacing until eventually they were forced to retire to their own lines, a spent force.

With the cavalry finally gone, the French infantry redoubled its efforts, particularly at Hougoumont, the defence of which appeared very close to collapse once again. The division, minus those already caught up in the fighting in Hougoumont orchard, was therefore pulled back to more protected positions, behind the main ridge. When initially ordered by an aide-de-camp to retire, Colonel Colborne replied that if the Duke had ordered the move because he believed that they were suffering from the artillery fire, then he might be informed that as they stood in a little dip in the valley, they were not presently in any danger where they were. However, because of the swarm of French skirmishers seen approaching, it seemed that the orchard of Hougoumont would soon be lost to the enemy. Consequently, Colborne quickly reconsidered his position and ordered his regiment to move into a more protected position, behind the allied crest line. The British Light Brigade retired in a four-deep line[30] behind the ridge and formed up to the right of Maitland's Guards Brigade and the few of Byng's Guards Brigade which had not been sent to bolster the defence of Hougoumont:

> Colonel Hervey, one of the Duke of Wellington's aides-de-camp, brought an order from the Duke for the 52nd to retire up the hill. I mentioned to him that if the Duke had ordered us to retire with reference to our exposed position, that we were protected by the ground in front. 'Very well' he replied, 'I will mention this.'
>
> However, soon after I had received this order I heard a great noise and clamour in the direction of Hougoumont, and observed the Nassau regiments, I believe, running in disorder out of the wood; and supposing that Hougoumont would be abandoned and our flank would be exposed, I formed columns from squares, and wheeled into two lines, and this formation being completed, we faced about and retired in two lines through the Belgian guns under the command of Colonel Gould.[31]

The heavily depleted KGL battalions retired slightly towards the 23rd Fusiliers, away from the nipping fire from Hougoumont, although the Light and 2nd Battalions continued the contest for the orchard. The Salzgitter and Osnabrück Battalions were also moved onto the ridge top to further bolster the defence in this area, as Major Dreves recorded:

> The battalion remained here until the French Guard attacked later on. Although protected by a ridge in front, it suffered considerably from the enemy artillery fire. To the left one could see English infantry advancing, although its further moves could not be observed from the battalion's position.

> At about half past 6 [8] o'clock, the battalion moved up to the crest of the ridge and was assigned a position to the right of the battery mentioned earlier.[32] To the left of the battery were battalions of the brigade of the English Colonel Adams; no troops could be observed to the right of the battalion.[33]

The 23rd Fusiliers formed an extension to the right of the British Light Brigade along the ridge line, forming the corner of the line. The 14th and 51st retained their previous positions behind them overlooking the Nivelles road.

> After the cavalry attacks had been disposed of, and subsequently when the enemy's infantry were again about attacking Hougoumont, the right of the brigade was judged to be too near the enclosures of that place, and had it remained, would have been exposed to being taken in flank from thence. It was therefore, at the suggestion of Sir J. Colborne, retired, and again brought a little further back in order to be screened from the fire of the enemy's artillery by the fall of the slope.[34]

Having reformed and substantially strengthened this sector, the troops lay on the ground whilst retaining their formations, both to protect them from the incessant cannonade and to gain some well-needed respite.

> On our arriving near the cross road on the summit of the hill, near the Belgian guns, I halted the 52nd. Many of our wounded were lying a few paces in our front. My anxious attention had been attracted to the dense columns moving on the Genappe road towards the centre of our position, and observing their rapid advance I ordered our left hand company to wheel to the left, and formed the remaining companies on that company.[35]

Whilst retiring, they became a target for the French guns, and the 52nd temporarily lost one of its colours. Ensign Leeke describes the chaos:

> Whilst the movement was taking place, the fire of the French artillery was more furious than ever, and several casualties occurred. In the left square Colonel William Rowan was wounded in the elbow by a shot which passed through his horse's neck and killed it, bringing its rider heavily to the ground. Poor Nettles, who carried the King's colour, was killed just before reaching the summit of the position, by a cannon-shot through his body; and it was said that his colour-serjeant was killed at or about the same time; and in some unaccountable way, the colour was left under the body of poor Nettles

Cavalry Attacks 4pm

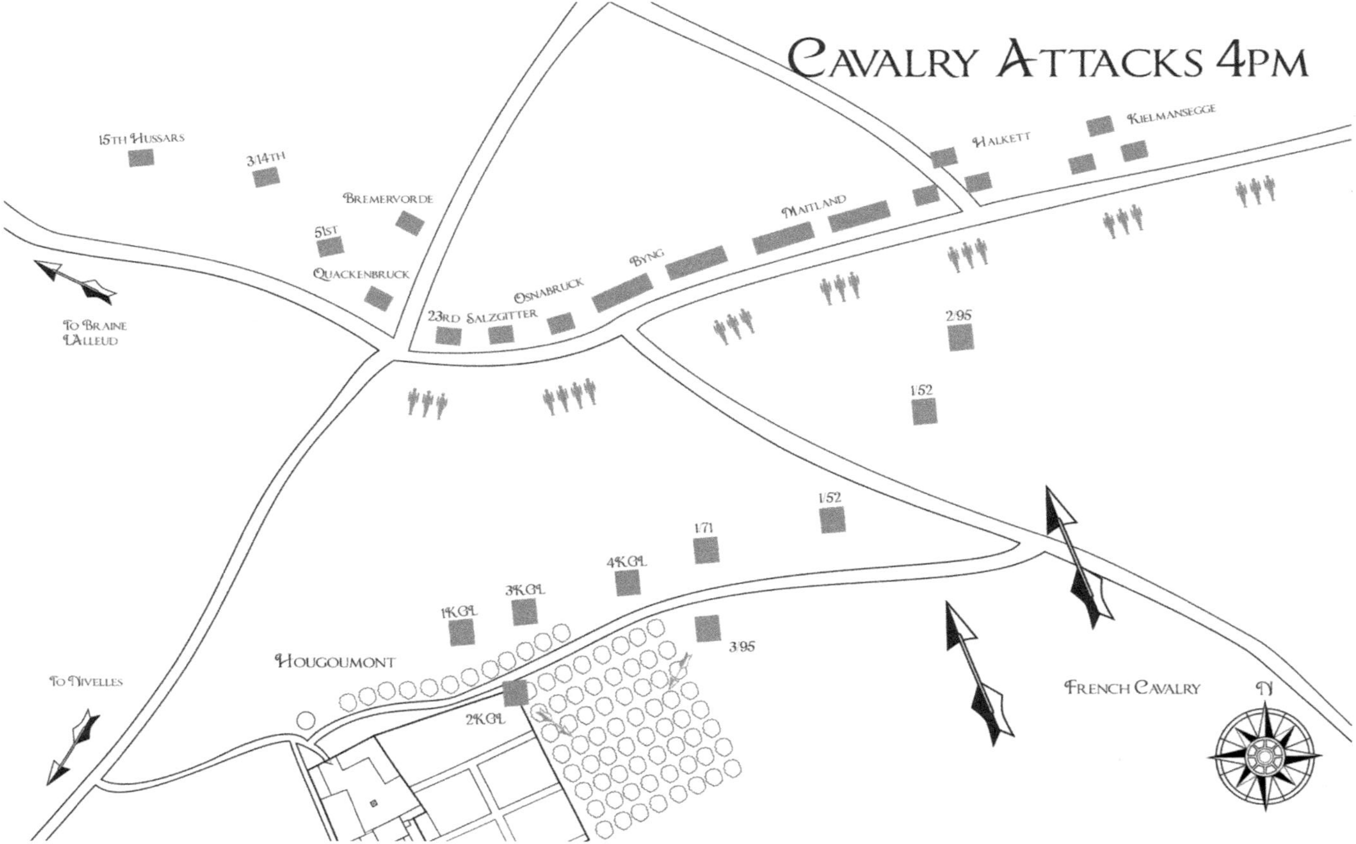

> till the next morning, when it was discovered by a serjeant of Captain Mercer's troop of horse-artillery. ... It certainly was a pleasant relief ... when, on passing the crest of the position, we found ourselves, at forty paces from it, out of fire on its reverse slope.[36]

The sounds of battle far to their left foretold the arrival of the Prussians on Napoleon's right wing. They had been expected since morning and some must have doubted that they were ever coming. Second Lieutenant Richard Cocks Eyre of the 2/95th recorded that:

> About four o'clock we found that some divisions of Prussians had come up, made an attack, and turned the left flank of the enemy. Things then began to wear a more favourable appearance. The whole British and Belgic army came up in squares; the French cavalry which had by this time got into a little order, then made another charge and were beaten back with an immense loss without doing us any harm. As soon as they had cleared the way a second time our whole army formed line.[37]

Certainly better late than never, their influence on the battle was now going to be unquestionably decisive. For, as Sir Henry Clinton, wrote:

> About this time an officer of French cavalry came over & stated that Bonaparte was himself opposed to us & that Grouchy was attacking the Prussians & had reported that he had beaten them & that he was making prisoners *a volonte*. The advance of the enemy upon our left seemed to confirm this report, but at half past 5 the fire upon our left redoubled (this was the first attack of the Prussians) & it was observed to advance upon the enemy.[38]

But did Napoleon still have anything left to give?

Chapter 14

The Guard Advances

Unsure of Napoleon's next move, but certain he was not finished yet, the allied officers anxiously watched for signs of troop movements. But whilst they wondered a lone French cavalryman approached them and immediately warned them of the final attack. Colonel Colborne states:

> as we were ascending the hill a French colonel of the cuirassiers galloped out of the French ranks, holloaing out *'Vive le Roi'*, repeatedly, and rode up to me, addressed and said *'Ce ____ Napoleon est la avec les Gardes. Voila l'attaque qui se fait'*. This officer remained with me for some time.[1]

Whether by the same French cavalryman, or another, it is not certain – because they are described very differently – but Major Hunter Blair got a very similar warning of the imminent attack of the Imperial Guard:

> I was in rear of the 52nd line in conversation with the late Sir Augustus Frazer, Horse Artillery, when the French Hussar officer, a deserter, mentioned by Colonel Gawler, rode up to me and joined us. He said we should be attacked by the French Guard within half-an-hour. Sir Augustus rode off to inform the Duke, then towards the left, desiring me to look to the deserter, whose information proved literally correct.
>
> The French cannonade commenced before Sir Augustus' return. I sent the French officer to the rear in charge of a sergeant of the 52nd Regiment.[2]

The battle was reaching its climax. Wellington's men had survived every assault and the Prussian army was bearing down on Napoleon's right rear at Plancenoit. With one enemy in his front and one closing in upon his flank and rear, Napoleon was in danger of being crushed.

But desperate times lead to desperate decisions and Napoleon prepared to send forth his Imperial Guard in one final attempt to smash through the much weakened allied lines. La Haye Sainte farm had fallen into French hands and Wellington's troops near the crossroads were clearly reeling under the intense pressure. Napoleon decided that the Imperial Guard were to be sent forward to smash through the feeble remnants of the Anglo-Netherlands line and the cavalry would exploit the gap made to the full. It would be Ligny all over again!

Sir Henry Clinton described the situation:

> Towards seven o'clock while the fire upon his right was still advancing, Bonaparte saw that he should be exposed to great danger & to the certainty of losing all his guns if he did not disembarrass himself from one of his opponents & having the greater force upon his left (that is opposite to the Duke of Wellington) probably determined him.
>
> He harangued his guards, who to that time had been in reserve, he pointed out the danger of his position & that his hopes were in them who had so often rendered him great service & that now they might become the defenders & saviours of their country. He increased his artillery, at that time the Duke of Wellington came to the right & though appearances were very favourable, he desired me to strengthen the right as he expected to be attacked by the infantry & cavalry (a French officer had just passed over & had brought the intelligence). The greater part of the division had been engaged excepting two battalions of Hanoverians which were still in reserve & upon the other side of the Nivelles road. The attack, which was formidable as to appearance was directed against the First Division's [position?], it was comprised of three masses of infantry (the Imperial Guards).[3]

General Adam was also on the spot and made his preparations for the crisis to come:

> While in this position a French officer deserted and came over to where the brigade was, and gave information that the Imperial Guard was forming to make an attack on that part of the position.
>
> It was not judged expedient to receive this attack, but to move forward the brigade and assail the enemy instead of waiting to be assailed, and orders to that effect were given.
>
> The brigade was at this time formed in line four deep from right to left 71st, 52nd, 2nd 95th; and the 2 companies of the 3rd 95th on the right of 71st.

> The first encounter with the Imperial Guard was a very sharp tussle with its tirailleurs, but this did not extend to our right farther than the right of 52nd, and hardly to left of 71st.[4]

The advancing columns were struck repeatedly by cannon fire, but still they continued to advance, determined to succeed:

> The enemy advanced in heavy close column, with the intention of penetrating the position at the right angle of the Foot Guards. They were within the angle formed by the battery and the Foot Guards before they went about, so that at last the right gun could not conveniently be brought to bear upon the head of the column. The battery fired case shot from the moment they appeared on the crest of the hill (about two hundred yards), and during the advance along the plateau, from which they suffered severely, the column waving, at each successive discharge, like standing corn blown by the wind.[5]

The first column of French Guard marched directly towards the British Guards of Maitland's Division and they were driven back after a severe firefight. As the Imperial Guardsmen recoiled, Maitland's men charged after them down the hill with the bayonet. As Lieutenant Pringle of the Guards recounts:

> In less than a minute above 300 were down. They now wavered, and several of the rear divisions began to draw out as if to deploy, whilst some of the men in their rear beginning to fire over the heads of those in front was so evident a proof of their confusion, that Lord Saltoun (who had joined the brigade, having had the whole of his light infantry battalion dispersed at Hougoumont) holloaed out 'Now's the time, my boys.' Immediately the brigade sprang forward. La Garde turned and gave us little opportunity of trying the steel.[6]

But suddenly the British guardsmen were brought up short. Through the smoke they became made aware of a second column of the Imperial Guard moving up in support. There was nothing for it, but to retire as quickly as possible to the ridge line and to reform their ranks:

> We charged down the hill till we had passed the end of the orchard of Hougoumont, when our right flank became exposed to another heavy column (as we afterwards understood of the Chasseurs of the Garde) who were advancing in support of the former column. This circumstance, beside that our charge was isolated, obliged the brigade to retire towards their original position.[7]

7.45 Defeat of Guard

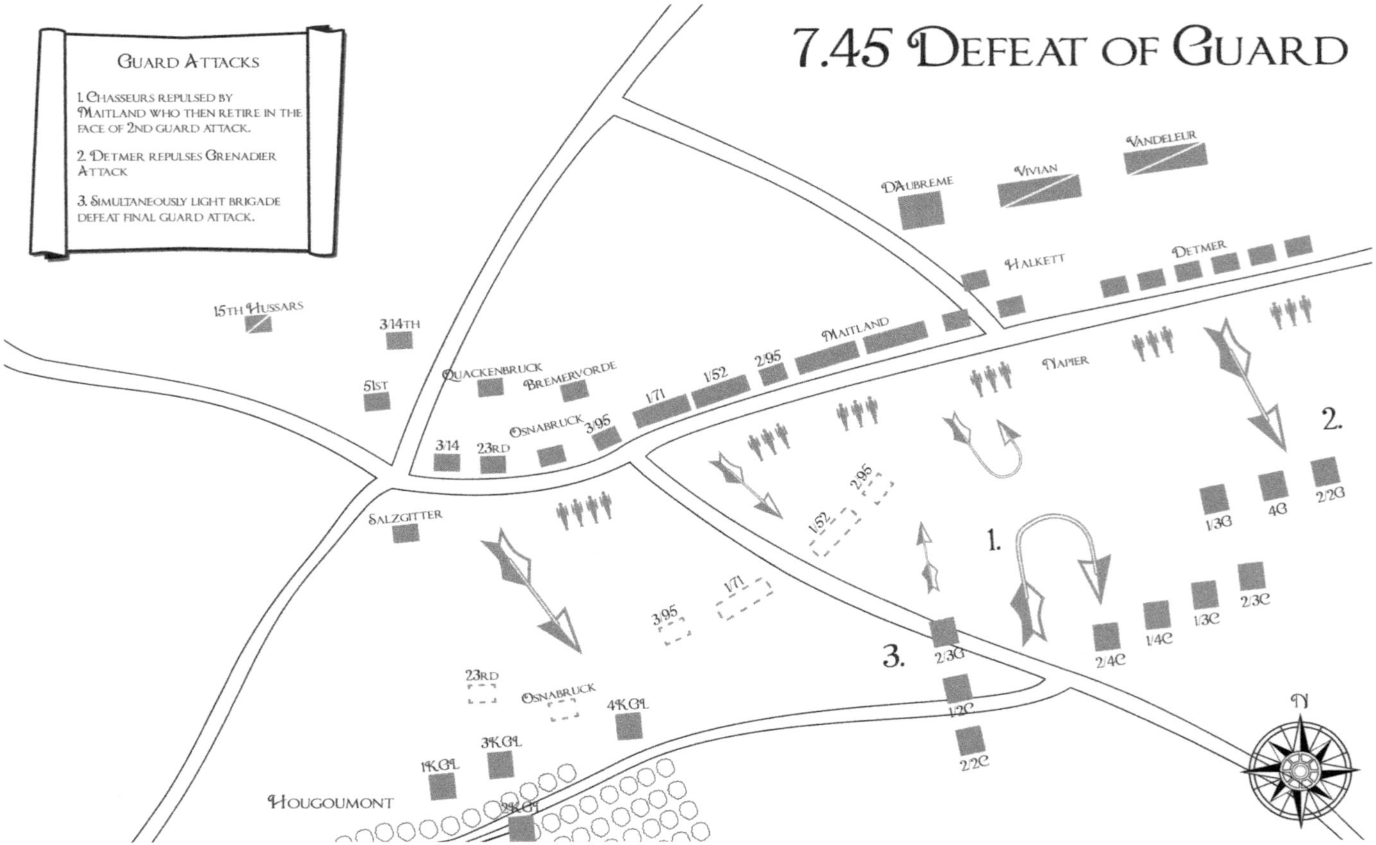

At this moment, according to Colonel Colborne, he manoeuvred his regiment without orders to alter its front by some forty-five degrees or so to the left, so that it faced the flank of the advancing Imperial Guardsmen. This is Colborne's account of this movement:

> This movement placed us nearly parallel with the moving columns of the French Imperial Guards. I ordered a strong company to extend in our front, and at this moment, Sir F. Adam rode up and asked me what I was going to do. I think I said 'to make that column feel our fire'. Sir F. Adam then ordered me to move on, and that the 71st should follow, and rode away towards the 71st.
>
> I instantly ordered the extended company of the 52nd, about 100 men, under the command of Lieutenant Anderson, to advance as quickly as possible without any support except from the battalion, and to fire into the French column at any distance. Thus the 52nd formed in two lines of half companies, the rear line at ten paces distance from the front – after giving three cheers, followed the extended company, passed along the front of the Brigade of Guards in line, commanded by Sir John Byng, and about 500 yards in front of them. ...
>
> I observed that as soon as the French columns were sharply attacked by our skirmishers, a considerable part of the column halted and formed a line facing towards the 52nd and opened a very sharp fire on the skirmishers and on the battalion. ...
>
> Three or four companies of the 95th were formed on our left rather to the rear of our line; the remainder of the brigade, the 71st, must have been at least six hundred yards to the rear when the 52nd commenced its movement towards the Imperial Guards; but I think I observed the 71st moving on, as well as the whole of Sir H. Clinton's Division, when we had advanced a few hundred paces. ...
>
> The 52nd suffered severely from the fire of the enemy; the loss of skirmishers was severe, and the two officers of the company were wounded. The right wing of the 52nd lost nearly one hundred and fifty men during the advance; the officer carrying the regimental colour was killed.[8]

General Adam, however, stated that the 71st moved in support of the 52nd immediately: When their tirailleurs were disposed of, the 52nd were right shouldered forward by Sir J. Colborne, and the 71st conformed.[9] His *aides-de-camp* saw Lord Hill with the 52nd at this moment:

> The cannonade continued without intermission, and about 6 [8] o'clock we saw heavy columns of infantry supported by dragoons forming for a fresh attack, it was evident it would be a desperate and, we thought, probably a decisive one; everyone felt how much

depended on this terrible moment. A black mass of the grenadiers of the Imperial Guard with music playing and the great Napoleon at their head came rolling onward from the farm of 'La Belle Alliance'; with rapid pace they descended the opposite heights, all scattered firing ceased on both sides, our little army seemed to collect within itself, the infantry deployed into line, and the artillery, charged to the muzzle with grape and canister, waited for the moment when the enemy's columns should commence the ascent of our heights; those spaces in our lines which death had opened and left vacant were covered in appearance by bodies of cavalry.

The point at which the enemy aimed was now evident; it was a re-entering angle formed by a brigade of Guards, and the light brigade of Lord Hill's corps, Lord Hill was there in person. The French moved on with arms sloped *'au pas de charge'*; they began to ascend the hill, in a few seconds they were within a hundred paces of us, and as yet not a shot had been fired. The awful moment was now at hand, a peal of ten thousand thunders burst at once on their devoted heads, the storm swept them down as a whirlwind which rushes over the ripe corn, they paused, their advance ceased, they commenced firing from the head of their columns and attempted to extend their front; but death had already caused too much confusion among them, they crowded instinctively behind each other to avoid a fire which was intolerably dreadful; still they stood firm, *'La Garde meurt mais ne se rend pas'*.[10, 11]

The French stood their ground, however, and

opened a fire the most tremendous ever known, I believe, in the annals of war, 250 pieces very close, throwing shells & round shot, grape & every instrument of destruction. It is really not exaggeration to say one could not ride quick over the ground for the bodies of men & horses. Under cover of this cannonade advanced Bonaparte at the head of his Imperial Guard. Cavalry in a column on the left flank, the Grenadiers of the Guard on their right flank. They advanced most steadily up to our line in the great mass. They halted & commenced firing, their troops were literally mowed down. The fire was so great, nothing could stand. Our guns were moved close up to the flank of their column foudroyer [to strike down] with grape into it. Lord Hill moved a brigade (our elite) round the flank. I brought up, six squadrons of cavalry & we made a general charge. The cuirassiers of the Imperial Guard had their ranks much thinned by our artillery. They went about, we with the cavalry pursued them, leaving the French infantry steady in our flank.[12]

Then, at last, the French Guard broke and ran. Digby Mackworth continues:

> For half an hour this horrible butchery continued, at last seeing all their efforts vain, all their courage useless, deserted by their emperor, who had already flown, unsupported by their comrades, who were already beaten, the hitherto invincible Old Guard gave way and fled in every direction.[13]

In the confusion Lord Hill disappeared and for a while his aides-de-camp feared that he had been hit. As Horace Churchill recalled:

> Currie was killed by a grape shot close to me, Lord Hill in the grand melee with the Imperial Guard, had his horse killed & was rode over. We lost him for an hour[14] & I thought he must have been killed, I saw him at last knocking about a fresh horse.[15]

The 2nd Battalion 95th on the left of the 52nd moved correspondingly with them – apparently on the direct orders of the Duke himself. According to Captain Joseph Logan:

> Lord Wellington rode up to me & ordered I should attack them immediately. I marched with the 52nd & 71st Regiments on my right & such a carnage I never before beheld. The firing of guns &c was so great that the man next to me could not hear my orders. After some desperate fighting the French began to retire & you may be certain we stuck to their breasts. That noble fellow Lord Wellington moved on with the 95th & frequently cried out 'Move on my brave fellows'. I feared for his safety; myself I did not care about. My God! Had he fallen what a bitter day it would have been for England.
>
> Lord Hill & Sir H Clinton & General Adam were also with us & conducted themselves like heroes.[16]

The presence of the Duke of Wellington is corroborated by Private Lewis of the same regiment:

> when Wellington rode away from our regiment & then we advanced like Britons, but we could not go five steps without walking over the dead & wounded & Boney's horses of the Imperial Guards [cuirassiers] that the men was killed was running loose about in all directions.[17]

The fire-fight was intense, with the left flank of the Imperial Guard column turning to return fire. The skirmishers of the 52nd suffered severely, as did the formed ranks moving up in their support. Ensign Leeke recounts that:

> Here I saw Winterbottom badly wounded in the head, and brought by his horse through the line, without his cap, the blood streaming down him; the poor fellow managed to hold on by the pommel of his saddle. Captain Diggle, commanding No. 1 company, had been desperately wounded just before on the left temple. Lieutenant Dawson was shot through the lungs; Anderson lost a leg. Major Love was severely wounded in the head, and afterwards, as he lay on the ground, in the foot and in two other places. Lieutenant Campbell, who had been skirmishing, came through the line severely wounded in the groin; General Adam was severely wounded in the leg, but did not quit the field. Colonel Charles Rowan was also slightly wounded; Sir John Colborne had his horse killed under him, and was grazed in the hand and on the foot. Several of the other officers were very slightly hit, but were not returned as wounded; I consider that about 140 of our men were killed or wounded at this time, in the course of five or six minutes.[18]

Finally the Imperial Guard broke, turned and fled, and the Duke of Wellington ordered the line to advance – but that was not as easy as it sounded:

> The French Imperial Guards and the whole of their infantry advanced and (we flatter ourselves) were met in the most glorious style. The action was now become general and at its height. The fate of the day was at length decided by a charge of our whole army in line four deep. After a conflict which I cannot attempt to describe to you the French Imperial Guards gave way and their whole force were thrown into the utmost confusion.[19]

As the brigade advanced it suddenly became aware of the 23rd Light Dragoons trying to take advantage of the situation and attacking some French cavalry in their front. The 23rd was beaten back and nearly driven in on the 52nd, who stopped to fire. However, the confusion was quickly sorted out and the Duke soon appeared to urge the brigade to continue its movement:

> At this moment two or three squadrons of the 23rd Dragoons appeared, directly in front of the line of the 52nd, approaching rapidly towards the line. The two companies on the left halted and fired into them, supposing them to be enemy cavalry. My horse was wounded; I called out to the Adjutant to stop the fire, and whilst we were

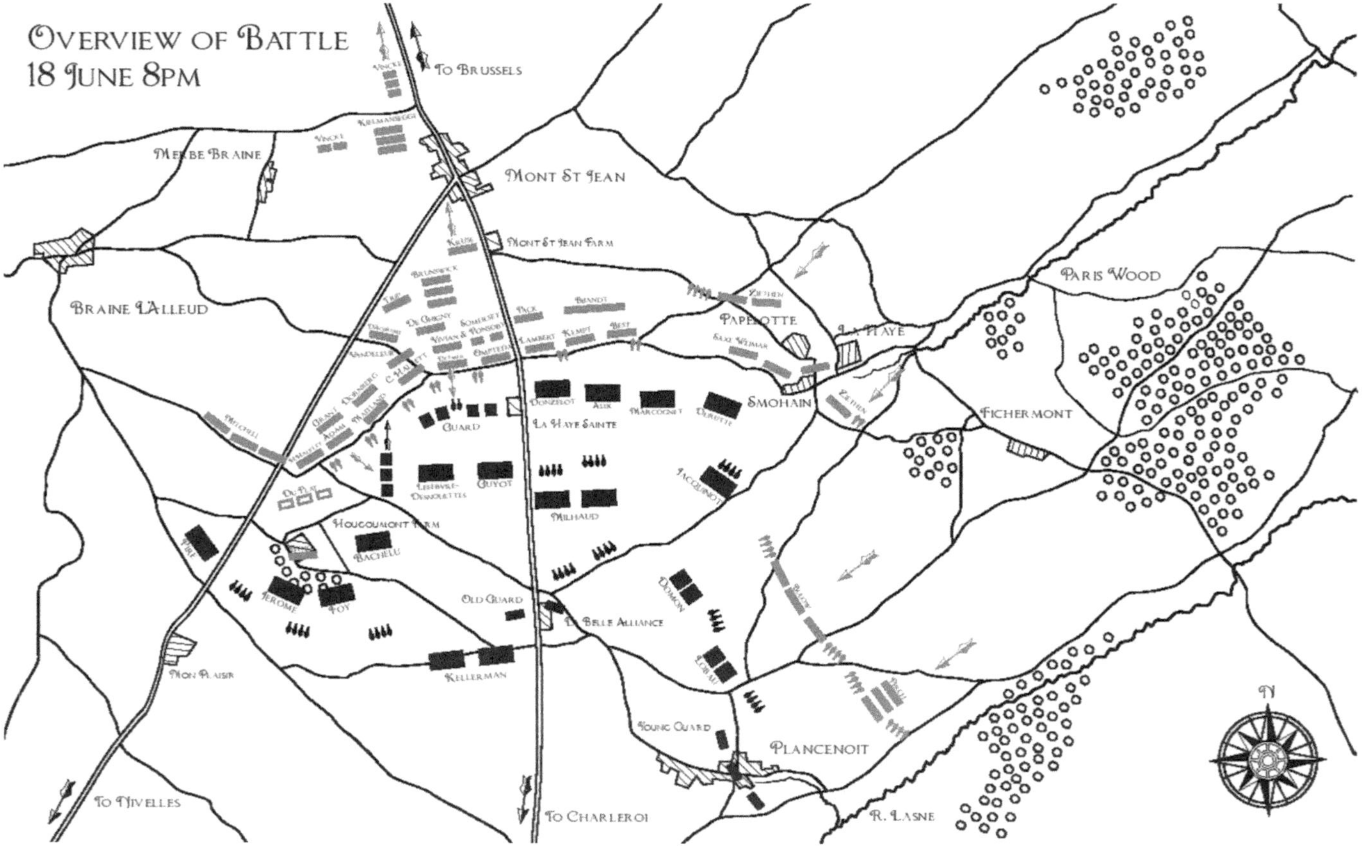
Overview of Battle
18 June 8pm
To Brussels
Vincke
Kielmansegge
Merbe Braine
Mont St Jean
Mont St Jean Farm
Kruse
Brunswick
Braine L'Alleud
Trip
De Ghigny
Somerset
Vivian & Ponsonby
Pack
Brandt
Lambert
Kempt
Best
Ompteda
Vandeleur
C. Halkett
Dornberg
Maitland
Adam
Mitchell
Papelotte
Saxe Weimar
Ziethen
La Haye
Smohain
Paris Wood
Fichermont
Donzelot
Alix
Marcognet
Durutte
Guard
La Haye Sainte
Jacquinot
Lefebvre-Desnouettes
Guyot
Milhaud
Du Plat
Hougoumont Farm
Bachelu
Pire
Jerome
Foy
Old Guard
Belle Alliance
Domon
Bulow
Lobau
Kellerman
Mon Plaisir
Young Guard
Plancenoit
Pirch
R. Lasne
To Nivelles
To Charleroi
N

> rectifying this mistake ... the Duke of Wellington came to the rear of the left of our line near the two companies which had fired. I said to his Grace 'It is our own cavalry which has caused this firing'. His Grace replied, 'Never mind, go on, go on'.[20]

Captain Aldridge of the 2/95th also saw the confusion:

> Joined immediately with the 52nd pursuing the enemy. Almost immediately after saw a small body of English light cavalry pass to his left and go to the front. Saw these dragoons charge. Saw the French cavalry drive them towards the front of the 52nd. Very soon after this a part of the 95th extended to skirmish.[21]

The cavalry, though, were more of a nuisance than Colborne admits and caused some confusion in the ranks of the 52nd. According to Ensign Leeke, the cavalry:

> rode at the centre of the regiment, and, when they were about twenty yards off, the line opened about six or eight feet in the centre to let them pass. I thought at the moment that the men were not right in making an opening for those whom we regarded as enemies, and should have received the charge on their bayonets; I, therefore stood to the front ... against the leading horseman. The poor fellow was, however, shot dead by our men ... The horse passed through the centre of the interval ... There was a cry 'They are English' and the firing ceased.[22]

The 71st had also moved forward in support as Colborne says: 'At this time the 71st formed on our right flank, and I ordered the bugles to sound the advance, and the whole line charged up the hill'.[23]

Colborne was aware of French infantry on his right flank as he pushed forward, but not close enough to worry him and he trusted to the supporting troops to deal with them:

> Although there is reason to believe that the enemy's second corps was advanced to cover the left flank of his attack with its own left resting on the hedge of Hougoumont, yet no part of it came near enough to menace seriously the right flank of the 52nd regiment during the whole of the forward movement and charge. This right flank appeared entirely clear of the enemy for at least 300 yards.[24]

The discomfited British Guards now became aware of the movement of the Light Brigade and they reformed and followed it down the hill, but they went no further than the floor of the valley:

> Opportunely, Sir F. Adam's light brigade had in the meantime come round the knoll between the position and Hougoumont, when we had been ordered to take ground to our left, and were advancing under the hedge and blind line along the northern side of the orchard at Hougoumont. As soon therefore as we had uncovered their front we halted and formed.
>
> The two brigades now returned to the charge which the Chasseurs did not wait for, and we continued our forward movement till we got to the bottom of the valley between the positions. Here our brigade halted to restore its order ... Whilst we were halted in the valley the light troops and cavalry had passed us and gone in pursuit.[25]

As the Light Brigade advanced, the interval between the 52nd and 71st grew wider. The 3/95th tried to plug the gap but was not numerous enough. There were also urgent requests made for reinforcements to cover the right flank of the 71st as the brigade advanced:

> ... but it being considered that the interval between the right of 71st and the enclosures of Hougoumont left the right of the brigade exposed, request more than once made for troops from the other part of the division to occupy this space and cover the flank of the 3rd Brigade, and at length Lieutenant Colonel Halkett, with a part of his Hanoverian Militia Brigade was sent for this purpose, and as it came forward the 3rd Brigade advanced, the Imperial Guard was driven back, and the brigade, continuing to advance, crossed the Genappe chaussee.[26]

General Clinton had already observed the movement of the Light Brigade and had immediately ordered the Osnabrück Battalion and the 23rd Fusiliers forward in support:

> The attack which was very formidable as to appearances was direct against the First Division, it was composed of 3 squares of infantry, the Imperial Guards. Our Guards advanced to meet it. Adam's Brigade also advanced & brought up their right, the cavalry was still very strong & ever had had the best in every meeting with that of the enemy, I supported the attack by an Hanoverian battalion in column at quarter distance, the squares in echelon with the 23rd Regiment which formed part of a brigade of the 4th Division & was placed under my orders. The enemy gave way & was pursued across the plain, our cavalry came forward & from this moment the ease in which we drove him across the road to Genappe, in which direction the Prussians were pursuing & pressed him as long as we could see. The road was absolutely choked with his artillery, many of the guns & tumbrils horsed, I never saw a more complete rout ...[27]

The Duke had set every battalion he could find in motion following the movement. He rode to the KGL Brigade to order them to follow:

> Duke of Wellington rode up and ordered the brigade to advance in line. The outcome of the battle now seemed to have been decided. Accompanied by our cavalry, we advanced towards the French batteries which kept up their heavy fire, but their guns then were abandoned, one by one, and were left standing where they were.[28]

The 1st Line Battalion KGL also joined the effort:

> Towards 8 o'clock, the Duke of Wellington rode up and ordered the squares to form line of 4 ranks and advance in line against the enemy Guards; these, too, were beaten, and victory had been won. The enormous exertions, the men had eaten little or nothing during the past 3 days, made it impossible to take part in the pursuit of the enemy, and camp was set up one hour away from the battlefield. The Prussians, who had just arrived, now pursued the defeated enemy.[29]

Colonel Halkett sent orders to his other battalions to join him, but unbeknown to him, Captain Saffe, the Brigade Major, who was sent to bring the other battalions up was killed en route and the message was never received. The Osnabrück Battalion, however, moved quickly to come up with the advance and soon caught up with a rapidly dissolving Imperial Guard battalion:

> Opposite our position, very strong enemy columns stood in the background, of which four battalions of the French Guard were nearest to us. These then attacked in columns, while their skirmishers moved up to within a short distance from us. After the skirmishers had been driven back by the English and the battalion's riflemen, the battalion attacked in column in coordination with the English to the left, who advanced in line, against the French columns approaching through a depression in the terrain. After putting up a strong resistance, they began to retreat.[30]

During the advance, a French general officer was seen to be injured by an exploding shell and was left for dead by the retreating Imperial Guardsmen. Raising himself, but still dazed, he tried to escape. Colonel Halkett immediately rode forward and seized the general and captured him after a short struggle. He was General Cambronne, the very same man whom the myths state stood in the final square of the Imperial Guard and defied death by saying '*La Garde meurt mais ne se rend pas*' or the expletive '*Merde!*' If these words were ever said, they were not said by him:

> As the French Guard retired in some disorder, a French general (whose name, I believe, was Cambronne) was energetically engaged in attempting to halt and reform the battalions. He succeeded several times; but their retiring continued, however, as they were forcefully driven back by our pursuing battalions. Our brigadier, the then Colonel Halkett, had observed that action and, with unequalled intrepidity, rode through the French skirmishers, who covered the retreating columns, to that general and, with great luck, brought him back before the entire line, through the enemy skirmishers, and made him his prisoner,[31] notwithstanding [the man's] forceful resistance.[32]

As the Light Brigade marched across the valley, the British light cavalry saw their moment. Vivian, followed by Vandeleur, Grant and Dornberg launched their regiments against the disordered French line. The cavalry charged straight across the valley passing across the rear of the Light Brigade, the men of which were seemingly oblivious to their movement. Some French units formed square and beat off the frenzied attacks of the cavalry, but most units simply crumpled and fled, allowing the light cavalrymen to cause havoc, with their slashing sabres even attacking some unlucky Prussian troops in the gathering gloom. Sir Hussey Vivian describes the cavalry charge:

> No words can give any idea of it (how a man escaped is to me a miracle), we every instant expecting through the smoke to see the enemy appearing under our noses, for the smoke was literally so thick that we could not see ten yards off. But we at last began to find that the shots did not come so thick, and I discovered that the enemy were, instead of advancing to gain our position, retrograding on theirs. The moment to attack was arrived, and I received orders to advance …
>
> I led the head of my brigade diagonally across the ground for the left body of cavalry … the 10th cut down the French in their ranks, some few then escaped under cover of a hedge, but from this time every man was in retreat, and eventually every man was taken during a pursuit which lasted as long as we could see, so long, indeed, until from actually having cut down some Prussians, we were obliged to desist and give them the pursuit.[33]

But the fighting was far from finished. General Adam records that:

> While advancing, the Duke of Wellington being with the brigade, some battalions of the enemy were reformed, and appeared inclined to stand. The Duke ordered them to be attacked, but it was suggested to his Grace that the brigade, which from its rapid advance was somewhat loose in its formation, had better be halted and the files

> closed in. The halt was ordered accordingly, but after a few moments the Duke said 'They won't stand, better attack them',[34] and the 3rd Brigade was accordingly again put in motion, and the battalions of the enemy withdrew, and fell into the mass of confusion which existed in our front.[35]

The Duke had judged the situation perfectly. Those French units which still appeared to offer resistance generally collapsed as the Light Brigade approached.

As it gained the main road the right wing of the 52nd came under heavy grape shot from three guns to its right. Lieutenant George Gawler now commanded this company since Captain Diggle was wounded, and was ordered to detach a section and to drive them off, which it did successfully.

Having crossed the floor of the shallow valley in the direction of La Belle Alliance, the 52nd actually crossed the main road, but then turned to push on parallel to the road towards the few remnants of the French army that still stood firm. The battalion overran French gun batteries and infantry units as they pushed on. The supporting troops of Adam's Brigade also altered their line of march to march parallel to the 52nd but on the other side of the road:

> I ordered the 52nd Regiment to 'pass the road' and the whole passed through the guns & carriages &c and we formed columns of companies, our right resting on the road to Genappe. We moved on in column and passed, I think, eighty guns or carriages in about ten minutes after this new formation.
>
> ... The 71st did not cross the Genappe road, but moved to the right, as well as part of Sir H. Clinton's Division.[36]

The troops now passed batteries of guns, abandoned by their artillerymen in an effort to escape. Some were still loaded and were turned to fire into the fleeing throng: 'The gun fired there by Captain Campbell, aide de camp to Sir Frederick Adam, was turned by some men of my own company under the command of Lt. Torriano'.[37]

The Osnabrück battalion to the right, similarly overran a great number of guns, as Major Dreve's recounts:

> The retiring Guard still halted several times after that general had been taken prisoner and, by taking every advantage of the terrain, attempted by their fire to stop their pursuers. They eventually had to yield to the forceful advance of the pursuing troops and dissolved into a disorderly mob.

> In its pursuit of the enemy, the battalion drove in on four French batteries, one by one, of which two kept on firing. After several rounds of fire from the head of the battalion and from our riflemen, they were seized in our subsequent attack. The third battery was about to retreat and was then taken, and, upon the approach of our battalion, the artillerymen of the fourth battery left their cannon, which were then captured.[38]

Some of the French cannon still fired on them, much of the shot going over their heads. Indeed it is believed that grape shot from one of these cannon firing at this moment struck Lord Uxbridge whilst riding with the Duke just behind the 52nd:

> The three guns which had been driven off by the right section under Gawler, and had retired to the higher part of the French position, again fired grape at us, which passed over our heads, but wounded Lord Uxbridge in the knee about twenty yards in the rear of the centre of the 52nd.[39]

They drove on with the fury of soldiers who had been assaulted all day without being able to fight back. Now they had been unleashed, nothing would stop their mad rush:

> The shout was then universal, we charged them at a steady pace, they formed on the hill in solid square but the bayonet soon drove them to the devil, they threw down their knapsacks & arms, left wagons, horses etc & fled.[40]

Here they started to encountered Prussian troops:

> At the junction of the Genappe road and the road leading, I believe, from Wavre to Nivelles, the skirmishers of the 52nd and the advance of the Prussians under General Bulow mixed ... We halted a few hundred yards from it, and the whole of General Bulow's Corps passed our right on the road leading to Genappe.[41]

The troops drove on until it was too dark to see, when the dangers of a clash with Prussian forces became too great:

> We drove them across the road to Genappe in which direction the Prussians were pursuing & we pushed them as long as we could see. The road was absolutely choked with his artillery, many of the guns & tumbrils horsed. I never saw a more complete rout. ... The Prussians continued the pursuit during a great part of the night & the

> next day (the 19th) Blücher was at Gosselies. By pressing the enemy he took an immense quantity of artillery & baggage, Bonaparte's carriage amongst the rest.[42]

The scenes of chaos were everywhere:

> We followed them (shouting and keeping up a tremendous fire of musketry, shells and rockets) about seven miles during which pursuit a scene presented itself which I think hell itself could not surpass; about dusk we came up to two villages which our rockets had set fire to, here the French thought they may easily check our pursuit and with that idea brought about their whole artillery which they commenced loading with grape and round shot and poured them in on us from all quarters, their infantry likewise kept up a destructive fire of musketry. If anything in the world would have damped the ardour of British troops this would have done it but their confidence in their general and encouraged as they were by success the devil himself would not have stopped them. They continued their huzzas and dashed through everything that opposed them. We now came to an immense hill where we found the consternation of the routed enemy so great that all classes of them, dragoons, infantry and artillery were mixed in one immense and confused mass. The greater part of their infantry threw down their packs and arms to be able to mount the hill they were then endeavouring to get over. Those we came up to ran into us as prisoners. Our lines then shortened pace to allow our cavalry and light troops to make a flank movement and get round to the other side of the hill, by this we succeeded in taking a great number of prisoners, a great part of their artillery and the whole of their provision and ammunition wagons. It however gave us some hard work as the part of the French army we had cut off fought hard with the idea of joining their companions who were better at running than themselves. In this however they were foiled, and in this last movement (about half past nine at night) which gloriously concluded a well and hard fought day.[43]

Private Smith charged for as long as contact could still be made with the fleeing enemy: 'At night when their army gave way they heaved their knapsacks and arms from them in all directions and run, our brigade cheered and charged them as long as we seed a mass of them for dark night'.[44]

The Osnabrück Battalion drove on alongside the 52nd until exhaustion also brought the battalion to a halt:

> The battalion pursued the enemy jointly with English and Prussian troops, eventually intermingled with them, on and along the side of the Genappe highway, until about 10 o'clock at night. The remnants of the battalion gathered near some houses, probably Maison du Roi or Le Caillou.
>
> The battalion pursued the enemy jointly with English and Prussian troops, eventually intermingled with them, on and along the side of the Genappe highway, until about 10 o'clock at night. The remnants of the battalion gathered near some houses, probably Maison du Roi or Le Caillou.
>
> The battalion was unable to continue its advance further, due to the extraordinary exertions on this day. Having thus become separated somewhat from the other troops, I was charged at 11 o'clock at night by the brigadier, the then Colonel Halkett, with a reconnoitring assignment, with as many of the battalion's men as I was able to put on the road. I undertook this with the greater part of the remnants of the battalion in the direction of Genappe. While faced with great difficulties due to the extreme exhaustion of the troops and the darkness of night, I executed this assignment to the satisfaction of the brigadier.[45]

Captain Horace Churchill records that:

> The enemy were now beat back, Bonaparte had led his own Guards & been beaten. The Prussians now came up on the enemy's flank & this obliged them to hurry their retreat. Our cavalry & artillery then advanced. The enemy were pursued & began a precipitate retreat. The fruits of this victory were about 200 pieces of artillery taken in the pursuit, 4 eagles,[46] the baggage of Bonaparte & his army.
>
> It is needless to enlarge upon the conduct of the troops of the two armies. Lord Wellington calls it the battle of the giants & he says that there is no hell for any fellow that escaped that cannonade. I believe in the whole army Lord Wellington was the individual who fought hardest & the only individual not touched.[47]

Slowly the firing stopped and the pursuit ended for the 2nd Division:

> All firing ceased as darkness set in. Our brigade advanced to a place near where the French camp had been, and there bivouacked for the night. … It was said that 150 guns had been captured, not counting 60 that had been seized by the Prussians. They had arrived in the evening on our left flank and had supported the attack against the French right flank, thereby frightening the terror stricken French even more.[48]

Ensign Jack Barnett of the 71st recorded the thanks of Sir Henry Clinton and Lord Hill on the battlefield:

> The Prussians pursued them all night & slew them without mercy. We bivouacked at 2 miles from the field, since that, we have marched constantly & without interruption until we arrived here.
>
> We lost 250 men killed & wounded, out of 800 & very few wounded will ever serve again, all shells & cannon.
>
> The regiment was thanked on the field, by Sir H Clinton & Lord Hill & I heard General Adam says he would rather have commanded the regiment than have been a king. This was in the heat of the battle.[49]

Meanwhile, the French within Hougoumont wood had no idea of what had occurred elsewhere on the battlefield and they continued to fight on until overwhelmed by the additional troops now pushing through the woods. These included Brunswick troops and the Salzgitter Battalion:

> When about 8 o'clock in the evening the attack of the Imperial Guard was beaten back, only the smaller part of our much weakened rifle battalion happened to be near Captain Beuermann, who was in command. He ordered me to search for any of our men in the walled garden, the chateau building, the farm buildings and the adjoining spaces and to gather them and bring them back.
>
> My prompt and eager efforts had no significant success. I found only a few men who had brought up from the basement of the chateau a drink of beer, where some was still available. I do not dare describe the scenery that I faced on the inside of the estate: it would be a picture full of blood, with burned and mangled corpses, with dying, wounded and fatigued warriors, surrounded by burning and smoking ruins. This scene of a contest fought most bitterly for long hours I left as fast as I could and rejoined Captain Beuermann.
>
> Of the advancing British troops on the extreme right wing, who passed by Hougoumont, a number also moved into the environs of the estate. With their help, the enemy tirailleurs who still resisted energetically, ignorant as they were of what had happened elsewhere, were now completely driven out of the wood. Beuermann, with all the men of the battalion he had been able to gather, now rushed on with the tumult of the advancing troops; the other part of the riflemen had joined the 2nd Line Battalion. In the vicinity of the tavern of La Belle Alliance. … the British troops were told to halt. The daylight already began to yield to the darkness of night. Most of our totally exhausted men sank down on the wet ground not far from the well known observatory, and let themselves be embraced by the god of

> sleep, to the extent this was possible, so did I myself. But as is easily understood, this rest would not remain undisturbed. Apart from the incessant monotonous noise peculiar to such scenes of war, there was here and there a thunderous blowing up of a powder wagon or a limber. In their anger and utter despair, badly wounded enemies would fire their muskets at groups of our men who had gathered around camp fires; or there was small arms fire for other unknown reasons. Added to that was the moaning and groaning of innumerable wounded who were imploring in different languages for a drink to still their terrible thirst, or for any help, even often for their deaths. A large number of horses without their riders were running loose and caused unrest, not to think of the disturbances that were visited upon those, who had lain down, by scavengers and other vagrants crawling about, and not least of all by one's own excitable state of mind.[50]

The men fighting in the wood were supported by the Salzgitter Battalion and units of the Brunswick Corps. Finally the allied troops drove the enemy back and cleared the woods:

> Our two squares now marched forward, more to the right and up an elevation at battalion distance apart, and deployed while under a severe cannonade: a deployment which redounds a particular honour to the battalion in having it executed in outstanding order while exposed to heavy fire. Here we stood in line for a short time only, because the enemy seemed to have made some gains on his left wing; also, we had to reform in squares because of the enemy cavalry. The assigned position was on the far side of a deep hollow way, from which the men could climb up only singly and under heavy fire of case shot. They reformed calmly, as always, and marched in close column far enough under the gun range that their fire became almost ineffective. It was now necessary to seize the wood and the Chateau [Hougoumont], for the possession of which a battalion of English Guards, the 2nd line Battalion [KGL], and 2 battalions of Brunswickers had fought all day in vain. Only small detachments of these battalions were still in the wood; as to the enemy, there were skirmishers of different corps in the wood, particularly of the [Imperial] Guards, whose strong solid columns to the left [of the wood] seemed to threaten our flank. My battalion was assigned this challenging task at around 7 o'clock in the evening. The Osnabrück Battalion and the 95th English regiment faced the [French] columns, and we thus protected each other. Massed columns of enemy infantry and cavalry also stood to our right. The enemy held on most tenaciously. We moved forward by companies; my men had also run out of ammunition and began using the enemy's cartridges.[51] The

small Brunswick detachments remained behind. Our advance was made extremely difficult by the enemy who had protective ditches on both of his flanks. Under these circumstances, and because dusk was setting in, nothing seemed to be more effective than an attack with the bayonet. Shouting 'Hurrah!', we were quick enough and fortunate to gain possession of the wood, certainly a most important position. The battalion rallied immediately upon leaving the wood and advanced up the elevation in closed column. It was night by this time. We were followed by the 2nd Line Battalion, and were later joined by a battery of horse artillery.

Everything was quiet now, and camp fires were being lit. I was in doubt as to which direction to follow to find the brigade, took a left turn, and at 10 o'clock at night came up to Maison Rouge [Roi?] on the highway to Genappe. Two battalions of Vincke's Brigade had already gathered here, and that was where I set up bivouac as ordered by General Maitland.[52]

Reaching the position of the former French lines, they halted and stopped for the night:

Between 7 and 8 o'clock, several battalions marched by the rear of, and through, the wood; I noticed Major General Hugh Halkett among them. I believe they went to the area of Belle Alliance, which appeared to be located a little more than a quarter of an hour to the left of us. The fighting soon ended in our area, and between 8 and 9 o'clock I was ordered to advance. The brigade had moved to the right; the battalion advanced without meeting an enemy straight ahead through cornfields, where there were a number of dead enemies. It was already quite dark when the battalion arrived at the N. N. village[53] and met a strong Prussian column. This was the site where the English Dragoon Guards fought their last action against the enemy cuirassiers. Since there was no way to pass through at this point, I was ordered by General Sir Henry Clinton to remain here during the night and join the division in the morning.[54]

The sun had finally set, darkness plunged the battlefield into a gruesome moonlit nightmare. The French had fled the field, their heels nipped by the Prussian cavalry. Wellington's men advanced to just beyond La Belle Alliance where, without an enemy to pursue, exhaustion overwhelmed them and they sank where they stood, little caring for sustenance, simply desperate for rest.

I never saw such a scene; & our regiment as you will see (if justice is done) distinguished itself above all. The Duke of W[ellington] at least

> came & told us so on the field. We took an immensity of cannon, particularly the Light Brigade; in all (226). It was the most beautiful sight I ever saw; we advanced in square of regiments; the French cavalry charged us, & we drove them back with immense loss. We then charged them, & in fact we had every description of fighting, but their guns did great havoc with shells & grape, & we lost just half our corps, and I am sorry to say the wounded are nearly all bad.[55]

The Quakenbrück and Bremervorde battalions apparently remained in their positions on the battlefield and did not advance at all:

> and now the entire line of the English army advanced in pursuit of the fleeing enemy. The brigadier, Major General Halkett, now took the Osnabrück and Salzgitter Battalions under his personal command, and put the remaining two battalions to the disposition of Lieutenant Colonel von der Schulenburg, (now deceased). The Bremervorde and Quakenbrück Battalions were then separated from the two already mentioned ones and advanced to the height of the Hougoumont farm without meeting an enemy. During the night from 18 to 19 June, they camped on the battlefield near the border of the small wood at Hougoumont. On the next morning they united again with the other two battalions.[56]

It was all over so quickly, as Digby Mackworth recorded that night:

> One spontaneous and almost painfully animated 'Hurra' burst from the victorious ranks of England, the line at once advanced; general officers, soldiers all partaking of one common enthusiasm. The battle was over, guns, prisoners, ammunition wagons, baggage, horses successively fell into our hands; night and fatigue compelled us to halt, we halted on each side of the Genappe road, and in a short time we saw numerous columns of Prussians advancing along in pursuit of the enemy, each column cheered us in passing, the officers saluted, and many embraced us; never was witnessed a more enthusiastic moment; we felt amply rewarded for the exertions of the day. We retired to take a little most welcome repose while the Prussians continued the pursuit without intermission, and thus ended this ever memorable day.[57]

Chapter 15

The Aftermath

The confusion and uncertainty in Brussels concerning the result of the battle is made clear by Henry Clinton's wife, Susan, who remained in the city eagerly awaiting news of the fighting and of her beloved husband. Susan records how the news from the battlefront varied wildly throughout those anxious hours:

> About 6[pm] there was a very nervous moment, the enemy got possession of some strong ground & their cavalry was formidable. It was this I suppose that induced Henry to order all his baggage to Brussels. Between 11 & 12 that night after my having put up the best way I could 11 of his horses & a mule in my stables, coach house & yard, also the horses of some of his Staff, a friend received what he considered certain intelligence that my poor fellow was wounded so he hurriedly came & ordered off 3 servants horses with blankets, I knew nothing of this till the morning although I was up till 2 expecting him every minute, I suppose General Adam had been taken for him.[1]

Henry Clinton survived uninjured and had been fortunate to get some food in the village of Waterloo, but few of his men would be so lucky:

> Henry was well at 12 o'clock last night in the village of Waterloo & in the house of hospitable people who were engaged in getting him something to eat, for he had had nothing since morning, his baggage & all his horses & servants came in here late last night, having been sent away at about 6 when the action was still going on & result doubtful. I sat up till 2, every moment expecting poor Henry himself & dreading the worst.[2]

She also reported that Henry was particularly happy with the conduct of his troops and that he had personally thanked the regiments on the battlefield:

> Some wounded soldiers of the 52nd report that Henry was much pleased with their regiment & made them very happy by riding up to thank them after the action. The young Hanoverian Brigade [that] was under Halkett behaved I am told admirably, they took 12 pieces of cannon & Halkett took himself a French general officer. Of the Germans I have not yet been able to pick up anything except that they were equally engaged with the rest.[3]

In the cold light of day, the battlefield that morning was a terrible sight. The immediate business for the regiments on the morning of 19 June was to take a full roll call, to aid the injured, bury the dead, to partake of some nourishment and to repair their equipment in preparation to march in pursuit of the French.

> The troops took up arms early in the morning of 19 June. This served the purpose of facilitating the reassembling the men, who had been scattered, partly due to helping back the wounded – a duty that an undeniably larger number than necessary had engaged in – partly from the fighting as such, as well as from the search for a more comfortable place to rest in the dark or for something to eat or for other kinds of things …
>
> Entire ranks of fallen warriors all over the vast field indicated those well recognizable places where the most violent fighting had occurred: a horrifying, heart-rending scene met the terrified eye, of mutilated and often already nude corpses, of fallen and mortally wounded horses, which wrenched the stomach almost more than the gnawing hunger could do. In our brigade, that hunger was eased somewhat by the distribution of frugal portions. As we were eating the food we had just received, a part of the Prussian army was passing by our camp ground in its pursuit of the French. Not much later, our own army also marched off to take part in its turn in the pursuit of the remains of the enemy army.[4]

The British and Hanoverian contingents of the army at Waterloo suffered a total of 9,263 killed, wounded and missing (most of the missing were eventually found to be dead) from a total of 44,000 men. This equates to an average casualty rate of 21%.

Although casualty rates alone are not a reliable comparison of a unit's involvement in a battle, they are useful as a general indicator. From a total of 6,450 officers and men who were at Waterloo[5] with the 2nd Division, they suffered in total 211 killed, 1,118 wounded and 234 missing. This equates to about one in four or a 25 % casualty rate. This rate is quite high for a unit that only saw serious action in the final four hours of the battle. These numbers were not consistent across the division, as would be expected, given that their individual roles differed so much. Although it will be noted that there are some very strange anomalies. Some regiments did not believe they had suffered as severely as others and there was much confusion regarding the casualty rates:

> I can't account for it but the 71st Regiment was certainly as much in the thick of it as any but fortunately got off with smaller loss in comparison with some other regiments, probably from being more moved about, for I assure you the Light Brigade was not left long stationary. Our General Adam is a fine fellow indeed, and Reynell though a fidget in quarters is a soldier in the field.[6]

As would be expected, because of their roles, the Light Brigade suffered the highest casualties, amounting to some 45% of the total casualties of the entire division. However, on checking the casualty rates in detail, the 71st suffered a disproportionately greater number of casualties than the 52nd, with losses of 26.1% versus 21.6% respectively. In fact the dubious honour for the highest proportion of casualties in the Light Brigade must actually be given to the 2nd Battalion 95th who suffered a massive rate of 43.2%.

Du Plat's Brigade also suffered a disproportionately higher casualty rate at 27.6% and their loss amounted to fully 30% of the total loss of the division. Losses of the individual battalions was remarkably consistent, however, the 3rd Battalion suffering the worst at 29.7% whilst the lightest casualty figure was that of the 2nd Battalion at 25.5%, perhaps because they were in the orchard and therefore both more spread out and to some extent protected by the trees.

This means that the Hanoverian Brigade suffered a significant loss of 25% of the total for the division, even though these troops had remained in reserve, only under distant cannon fire for the greater proportion of the battle. Surprisingly, the losses suffered by the Osnabrück Battalion are not the highest in the brigade, despite the fact that it alone joined the final advance. This dubious honour, at a casualty rate of 29%, goes to the Salzgitter Battalion, which was tasked with clearing out Hougoumont woods. Perhaps this was a more dangerous task, as the French defenders within had little indication of the complete rout of the French army in progress outside the wood and presumably fought on with greater tenacity. However, this figure is skewed by a high number of missing in the Salzgitter Battalion at eighty-three men (nearly 15% of the total battalion). However, in the later Official Return, it shows only one missing with the number of dead and wounded having increased to thirteen, therefore the other seventy must have returned to the battalion over the next day or so. Taking this into account, the battalion's casualty rate is a more realistic 17%.The highest actual casualty rate thus appears to be that of the Osnabrück Battalion at 18.6%. The other two battalions perhaps unsurprisingly suffered the least, the Bremervorde suffering a 15% and the Quakenbrück a remarkably low 7%.

With regard to the troops of the 4th Division temporarily attached to the 2nd Division at Waterloo, their losses according to the Official Returns were: 23rd Fusiliers 15.3%, 51st Foot 5.6%, and 3/14th 5.0%. Given the more prominent role played by the 23rd in both defending against the cavalry attacks and joining in the final advance, this is much as expected and very similar to the losses of the Hanoverian troops who had also spent long periods of the action in reserve.

The wounded were collected and transported to Brussels, where the inhabitants did everything in their power to ease their plight. This, however, took days to achieve completely, with some French wounded being left on the battlefield for four days or more. Indeed, it is undoubtedly a fact that large numbers of the wounded died on the battlefield many hours, if not days, after the actual battle from the lack of medical aid or simply water:

> I was fortunate enough to get wounded! A musket ball entered just below the wrist in my left hand, the bones leading to my thumb and forefinger are a good deal smashed, the ball is still in my hand. Some leather and velvet which was driven in from my sleeve and glove have been already extracted but there is too much inflammation to allow them to cut out the ball. I am however assured that there is no danger of losing the hand and that I shall in great measure recover the use of it ... When I was wounded it was dark, my friend Drummond (who you have heard me mention) got a man of the band to assist me to the rear in quest of a surgeon but after wandering as far as my strength would allow me I found the attempt to find one useless and therefore got the man who was with me to search for some blankets among the packs of the unfortunate fellows who were pretty thickly scattered about us and after getting well wrapped up laid down for the remainder of the night. In this situation I suffered the most excruciating pains. In the early part of the fight I was struck in the left knee by a piece of shell; whilst I kept myself in motion I felt very little from the blow which did not penetrate but after I had lain some time on the ground it gave me an immensity of pain as it was much swollen and perfectly stiff. At day break on 19th Drummond found me out and to my unspeakable joy procured a dragoon horse that was slightly wounded to take me to Brussels. I shall not attempt to describe the scene which presented itself in retracing the ground we had fought over. ... I am now in a very good billet. The people are very kind to me, they give me linen and clothes when I can get up. ... As soon as the ball is taken out of my hand I shall go to the regiment.[7]

Others, despite their own wounds, were more aggrieved at the loss of their favourite horse:

> The 4¾ ounce ball (iron grape) entered under the collarbone & came out through the blade bone behind. The wound behind is beginning to heal & the discharge is trifling, the front wound still continues to discharge very much, he is a most confounded ugly fellow, with a nasty red & bosomed face as big as a tea cup. I have had a great deal to do to keep body and soul together, & have never yet been out of bed, accept when assisted by these people, for the doctors to dress me twice a day. It was generally thought in the army that it was impossible for me to survive, but I hope the people not wounded, were so much employed in the pursuit that none of them wrote home. In fact I am put down as dead in one list. It was impossible for Bonaparte & Honesty to agree, his faithlessness was enough to get him sacrificed, [I] mentioned before to my mother my servant [had?] him buried. A very short time after I was wounded Honesty got three shot, two [from] cannon, one round carried off a fore leg, a shot destroyed the saddle but did not kill, he got also a musket shot in the chest & poor fellow he bled to death, he carried me beautifully when sent on a message through a rye field [six?] feet high, he was in the most beautiful condition you can imagine, we never had exactly a squabble, I was one day forced to tell him who was master & he always believed it after. You cannot imagine how much I regret Honesty. When I was wounded, I was not on him, but had gone up to him in the middle of the square & took something I wanted out of the holsters. While I was doing this a musket ball struck in the boat cloak strapped in front. I know not exactly if this ball went into him, I almost think not, however I stept [sic] a few paces aside & said 'If you are hit old fellow do not think I did it', from thence I went to the front face of the square, in order to bring some musket fire to bear on the enemy; in endeavouring to get through the closed ranks I got the grape shot in my shoulder & five other wounds in my face. I knew when I got the bullets in my face but do not [know?] when the grape hit me. When I fell & they came round me & said 'He has got a ball through his right eye'. Colonel Dalmer asked me some questions, I said I had got just as much as I could carry off, & that I thought pretty nearly enough to finish me.[8]

Susan Clinton was also grieved to learn that the initial reports of du Plat's escape without injury were misplaced:

> I thought my information good when the A.D.C. of General Adam, Captain Yorke assured me that Colonel du Plat was well & remained with the army, I was doubly shocked today when from still better authority I was

informed that he was mortally wounded & died on Monday, this excellent man will be a serious loss to poor Henry, he wanted some experience in the command of a brigade but what he wanted was made up by his zeal & his desire to please, at the same time so mild & so much of a gentleman, this poor man has been almost living with us at Ath & at Beloeil, General Adam is doing well but the ball was still in his leg yesterday, however being the general officer of least suffering here, he has the superintendence of the military business since the removal of headquarters, this gives so much trouble & vexation that it is prejudicial to his recovery.[9]

Commanding officers began their reports to their brigade commanders, recommending those who had shown particular valour:

> I cannot praise enough the good conduct of my officers and men on this day. The following have excelled in particular by their calm intrepidity: 1.) Major Rudorff, 2.) my brother, Captain von Hammerstein, 3.) the rifle officer, Ensign Mull, 4.) the two Sergeants Werner and Brand of the 1st Light Battalion, 5.) the soldiers NCO Fritze of No. 1 Company, Franz Lierat of No. 2, Corporal Schulze of No. 3, NCO Beker of No. 4 Company.

As well as praise for those who had performed well under fire, there was condemnation for one German officer:

> Finally, I regret to have to add that Lieutenant Tospau of my battalion had absented himself on the day before the expected battle, and returned on the following morning. With your permission, my dear colonel, I had to separate him immediately from the battalion before the battle for that reason, and because none of his fellow officers would serve any longer in his presence.[10]

Those whose units had remained in reserve and had few casualties were almost apologetic for it:

> Since we were part of the reserve, we did not become involved in a fire fight. But during 18 June our brigade was exposed to an almost continuous heavy cannonade, ... Without doubt, the number of killed and wounded would have been much higher, had not the earlier rainy weather softened the soil, so that the cannon balls etc. had lost much of their lethal force that these could have kept by bouncing off a hard soil surface.[11]

Henry Clinton wrote a fulsome report on the actions of the 18 June praising all of his troops, even his raw Hanoverians who had had to endure such a ferocious cannonade. This was sent to Lord Hill with the report from General Adam on the actions of the Light Brigade attached:

My Lord,

I have the honour to report to your lordship that the conduct of the Second Division during the action of yesterday in as such as to entitle it to the approbation of your lordship and to that of the commander of the forces, the steadiness with which the young Hanoverian Brigade under Colonel Halkett sustained the effect of a lasting cannonade during the several hours which that brigade continued to be in reserve, would have been creditable in veteran troops.

From the moment at which the 2nd Division was called upon to take a more active part in the action by relieving some of the corps in the first line, the good conduct of the whole could hardly be surpassed.

The brigade of Colonel du Plat was the first employed in this manner, and it was not long before its valuable commander received a dangerous wound, which will long deprive the army of the benefit of his services. It then fell to Major General Adam's Brigade to take its share of the same honourable service, the manoeuvre in which the several regiments, the 52nd Regiment under Colonel Sir J. Colborne, the 71st under Colonel Reynell, and the 2nd and 3rd 95th under Colonel Norcott and Lt. Colonel Ross have discharged their duty was witnessed & admired by the whole army. It was late in the day when I brought forward the brigade under the command of Colonel Halkett, the activity with which this move was performed by every battalion of the brigade, the regularity of its movements and the correctness of its formations under a destructive cannonade were very praiseworthy in these young troops, the Salzgitter Battalion under Major Hammerstein I employed by reinforcing the post of Hougoumont, at that moment vigorously attacked, and the Osnabrück Battalion under Lt. Colonel Count Munster advanced with the first line, while the battalions of Bremervorde and Quakenbrück under Lt. Colonel Count Schulenburg and Major Baron Bussche continued in reserve as a support to the right of the line where the handsome repulse of the enemy's last attack by the Imperial Guards, afforded the opportunity to become ourselves the attacking body, so judiciously taken advantageously of by Major General C. Adam's Brigade under your lordship's immediate direction. I directed Colonel Halkett to reinforce the attacking line with the Osnabrück Battalion under Lt. Colonel Count Munster and I added to it the brigade of the German Legion, the command of which had now devolved upon Lt. Colonel Wissell, the 23rd Regiment under the command of Major Dalmer in consequence of Lt. Colonel Sir H. W. Ellis being wounded, advanced as a support to the right of the attack. The gallantry with which this service was performed, by every corps which had the good fortune to be employed in it I am sure attracted your lordship's notice, and I think without claiming too large a share of merit for these several corps, I may say that the result of these noble efforts greatly contributed to the complete success of this glorious day. Though the whole of the artillery and numerous trophies taken from the enemy, may belong in consequence to every corps engaged, as the effect of their exertions, I must report that the enemy was driven from four pieces of cannon which he was attempting to carry off upon the right of the Genappe road, by the Osnabrück Battalion which also during its advance got possession of two pairs of colours.

Major Sympher's troop of horse artillery and Captain Bolton's Brigade conducted themselves entirely to my satisfaction, the service has lost an excellent artillery officer in Captain Bolton, who was killed near the close of the day after usefully exerting himself during the whole of it. Major Sympher's troop followed in support of the cavalry until the darkness put an end to the pursuit of the enemy.

The brigade of the 4th Division commanded by Colonel Mitchell having been placed for the moment under my orders, I am happy here having to make the same favourable report of the conduct of every corps composing this brigade, the 51st Regiment under [blank – Lt. Colonel Mitchell] having been most usefully employed during the whole of the day with one squadron of the 15th Hussars in keeping in check a considerable body of the enemy's cavalry supported by infantry which menaced our right and the 14th Regiment under Lt. Colonel Tidy having acted as a support to the 51st Regiment and latterly as a support to the right of the post of Hougoumont. I have also to acknowledge the assistance which I had from Lt. Colonel Sir Jeremiah Dickson the Assistant Quarter Master General and from Captain Bentinck acting as Assistant Adjutant General as well as from the officers of my personal staff. I beg that your lordship in making your report to the commander of the forces will have the enclosed letter from Major General Adam laid before his Grace. H.C.[12]

Henry Clinton was also soon reporting to Lord Hill those of the division whom he believed should be recognised by a step in rank for their actions:

My Lord,

I have the honour to enclose a list of the officers who commanded the battalions or at least companies on the 18th instant, and of those who during the action succeeded to such commands in consequence of others being disabled; and I beg leave to add the names of other officers which from the favourable reports made of them by the officers commanding brigades, it is my duty to request you will lay

before the commander of the forces, in the hope that His Grace will recommend them for promotion. The names of these officers:
Brevet Major Blair 91st Foot.
Lieutenant Campbell 7th Foot aide de camp to Major General Adam.
Lieutenant Rantzau 4th Battalion KGL who acted as aide de camp to the late Colonel du Plat, and is now doing the duty of Major of Brigade.
Captain Saffe, 1st Line Battalion KGL, Major of Brigade to Colonel Halkett's Brigade.
Brevet Lt. Colonel Rowan.
Brevet Major Chalmers and Lieutenant and Adjutant Winterbottom 52nd Regiment.
Captain Reed, Lieutenant Barailler and Lieutenant and Adjutant Anderson 71st Regiment.
Captain Logan, Lieutenant Humbley, & Lieutenant and Adjutant Smith 2nd Battalion 95th Regiment.
[Brevet] Major Fullerton, Captain Eeles, & Lieutenant Hope 3rd Battalion 95th Regiment.
Captain Goeben 1st Battalion K.G. Legion, Captain Rettberg ditto.
Captain Purgold 2nd Battalion KGL Captain Beurmann 2nd Battalion KGL who succeeded to the command of the flank companies after Captain Hesse was wounded.
Lieutenant Dehnel, 3rd Battalion KGL
Captain Heise, Lieutenant Freudenthal 4th Battalion KGL
Major Count Munster, Captain Gotthard, Lieutenant Winckler Osnabrück Battalion.
Major Baron Hammerstein, Captain Baron Hammerstein and Ensign Mull Saltzgitter Battalion.
Major Rudorff, Captain of the 1st Light Battalion KGL doing duty with the Salzgitter Battalion.
Captain Appuhn 3rd Battalion and Lieutenant During 1st Battalion KGL doing duty with the Osnabrück Battalion.
I beg also to recommend Captain Bentinck of the Coldstream Guards who has been doing duty as Assistant Adjutant General to the Second Division from its first formation, and who is a zealous and active officer.[13]

However, it would seem that the lists of recommendations to the Duke were far too large and the list had to be revised:

Sir,

In obedience to the General Orders of the 2nd [July] instant I have the honour herewith to enclose the names of those officers belonging to the 2nd Division of Infantry whom I wish to submit in order to their attracting brevet promotion. H.C.

List of Officers of the 2nd Division whose names are submitted for obtaining a brevet promotion.

<u>52nd Regiment</u>
Brevet Lieutenant Colonel Chalmers
Captain C. Diggle
*Lieutenant & Adjutant J. Winterbottom

<u>71st Regiment</u>
Major Walker
Captain Reed
*Lieutenant Barrailler

<u>95th Regiment 2nd Battalion</u>
[Brevet] Major Miller
Captain Logan
*Lieutenant Humbley

<u>95th Regiment 3rd Battalion</u>
Major James Fullerton
Captain Eeles
*Lieutenant J. C. Hope [2nd]

<u>1st Battalion King's German Legion</u>
Major Robertson
Captain A. de Saffe Major of Brigade
Captain F. Baron Goeben
*Lieutenant H. During

<u>2nd Battalion King's German Legion</u>
Major Muller
Captain W. Baron Decken acting Major to Bremervorde Battalion

<u>3rd Battalion King's German Legion</u>
Major Luttermann
Captain Louis de Dreves, acting Major to Osnabrück Battalion

<u>4th Battalion King's German Legion</u>
Major Reh
Brevet Major Meyer
Lieutenant W. B. Rantzau acting as Aide de Camp to the late Colonel du Plat and from Major Wehmann's death (former Brigade Major) as Major of Brigade

Bremervorde Battalion of Hanoverians
Captain Frederick Scheuch
*Lieutenant Augustus Wahrendorff 1st Light Battalion King's German Legion acting as Major of Brigade

2nd Battalion Duke of York Osnabrück
Major Count Munster
Captain Frederick Gotthard [von Quernheim]

3rd Battalion Duke of York Quakenbrück
Major Baron W von dem Bussche[14]
Lt. Colonel Hunefeld
Captain Hulsemann 1st Light Battalion King's German Legion acting as Major
*Lieutenant and Adjutant Mackeprang

Salzgitter Battalion
Major Christopher Hammerstein
Captain George Rudorff 1st Light Battalion King's German Legion acting as Major
Captain Hans von Hammerstein

Staff
Captain Bentinck Coldstream Guards acting Assistant Adjutant General
Brevet Major Blair got Brevet Major of Brigade to the 3rd British Division
Captain Saffe 1st Battalion King's German Legion, Major of Brigade to the 3rd Hanoverian Brigade.

Those whose names have * marked to them were omitted from understanding that it is not usual to grant to officers of this rank promotion by brevet.[15]

General Adam, who had gone to England to recuperate from his wound, also sent a letter to the Light Brigade:

> I request you will express in my name to the officers, non-commissioned officers and men of the brigade (52nd, 71st and 95th Regiments) how much I regret my separation from them. The expectation of being early enabled to rejoin, and the hope of doing so, (which till within these last few days I have continually entertained),have alone prevented my sooner expressing to the several corps of the brigade the admiration I shall ever entertain of

their intrepid and noble conduct in the battle of the 18th of June. To have had the good fortune of being at their head on so glorious an occasion will be to me a subject of increasing satisfaction. In proportion as I have regretted being separated from the Light Brigade, I shall look forward with anxiety to resuming that which it will be my pride to have held.
Frederick Adam Major General.[16]

As regards the King's German Legion troops, a number were awarded the Guelphic Order of Hanover. This medal was instituted on 12 August 1815, for non-commissioned officers and soldiers who had distinguished themselves in battle, and provided its bearer with an annual cash stipend of 24 thaler. Entitlement to this medal was examined by a special commission and had to be supported by actual facts, which had been authoritatively certified (almost always by officers).[17]

Their citations read:

2nd Line Battalion, KGL, action at Hougoumont

Private Christian Hallego
When the garden [orchard] of Hougoumont, strongly occupied by the enemy, was retaken by the allies, Hallego particularly distinguished himself, being the first who rushed in, seized two Frenchmen and made them prisoners, and with powerful blows of the butt end of his musquet, cleared the way before him.[18]

3rd Line Battalion, KGL, action at Hougoumont

Corporal Christian Brinkmann
He was with the specially formed light battalion. After seizing the Hougoumont orchard, this detachment had been engaged from behind a hedge in vigorous skirmish fire with enemy tirailleurs. An enemy Staff officer was coming close to the hedge. Brinkmann quickly jumped through the hedge into the open and took him prisoner right in front of his men.

4th Line Battalion, KGL, action at Hougoumont

Sergeant Cristoph Brandt
The four light companies of the first four battalions of the legion had been combined into a battalion of its own. It had severe losses; its commander and the four captains had been killed or wounded within a very short time. The same fate eventually happened to the Adjutant,

Return of Killed, Wounded & Missing of the Allied Army under the Command of Field Marshal His Grace The Duke of Wellington K.G. & G.C.B. in Action with the Enemy On the Plains of Waterloo on 18th June 1815

KILLED Regiments	Colonels	Lt. Colonels	Majors	Captains	Lieutenants	Cornets/Ensigns	Staff	Troop Quartermasters	Sergeants	Drummer/ Trumpeter	Rank and File	Total
1st Batt 52nd						1					16	17
1st Batt 71st						1			1		23	25
2nd Batt 95th									2	1	31	34
3rd Batt 95th											3	3
Total Loss of British						2			3	1	73	79
1st Line Batt KGL				1					2	1	19	23
2nd Line Batt KGL				1					1	1	16	19
3rd Line Batt KGL				1					1		16	18
4th Line Batt KGL			1						1		12	14
Total Loss of KGL			1	3					5	2	63	74
Batt Bremervorde					1	1					16	18
Batt Osnabrück					1	1			1		15	18
Batt Quakenbrück											1	1
Batt Salzgitter											21	21
Total Of Hanoverians					2	2			1		53	58
General Staff of 2nd Division												
Total 2nd Division			1	3	2	4			9	3	189	211

WOUNDED Regiments	Colonels	Lt. Colonels	Majors	Captains	Lieutenants	Cornets/Ensigns	Staff	Troop Quartermasters	Sergeants	Drummer/Trumpeter	Rank and File	Total
1st Batt 52nd			1	2	5				8	1	182	199
1st Batt 71st	1	1		4	8				7	3	150	174
2nd Batt 95th		2		2	10				6	2	171	183
3rd Batt 95th		1	1		2				1	1	34	40
Total Loss of British	1	4	2	8	25				22	7	537	596
1st Line Batt KGL			1	1	2	1	1		6		63	75
2nd Line Batt KGL				1	1				4		75	81
3rd Line Batt KGL			1		4				2	1	90	98
4th Line Batt KGL				1	3	2	1		3		74	84
Total Loss of KGL			2	3	10	3	2		15	1	302	338
Batt Bremervorde					3	2				1	18	24
Batt Osnabrück			1	2	2	2			4	1	75	87
Batt Quakenbrück			1								8	9
Batt Salzgitter				1	1				2	1	59	64
Total Of Hanoverians			2	3	6	4			6	3	160	184
General Staff of 2nd Division												
Total 2nd Division	1	4	6	14	41	7	2		43	11	999	1118

MISSING Regiments	Colonels	Lt. Colonels	Majors	Captains	Lieutenants	Cornets/Ensigns	Staff	Troop Quartermasters	Sergeants	Drummer/Trumpeter	Rank and File	Total
1st Batt 52nd												
1st Batt 71st											3	3
2nd Batt 95th											20	20
3rd Batt 95th											7	7
Total Loss of British											30	30
1st Line Batt KGL										1	16	17
2nd Line Batt KGL									1		6	7
3rd Line Batt KGL											31	31
4th Line Batt KGL										1	13	14
Total Loss of KGL									1	2	66	69
Batt Bremervorde					1		1		2		44	48
Batt Osnabrück												
Batt Quakenbrück									1	1	22	24
Batt Salzgitter						1	2		6	1	73	83
Total Of Hanoverians					1	1	3		9	2	139	155
General Staff of 2nd Division												
Total 2nd Division					1	1	3		10	4	135	234

TOTAL Regiments	Colonels	Lt. Colonels	Majors	Captains	Lieutenants	Cornets/Ensigns	Staff	Troop Quartermasters	Sergeants	Drummer/Trumpeter	Rank and File	Total
1st Batt 52nd			1	2	5	1			8	1	198	216
1st Batt 71st	1	1		4	8	1			8	3	176	202
2nd Batt 95th		2		2	10				8	3	222	245
3rd Batt 95th		1	1		2				1	1	44	50
Total Loss of British	1	4	2	8	25	2			25	8	640	713
1st Line Batt KGL			1	2	2	1	1		8	2	98	115
2nd Line Batt KGL				2	1				5	1	97	106
3rd Line Batt KGL			1	1	4				3	1	137	147
4th Line Batt KGL			1	1	3				4	1	99	109
Total Loss of KGL			3	6	10	1	1		20	5	431	477
Batt Bremervorde					5	3			2	1	78	89
Batt Osnabrück			1	2	3	2			5	1	90	104
Batt Quakenbrück			1						1	1	31	36
Batt Salzgitter				1	1	2			8	2	153	167
Total Of Hanoverians			2	3	9	7			16	5	252	396
General Staff of 2nd Division												
Total 2nd Division	1	4	7	17	44	10	1		61	18	1323	1586

whose duties Brandt now performed with distinction. In the afternoon, this battalion, supported by the 2nd Line Battalion, had to drive the French from the Hougoumont orchards. As soon as this had been accomplished after fierce fighting, Brandt hurriedly saw to it that several gaps in the hedges were barricaded through which the enemy might have penetrated again.

4th Line Battalion, KGL, action at Hougoumont

Rifleman Henry Rohlfs
An officer attested to the bravery of this man as follows:

'After the combined light companies of the four line battalions (1st, 2nd, 3rd, 4th), together with the 2nd Line Battalion, had driven the enemy out of the orchard of Hougoumont on 18 June 1815, I and Rohlfs happened to be at the left wing of the skirmish line in a ditch behind a hedge. Apparently not noticing us, an enemy captain on horseback came close to us; I jumped up and grabbed the horse's bridle, but had to let go again if Rohlfs had not come to my aid and taken the captain prisoner. That man offered his watch and purse to Rohlfs, but he nobly declined to take them.

'During the brief period of our presence in that orchard, Rohlfs managed to shoot down some 12 to 14 enemy tirailleurs and two officers; before he fired he said to me each time: "Sir, now it's that one's turn" and each time the target dropped to the ground. But then he was wounded himself and fell down; he now, in a prone position from behind his knapsack, shot down a few more enemies. Soon thereafter we took part in the advance'.

1st Horse Battery, KGL (Captain A. Sympher)

Gun Captains Carl Heine and Henry Niemeyer
Before moving into action, this battery stood in the second line for a long time where it suffered some losses from enemy artillery fire. After several batteries had moved out of the first line due to lack of ammunition, it eventually advanced there and came under heavy artillery and skirmish fire. Here it assisted greatly in repelling the last heavy French attacks.

Heine and Niemeyer soon were the only active gun captains; they were kept busy hurrying from one piece to the next, taking care of the effective targeting of each gun. The crews also were taking losses; at Niemeyer's cannon five gunners had been killed or wounded. Niemeyer himself was struck by a canister ball in his lower left leg but remained active. In the evening, he brought back to the battery the ammunition reserve element, which in the general confusion had retired to one hour's distance from the battlefield ...

When the ammunition, particularly canister shot, was about to become depleted at a critical moment, enemy columns threatened to renew their attack. Heine on his [own] initiative with two gunners quickly searched out nearby abandoned and shot-up limbers and wagons while under heavy fire. Fortune was with him, and his volunteering was crowned with the best of success; the search turned up the desired ammunition which was then hauled to the battery and most effectively used at the very moment that the French Guard launched its attack.

Chapter 16

The March to Paris

Having been fed and watered, if the men had any food left to eat, or were lucky enough to scavenge some, orders were received for the army to march. Few were sorry to leave the horrid battlefield behind, for the stench of death was all around:

> The 52nd remained for several hours on the morning of the 19th near Maison du Roi, before they marched to Nivelles. Meat was served out, and the men cooked. I recollect having there first eaten 'beefsteaks fried at the end of a ramrod'. My servant brought water for us to drink from a pond in which he said there were the dead bodies of two French soldiers, and that he could not find any other water.[1]

The first day's march was not too strenuous, going only as far as Nivelles, but on the following days the marches became longer in an attempt to catch up with the Prussian advance. Henry Clinton was able to write to his brother one week after the battle with the route up to that time towards Paris. They had not encountered any resistance within France, but were forced to halt on 23 June simply because they had out-marched their supplies:

> On the 19th we marched to Nivelles, on the 20th the Prussians went to near Maubeuge, our army to Binche & Mons. In the night of the 20th Maubeuge was invested, on the 21st we marched to Bavay (headquarters Malplaquet), the Prussians beyond Avesnes which surrendered in the night. On the 22nd we marched to Cateau [Cambresis], the Prussians to Guise. Our First Corps is between Bavay & this place, Prince [Frederick] of Orange observes Le Quesnoy & Valenciennes. We are under the necessity of halting this day, having rather outrun our supplies & I should not be surprised if this should occasion a further halt tomorrow. This will be very useful to us in enabling us to get up our stragglers & bad marchers.

> Bonaparte is said to be at Laon with the remnant of his army, but I question if he will be able to get together [a] force sufficient to fight us again.[2]

As for the supplies, Commissary Tupper Carey had gone to Brussels during the battle to arrange for supplies to be loaded. With news of the victory arriving in the middle of the night, he immediately completed his loading and set out to join the division at Waterloo, but found that they had already moved on:

> A little after three o'clock in the morning we got on our legs again to attend to our duty. I received orders to take a convoy of provision wagons, with which I started before I could obtain any intelligence of my second horseman, who had no doubt been panic-struck, and with many others had started for Antwerp or Ostend. Our route lay through the Forest of Soignes. The chaussee road, from the recent heavy rains and immense thoroughfare during the last three days, was a mass of mud. My horse most unluckily cast a fore shoe in the midst of it, and in a short time began to get lame. What to do I did not know. To find such a thing as a resident farrier at that time was impossible. I could not lead my horse for long and walk, without doing him up as well as myself. I was therefore in despair at the idea that in not reaching the troops I should be considered as having neglected my duty. In this frame of mind and disagreeable dilemma, in a small nook of brushwood off the road [I saw] a farrier forge of one of the cavalry regiments. I at once went up and requested to have my horse shod. The farrier refused, being strictly forbidden to do so to any horse not of the cavalry. For a time all my remonstrances were ineffectual, until I thought of the only expedient which might probably overcome the difficulty. I pulled out of my pocket a Napoleon, which I offered him. For a time he hesitated what to do, but on my again telling him that the public service absolutely required it, he set at once about the work, and relieved me from a great load of embarrassment.[3]

He now came to the scene of the battle of the previous day and had to traverse the awful field. Nevertheless, he eventually arrived at Nivelles, where he was warmly received by the division:

> Our march was very slow, of course, and we passed through Waterloo, now a busy scene, the medical officers being fully occupied in collecting and attending to the wounded. Thence we proceeded to Mont St Jean, and arrived about nine o'clock at the fork of the road, leading on the one hand to Charleroi and on the other to Nivelles.

Here it was necessary to decide which to take, and I unfortunately took the wrong one, that leading to Charleroi. It was a great oversight on some officer's part, whose duty it was to do so, not to have stationed a person at that particular spot to point out to all going to the army the right path, in consequence of which the convoy, instead of reaching its destination at about one o'clock, only got there at night. We journeyed on a short distance and reached our position of battle. It was dreadful to see the numbers of the killed, both men and horses, on each side of the road. Many bodies were already stripped of their clothes. As we descended down towards La Haye Sainte, the scene of carnage was still more developed. All round the Haye Sainte and on the chaussee leading to the French position, the dead were innumerable, French and English intermixed. Those who had fallen in the road had been trampled upon by horses and wheels of artillery, into a mass of blood, flesh, and clothes, hardly to be distinguished one from the other. In the hollow between the two armies on each side of the road, there lay piles of dead Frenchmen and horses, among whom were many of the Imperial Guard. Their large bear-skin caps, which they had thrown away in the struggle, strewed the ground. To add to the numbers were many dead cuirassiers, still with their cuirasses on, some of which I could easily have brought away had I had time or someone to assist me in stripping the dead bodies. With the exception of a few parties wandering in quest of wounded men, as well as plunder, all was as quiet as a churchyard …

We followed the chaussee in the midst of this field of death, which, in addition to men and animals, was strewed with arms of every description, until we reached the foot of the French position, where it was said Napoleon took leave of his Guard moving on to the final attack. On ascending to the top of the eminence we came upon the French guns scattered in various directions, evidently in the way of being dragged to the chaussee from different positions. This attempt had failed owing to the muddy state of the ploughed land and the rapidity of our advance, which obliged the drivers of the gun carriages to flee for their lives by cutting the horses' traces. I perceived that some of the guns had engraved on them Egalite, Fraternite, and others with the letter N; many of the guns had the number of the English regiments which had captured them chalked on them; a mode usually adopted in the Peninsula. The carriages were sunk in the ground almost to the axle trees. As we proceeded, we fell in with the Prussian columns coming up from our left marching to join their army. They began to plunder the biscuit convoy most unceremoniously, and I had great difficulty in preventing it. Perceiving some troops to our right I rode up to them and found they were a part of our division; the 52nd Regiment,

> commanded by Sir John Colborne (now Lord Seaton), moving across the country towards Nivelles. I applied to him for a guard to protect the convoy, but he refused it with some unmeaning excuse, and I was therefore left to my own resources to get out of the difficulty as well as I could. The Prussians kept moving by us occasionally, and I would most certainly have been plundered by them of the best portion of the biscuit, had it not been for the opportune arrival of a detachment of our German cavalry (the King's German Legion). The commanding officer, seeing my dilemma, immediately ordered some of his men to draw their swords and accompany the convoy, and thus we moved on to Quatre Bras through Genappe. I there beheld, in addition to many other debris of the French Army, Napoleon's carriage on the spot where it had been overtaken and plundered. Around it were Prussian soldiers scraping and sifting the ground, in consequence of a report that some diamonds had fallen from their settings in the night scramble. When once past Quatre Bras we fortunately saw no more of the Prussians, and jogged on quietly until we reached Nivelles, not, however, before night fall, but in time for a most acceptable distribution to the troops.[4]

The 2nd Division was not involved in any major events on its relatively incident-free march to Paris. On 24 June the 4th British Brigade re-joined the 4th Division and ceased acting under Henry Clinton's command:

> We never seed a French soldier the whole of our advance after that night of the battle. Our advance was about 150 miles, very hard marching, we got the front in. Paris capitulated on the 3rd day after we made our appearance at Paris, the Prussians had a skirmish with them and drove them on to Paris, we never met to fire a shot at them. We marched in to Paris on the 7th July, [we] is encamped in the centre of the city on Boney's pleasure ground.[5]

The men looked on Paris as the end of their woes as many had lost everything they had during the confusion of the last few days. As Lieutenant George Horton of the 71st wrote:

> We hope to be in Paris in a week or ten days, as we are only distant 40 leagues. I must now tell you my grievances; I have lost the whole of my baggage, taken by the enemy; I have now only one shirt, now worn eight days, & other things which I happened to have on. I am quite at a loss to know what to do, & I am in a most miserable state, obliged to let the clothes dry on my back, & lying out in the rain, as we have very wet weather almost every night. We never had such long marches, ten

& twelve leagues without halting & I am obliged to walk the way. Do not think from all this that I want to get money from you, as I know it is out of the question, but if I thought it would answer I would write to Uncle George, as I have not a rag to my back.[6]

Many of both the regimental and the staff surgeons had remained with the injured, but this left the regiments on the march bereft of medical staff to treat the sick. It became necessary to request that some of the medical staff were sent back to their brigades. As Henry Clinton wrote:

Sir,

I enclose herewith a letter which I have just received from Lt. Colonel Wissell commanding the 1st Brigade of the King's German Legion forwarding a representation made to him by [the] senior surgeon of his brigade, who with two other surgeons & their assistants have been detained at Waterloo. In laying these papers before the commander of the forces I request you to mention to His Grace that Mr Maling, the staff surgeon attached to the 2nd Division who remained at Waterloo until all the wounded belonging to this division had been provided for previously to his leaving the wounded, did represent to Deputy Inspector Taylor the necessity there was that the surgeons of the regiments of the Legion should be allowed to join them (respective corps which are now without medical assistance and medical stores of any kind the surgeons having been required to keep their panniers at Waterloo, in these circumstances I trust that His Grace will give orders for the return of these surgeons to their regiments.[7]

After a second day of rest the army was put in motion again. Henry Clinton related each day's march in his diary:

Monday 26th

The 2nd Division of the English with the Nassau Brigade & the British cavalry marched by Vermand to Monchy, at Caulaincourt is the house & property of Mr de Caulaincourt. Here we crossed the Omignon River.

Wednesday 28th

A change was made in the direction of the march of some of the cavalry, that which had been moving upon the right by Montdidier was sent across to the Senlis road, & the Brigade of Hanoverians brought up from the rear & ordered to precede the 2nd Corps now composed of the 2nd & 4th British Divisions and of Colonel Estorff's Brigade of cavalry, the right column marched this day to Montdidier to Petite Crevecoeur & Montigny, the cavalry to St. Juste [en Chaussee].

Thursday 29th

The right column marched this day by St. Just where it fell into the great Amiens & Paris road, to the villages beyond Clermont, the 2nd Division encamped between the road & the village of Breuil le Vert, the cavalry towards Beauvais, the headquarters of the army were at Les Ageux near Pont St. Maxence.

Friday 30th

the order for our march did not arrive till past 5 this morning, at 6 the 2nd Division began its march & crossing the Oise at Creil reached Lamorlaye about 5 miles beyond Chantilly at 12 o'clock, the places which had been visited by the Prussians have suffered, the inhabitants are in a state of alarm & do not evince half that joy apparent in those where the Prussians have not been.

He added further details in a letter to his brother:

Luzarches 30th June 1815

We marched this morning about 6, crossed the Oise at Creil & my division is encamped at the little village of Lamorlay between this place & Chantilly. Firing has been heard all day in the direction of St. Denis, I think it likely that when the enemy who must be very weak shall see our whole force arrive, he will not attempt any defence. However, tomorrow will bring us to this point & I hope find an end to scenes of war.[8]

His diary continues:

Saturday 1st July

The 2nd Corps marched this day and encamped in position, the right on the height to the right of Pierrefitte sur Seine, the left on Le Bourget.

Sunday 2nd

Early this morning I received an order to occupy the village of Stains in place [of] some of the Nassau Division which was directed to be placed in reserve at Garges [les Gonesse], this extension, having to furnish pickets down to the Seine, made my position excepting the heights of Pierrefitte weak. About 12 I received orders to extend to my right & occupy with one brigade from Argenteuil to Epinay [sur Seine] inclusive, upon this occasion I directed a certain post to be furnished by the brigade under Colonel Reynell's command, but he observed that the distance was too great, and though I expressed disapprobation of this remark & repeated the order, I found on the following day that the picquet was furnished as Colonel Reynell had thought proper & not as I had ordered. How can business be conducted with any sort of regularity or even with security with the burdens of such practises?

His letter again gives further detail:

Sarcelles 2nd July

We advanced today to within half a league of St. Denis, which the enemy occupies & has entrenched. The Prussian army has crossed the Seine at the St Germain & will I conclude move on Paris on that side this day, what will be the course I know not, but if they do not surrender, it is probable then that we shall wait for the Russians & then storm them into a surrender, if the National Guards do not force them before.

But the news that day was of even greater consequence. Henry Clinton was quick to pass this on to Susan:

My dearest Susy,

I may now congratulate you upon the completion of the grandest event that the history of the whole world has furnished. The French army has submitted unconditionally & thrown itself upon the King's mercy. How perfect in every part has been the conclusion of this tremendous conflict, we flattered ourselves that with the reign of Bonaparte the mischief of the French Revolution had terminated, but the whole of what has since happened was something to perfect this great good & this would not have happened but for the insatiable ambition of that unprompted adventurer aided by some of the blackest traitors that the world ever produced. The king may now well be regarded and hailed as the saviour of Paris. But for him it is probable that it would have been carried by assault & fallen a prey to a serious plundering, a large part of the country has felt the scourge of war in all its horrors, many villages have been completely ransacked by these Prussians & that this would have been the case in Paris nobody can doubt, this is the horrid situation to which Bonaparte had exposed his own people & then he had the villainy to leave them, he will now be confined to the execration & contempt of

March To Paris
Wellington's Army
Blucher's Army
Fortress
Brussels
Scheldt
Waterloo
Wavre
Nivelles
Quatre Bras
Mons
Charleroi
Valenciennes
Bavay
Le Quesnoy
Phillipeville
Maubeuge
Cambrai
Landrecies
Givet
Avesnes
Cateau Cambresis
Peronne
Amiens
Somme
Vermand
St Quentin
Guise
Rocroi
Nesle
Villecourt
Ham
Roye
La Fere
St Just
Laon
Aisne
Oise
Clermont
Soissons
Compiegne
Rheims
Villers Cotterets
Senlis
Nanteuil
Marne
St Denis
Gonesse
Versailles
Vincennes
Paris
Seine
N

mankind, a more awful example by far than if he had fallen in the field or by the hand of an honest & independent Frenchman which certainly was to be expected.[9]

Returning to his diary, it is clear that there were some difficult moments as they prepared to enter Paris:

Monday 3rd

About 11 o'clock Lord Hill called & informed me that the Duke of Wellington had been met by an officer from Marshal Blücher at Argenteuil informing him that the enemy had surrendered unconditionally to the king, in consequence of this information I desired that the preparations for defending the villages of Villetaneuse, Pierrefitte & Stains might be discontinued. About two o'clock I received a letter from Colonel Reynell dated half past ten informing me that he had been ordered by the Duke of Wellington to cross the river for the support of a brigade of cavalry. In the afternoon I rode by Montmorency to Argenteuil crossed the Seine by the pontoon bridge & proceeded towards Courbevoie, here Colonel Reynell showed me an order written by the Duke of Wellington, saying that only posts which the enemy had upon the left of the river must be desired to withdraw. But the enemy was still in possession of a part of the village & had also a picquet in the road to the garrison, Colonel Reynell had been told that the French general had gone to Paris for instructions. Several hours had however passed and as night was approaching, I sent again to desire that the picquets might be withdrawn, in answer to this I received a proposal from the general to meet him which I acceded to, he expressed great unwillingness to remove his picquets & since if I attacked him he should defend himself, but upon my representing that we might both conform to the spirit of our instruction without risking any affair of blood, he agreed to withdraw his troops from the village & the road to St Germain & I placed those of the English cavalry so as to command a complete view of the bridge & the road to the barrier of Neuilly.

Rumours of French resistance still abounded:

Tuesday 4th

It is reported to me that the enemy began this morning about 6 o'clock to construct some works in front of their lines. At 12 o'clock I received the order to be in readiness to march at noon, yesterday a convention was concluded by Victor of which the enemy are to vacate the right bank of the Seine from Neuilly to St. Denis this day, the position of Montmartre tomorrow & the city of Paris upon the 6th, the French army is to retire beyond the Loire, this move is to be completed in 8 days. At four I received the order to march & immediately despatched to order to my division which however did not march by half an hour as early as it ought to have moved. The Nassau preceded our arrival at St. Denis round which we were obliged to file, the 2nd Division was to proceed to Neuilly & Villiers, the Nassau to Clichy and St. Ouen & the fourth to St. Denis. I was riding forward to examine our intended position when three French hussars attacked me & 2 or 3 officers with me, upon finding we did not alter our pace but rode steadily on, they halted, got off the road & fired, their shot being returned by some Prussian straggling hussars, the fire continued & I was constrained to find an officer with a trumpet to demand of the officer an explanation of this disloyal conduct. Several peasants coming in reported that the enemy retained possession of Neuilly. ... I was therefore under the necessity of remaining where I was, or by proceeding to open the communication to risk violating the convention & straying in some very serious accident. At daylight I examined myself the road & found a very good & direct road through the Borghese's garden.

Wednesday 5th

As soon as we could see past two [am] I occupied a position & made a troop encamp at Neuilly I heard that Colonel Reynell had met with similar opposition, confining him to the bare occupation of the village, which he had readily attempted to dispute. At ten o'clock I heard that the Duke of Wellington was to have his quarters at Neuilly, at 12 the enemy having left Montmartre it was occupied by our troops.

The allies were to take control of the gates of Paris, or *barrières*, but this was always likely to be fraught with difficulties:

Thursday 6th

By virtue of the convention, the barrieres of Paris are to be occupied this day at 12 o'clock by the allies, but when the troops were in readiness to proceed, a delay was occasioned by the enemy claiming that the National Guards should take the duties with us. To this the commanders refused their assent, but the National Guards would not retire until compelled to do so by the advance of our Guards, the gates taken by the 2nd Division, were those of Passy, on the Seine, St. Marie, Longchamps, Chaillot & Neuilly, at that of Neuilly I was obliged to order a British officer to remove the tricoloured flag which was waving over our heads & afterwards to take the arms from the gendarmerie at Chaillot & Longchamps, I was obliged to have the barricades removed, by setting fire to the palisades.

Henry Clinton reported his actions to Lord Hill:

> My Lord Hill,
>
> Major Churchill has reported that after some hesitation the National Guards stationed at the Barriere de l'Etoile were withdrawn, and I left it in the possession of a guard of the Legion. The Barriere of the Pont de Chaillot and Longchamp were built up, and the wall upon both sides closely loop-holed, believing this at first to be only the case with the Barriere of Chaillot I let the guard return, but I thought it better to have the barricade at Longchamps removed. I found here a post of the National Guards, which refused to withdraw until I desired the guard to take possession. This was also the case at the Barriere de St Marc, and while I was desiring the National Guard to remove from this gate, a party of Gendarmerie came galloping up, and in an unnecessary proud & authorative tone to me, ordered this National Guard at their peril to let any person of the Prussian or English army to enter, and to arrest any persons who should enter with a white cockade. At the Barriere de Bass Haussines, the same unwillingness to retire had been shown by the National Guards, the Barriere of Longchamps was opened, the guard posted there, but here again the National Guards reported that their orders from Massena required them to do the duty at the Barrieres in common with us. Upon my return to the Barriere de l'Etoile I found the sentries of the National Guards doing duty with us and the commanding officer advanced every objection to removing them, referring me also to an order of Massena in the building opposite to that in which a guard is lodged of over 50 Gendarmes with the tricoloured flag flying over our heads. Considering this an unnecessary ceremonial I desired that it might be removed, this they promised to do, but put it off, I therefore sent an officer to take it down, I thought it not correct that a corps of 50 Gendarmes armed should be lodged within the entrenchment in front of the Barriere, & therefore proposed to their commander to withdraw from this building entirely or to lodge their arms while they remained under charge of the Legion guard, but he proposed removing altogether. I have given orders for the opening the Barriere of Chaillot tomorrow morning. H.C.[10]

Orders were received for the troops to march into Paris and Henry Clinton's Light Brigade was given the undoubted honour of mounting guard in the city at the Tuilleries and outside Wellington's house. It is possible that this honour was bestowed on them, over the Guards, because of their actions in the Battle of Waterloo:

Friday 7th

In the night I received orders to send a brigade into Paris to encamp on the Champs Élysées where the Duke of Wellington was to have his headquarters. The rest of his army was to encamp in the Bois de Boulogne. After fixing upon the ground for the camp of my division, I went with the brigade and encamped them in the Champs Élysées.

Chapter 17

Paris

The Light Brigade was the first to march into Paris to mount guard and to camp on the Champs Élysées, a distinct honour.

> With respect to the troops that first entered Paris by the Bridge of Neuilly and the Bois de Boulogne – the brigade of General Adam passed the bridge of Neuilly the night before the Duke took up his quarters in Paris, and halted at Neuilly, after having had a sharp discussion with the French officer in command of the squadrons of cavalry at the bridge, who opposed our passage of the bridge in consequence of his having received no orders to give up his post.
>
> The next morning Sir F. Adam's Brigade, unaccompanied by any other, marched by the Barriere de l'Etoile to the Champs Élysées. The 52nd was posted near the Duke of Wellington's quarters.[1]

The very first unit to head the march into Paris was actually the 2/95th:

> I had the honour to command the first regiment of the allies which entered Paris. We marched up to the Tuilleries to mount guard over the palace. We are now encamped within twenty yards of the spot on which Louis & Queen were beheaded with about 20,000 others. ... I am recommended for a majority & Lord Hill thanked me personally as did also General Adams for the conduct of my regiment.[2]

Those were the sentiments of Captain Joseph Logan, but Private Lewis of the 2/95th summed up how most of the men were really feeling:

> yesterday the 7th of July that we entered Paris. But ever since the 15th of June till last night the 7th of July we have only laid down in the ground with our clothes on, so I leave you to judge if I am not fatigued out. Blücher rode by the side of Wellington yesterday when we entered Paris. As we was on the advance after the French army, every

town we came through the people was all fled to Paris & took away what they could & the British, Prussian & Russian army broke their houses open & plundered what was most good to them and set fire to some, but wine was more plenty than water for all their cellars was full of wine, the same as Squire Tucker's is full of cider and that was the first place all the soldiers broke open. I have often been in cellars & what wine we could not drink & carry away they would break in the head of the cask & let it run about, I was often over my half boots in wine. We marched through towns as large as Exeter & not a person to be seen but all locked up & window shutters fastened.

Direct as before, only left [sic] out Flanders and put France. There is at this present time more than 700,000 soldiers in Paris and round the suburbs, but Boney and all his army is gone, God knows where.[3]

The remainder of the allied army was encamped within the Bois de Boulogne, and the camp soon became a novel attraction for Parisians. The arrival of the allied soldiers was, nonetheless, marred by some misbehaviour from the Hanoverian troops whom Henry Clinton had caught on a foraging expedition. He wrote immediately to Colonel Halkett:

Dear Sir,

I have always remarked so good a disposition in the Hanoverian troops to obey orders & at the same time I observe so many instances of distribution of orders that I cannot believe that those which have been lately issued have been properly communicated to the soldiers, this could not only be a very considerable neglect of duty in them to whom it belongs to enforce obedience, but it is also of great importance to the soldiers who are hereby exposed to a disgraceful punishment without being aware of the transgression by which they became liable to it. Violation of the order that no soldier is to be out from camp without a pass, in violation of that order, which includes any article brought into camp but by a party under charge of an officer. I met this evening about 7 o'clock soldiers of the Osnabrück, Quakenbrück and Bremervorde Battalions at a considerable distance from the Bois de Boulogne proceeded as they alleged in search of forage, one amongst them declared that he had been sent by his master …

In the first place these men would not have been absent from the camp at this hour if the duty was regularly performed & all officers knowing that to send to fetch forage accepting through their commissary is a direct violation of the order of the Duke of Wellington & it is besides an encouragement to the soldiers to plunder or at least to every mischief. I beg you will communicate this letter to the

> commanding officers. Call upon the Adjutant of the Quakenbrück Battalion to explain the case of his battalion and mention to the commanding officers that if they do not succeed better in obliging their men to conform to the orders of the army, it will be my duty, & a duty which I shall discharge very unwillingly, to enforce restraint upon the whole to whatever extent it may be necessary in order to obtain a perfect obedience to any order which has been passed or will be passed for the good of the army. H.C.[4]

As soon as they had arrived in camp in the Bois de Boulogne, Henry Clinton began to inspect his troops properly for the first time since the Battle of Waterloo. On 8 July he began with the German Legion and Hanoverian troops and inspected 1st Line Battalion KGL which then consisted of 3 Captains, 11 Subalterns, 18 Sergeants, 9 Drummers, and 240 Rank and File:

> Since the battle of the 18th June this battalion has been commanded by Captain Goeben, I found it in very indifferent order & [he] does not appear to be at all qualified for improving it. I did not attempt to see it move, but the arms are dirty from neglect, the accoutrements as bad, the packs ill put together & all ill put on. There is an evident languor in the manner in which the officers go through their duty incompatible with any tolerable degree of order or discipline, the ammunition is not properly taken care of.[5]

He also inspected the 2nd Line Battalion KGL, which he found consisted of 1 Field Officer, 5 Captains, 14 Subalterns, 19 Sergeants, 11 Drummers and 294 Rank and File:

> Though too slow & otherwise not qualified to make a good commanding officer, the situation which Major Muller has directed to the improvement of this battalion has certainly placed it in point of excellence before the first battalion, the arms are not clean, nor are the packs generally properly put on, but the accoutrements are much cleaner and the ammunition in that state that some attention to the matter on the part of commanders of companies is apparent. Many bill hooks have been carelessly lost.[6]

The Bremervorde Battalion of Militia consisted of 2 Field Officers, 4 Captains, 12 Subalterns, 23 Sergeants, 6 Drummers and 517 Rank and File. Henry Clinton was impressed:

> In this battalion there is no appearance of its having been engaged in hard service during the last 3 weeks, the clothing though much worn

> is in good repair. The arms, accoutrements and appointments all evidently well looked after & taken care of, these young militia officers pay much more attention to the keeping of their men in order and fit for service than the officers of the legion. Count Schulenburg continues to command this battalion, if these young Hanoverians were to remain long enough in the field for their officers to acquire a good practical knowledge, they would very soon become amongst the most efficient of the Allied army.[7]

The Quakenbrück Battalion of Hanoverian militia consisted of 1 Field Officer, 3 Captains, 12 Subalterns, 16 Sergeants, 7 Drummers and 499 Rank and File and was not in such good condition:

> Major Bussche having been wounded in the action of the 18th June, the command of this battalion has devolved upon Major Hulsemann of one of the light battalions of the legion, the good system established by Major Bussche continues to be acted upon, though this battalion does not derive much benefit from the exertions of its present commanding officer. All that is wanting to this Hanoverian Battalion being in the state reasonably to be expected of them are a few repairs in their accoutrements and repacking some of their ammunition, owing to their soldiers being less experienced than their neighbours. They have idly lost their entrenching tools & many bill hooks also are wanting.[8]

Two days later he completed the inspection of the German troops. The Salzgitter Battalion consisted of 2 Field Officers, 3 Captains, 15 Subalterns, 20 Sergeants, 8 Drummers and 465 Rank and File:

> This is a small body of men as well as very young, upon the whole this battalion is not in so good order as the two of the same brigade which I inspected yesterday. The arms are dirty, the ammunition not generally well packed and the caps still put on in a slovenly manner. The action is considered as an unanswerable excuse for every irregularity.[9]

The Osnabrück Battalion contained 2 Field Officers, 2 Captains, 14 Subalterns, 22 Sergeants, 7 Drummers and 423 Rank and File:

> The share which this battalion had in the action of the 18th accounts for its losses & as in the former is brought forward as an excuse (by no means admissible) for every deficiency, with about 30 missing knapsacks were all shot away. The entrenching tools have most casually been lost as well as the bill hooks. It is true that the weather yesterday was very unfavourable but not bad enough to justify the

> bad appearance of the arms & accoutrements, the ammunition too is ill packed & has not been kept in the order desired.[10]

The 3rd Battalion KGL consisted of 1 Field Officer, 3 Captains, 11 Subalterns, 25 Sergeants, 11 Drummers and 367 Rank and File:

> This battalion as far as arms, appointments & general appearance of the soldiers is better than others of this brigade. The present commanding officer Major Luttermann is old & inactive, this battalion is quite fit for the field. The most apparent fault is in the looseness of the files.[11]

The 4th Battalion KGL consisted of 1 Field Officer, 4 Captains, 12 Subalterns, 19 Sergeants, 8 Drummers and 295 Rank and File:

> This battalion since it had the misfortune to lose its late excellent commander Colonel du Plat, has very much fallen off in its appearance. Major Reh who has lately commanded it & who is now retiring upon account of bodily infirmity, has neglected all those attentions necessary to keep troops in order, amongst other omissions he has allowed the paymaster of the battalion to be absent without ever reporting it. In forming up this battalion the files are much too loose, the arms are clean & packs well put on, but the ammunition has been neglected. The great failing in the legion is in the very evident indifference of a large part of the officers.[12]

It is clear that much work would be needed to bring the German battalions back up to perfection after the rigours of the battle and subsequent march on Paris. But Henry Clinton was particularly unhappy generally with the KGL battalions, where he noted a disinclination by the officers to apply themselves. Was it war-weariness or the spectre of imminent disbandment that appears to have led to a collapse in their morale?

A full week later, Clinton inspected the Light Brigade on the Champs Élysées. The 52nd Regiment consisted of 1 Field Officer, 8 Captains, 30 Subalterns, 47 Sergeants, 20 Drummers and 755 Rank and File. Henry Clinton recognised their excellent order but still questioned their laxity of discipline:

> This battalion is in good serviceable order, the excellent system introduced by Sir J. Moore continues its influence, indeed it has been in its full practise under its present good commander Sir J Colborne. The arms, ammunition & appointments are in good order, and as long as there is only a question of successful fighting however severe, the

> complaint may be this regiment will do its duty but in case unhappily this regiment shall be employed in assaulting a place or in any service in which its subordination shall be called in question to support the authority of its officers, all its good qualities will be of little accord. There is in this respect, a laxity of discipline which is very disgusting, an officer of whatever corps or rank receives from a soldier of this regiment no acknowledgement of respect. Upon a march, they used in the presence of this officer the most disrespectful language, nor do the officers pay the least attention to these instances of disrespect & insubordination, for the sake of security I would rather have in other respects a less efficient corps.[13]

The 2nd Battalion 95th consisted of 4 Captains, 11 Subalterns, 32 Sergeants, 11 Drummers and 348 Rank and File. This battalion did not impress Clinton:

> This battalion had been so much neglected by Colonel Wade that it still wears the appearance of a degree of looseness, the arms are not so clean, the ammunition taken so good care of or the packs so well put together as might be expected from a corps of so high a character, the present commanding officer however (Captain Logan) pays great attention to his duty. An action is supposed excuse to account satisfactorily for many deficiencies & particularly in such privileged regiments such as those composing their brigade. More camp kettles & bill hooks than the killed & wounded, were lost in the action, though properly these ought not to exceed one fifth of the casualties, but this is the way to be particular & that is a most mischievous but general pursuit of commanding officers.[14]

The two companies of the 3rd Battalion 95th Foot consisted of 1 Captain, 4 Subalterns, 8 Sergeants, 6 Drummers and 126 Rank and File. These troops were in a much better condition:

> But for the loss of the clothing which to this time is not satisfactorily accounted for, the detachment is in good order, I prefer its appearance to that of the 2nd Battalion, Captain Eeles having been taken from it to be placed upon the Staff, it has for the last short time been in rather incompetent hands, but Major Fullerton having joined, I have no doubt of its improvement. The same want of care is apparent in the state of the ammunition.[15]

The 71st Regiment consisted of 2 Field Officers, 6 Captains, 18 Subalterns, 46 Sergeants, 20 Drummers and 560 Rank and File. Henry was generally impressed:

> This regiment has improved greatly since I inspected it at Leuze on the 1st of May, the men are more steady & the late commencement of service has rather given them a more soldier-like appearance than affected their efficiency, the same remark in regard to losses in action applies & to a great degree in this battalion, but the arms are in good order, the ammunition is the most neglected & this in disobedience of a detailed order which I gave out upon the first formation of the division. Though not less celebrated as a fighting regiment it has not the appearance & instant prepossessing manner of the 52nd. I gave only a verbal caution to Colonel Reynell respecting the state of his ammunition & field equipment.[16]

On Thursday 20 July, Lord Hill inspected the entire 2nd Division. On paper it mustered 5,200 bayonets, but was only able to assemble a little above 4,000 men.

On 24 July, the Emperor of Russia reviewed the whole of the Duke of Wellington's army. The bulk of the cavalry, with the horse artillery attached to it, was formed in two lines extending from the end of the Champs Élysées to the Barrière de Neuilly. The infantry, with the foot artillery attached to it, was in contiguous columns of battalions from the barrier to beyond the bridge of Neuilly, A further two brigades of cavalry were in the rear of the infantry. By midday the Emperor had ridden along the line as far as the bridge of Neuilly and back to the Place de Louis XIV. The army then began to march past in quick time, the last regiment passing the royal gathering after 17.00 hours.

On Wednesday 9 August, Henry Clinton saw the Osnabrück and Salzgitter battalions at exercise in the morning and was apparently much struck with the improvement, particularly in the latter. On 22 August, Henry Clinton exercised his division by order of Lord Hill in the plain of Neuilly. The troops were apparently brought in confusion to the ground owing, seemingly, to the incapacity of the Assistant Quartermaster General.

This was an inauspicious final review of his troops – for two days later a General Order was issued changing the formation of the various divisions. The 2nd Division itself began to change beyond all recognition and this is where our story now comes to an end. There was no great send off, no final parting. In true army style it was done without any pomp and circumstance; it was a simple administrative exercise.

The changes in the Second Division at this time were as follows:

The British Light or 3rd Brigade remained virtually unchanged.

The 1st KGL Brigade was amalgamated with the 2nd KGL Brigade and transferred on 24 August to 3rd Division.

The Hanoverian Brigade remained unchanged.

To replace the KGL Brigade, the newly formed 12th Brigade consisting of 1/3rd Foot, 36th Foot, 38th Foot and 2/73rd Foot, commanded by Brevet Colonel Sir Charles Greville joined the 2nd Division. The 3rd Foot was added to this brigade at the request of Henry Clinton, who had been made their colonel.

As the KGL Brigade left his division, Sir Henry Clinton wrote to the men, wishing them luck, as this change was clearly in readiness for the final disbanding of the King's German Legion:

> Dear Sir,
>
> I have been directed to desire that you would report yourself to the general commanding the 3rd Division, in order to receive instructions. I assure you I do not send you this notice without feeling regret at the removal of your brigade from the 2nd Division. I have had satisfaction in observing the general good conduct of the brigade since we have served together, I sincerely hope the Duke of Wellington may be able to appoint you to some command, should it be necessary at this juncture to remove you from the command of the brigade, which may be not less agreeable to you, at any rate if you have lost a better appointment you have the satisfaction to reflect that this change has been brought about by a sense of duty in you. I beg you to accept and to assure your officers of my sincere regard and of my best wishes for their wellbeing and that of your gallant brigade. H. Clinton.[17]

King George III signed the official proclamation disbanding the King's German Legion at Carlton House on 24 December 1815. The troops marched back to Hanover to begin the reorganisation of the Hanoverian army, which would then incorporate elements of both the KGL and Hanoverian battalions. Orders for the Hanoverian Brigade to march home to Hanover also came in early December and Henry Clinton wrote of his sadness at leaving it:

> Dear Sir!
>
> I enclose to you the route for the march of your [3rd Hanoverian] Brigade to Brussels on your way to Hanover. The first day's march from your quarters would be too long; I therefore suggest that Count Schulenburg's Battalion be assembled between Le Chesnay and Rocquencourt and that the remainder of your brigade be entering Versailles on the 9th. I would have greatly regretted taking leave of your brigade without having seen your officers be appropriately awarded for their merits, had I not received the most satisfactory assurances from the Duke of Wellington of his high regard in which he holds your brigade and all Hanoverians who fought in the Battle of Waterloo, as well as of his approbation of their general good

> conduct. I am authorised to assure you that it has been, and still is, His Grace's desire that the Hanoverian army and those of the other nations receive due awards for their services. Since those foreign orders granted to him were intended exclusively for the British army, it was not in his power to use a part of these to reward the services of officers of the other nations. As to those awards that it is our government's prerogative to give, I know that it is the Duke's recommendation that they be conferred to the officers of the Hanoverian army as if they had served in the English army. I believe that this recommendation will certainly be considered, and I am convinced that a large part of these marks of esteem will be apportioned to your brigade at the time that they are granted. These details should not be made public, but I request that you pass them on to the commanding officers of your battalions.
>
> I ask that you express to them my thanks for their eagerness with which they without exception have supported me in the performance of my duties. Allow me to say the same to you, and let your brigade know that your outstanding leadership under any and all circumstances and calm bravery on this trying day of Waterloo have been such as to justly entitle you to the Duke of Wellington's fullest praise and to your country's gratitude. I wish you luck on your return to your homeland after your glorious service; as a soldier I much regret seeing you leave. I remain, dear sir, your obedient servant, Henry Clinton.[18]

Henry Clinton officially remained with his much altered 2nd Division, until the final return of the Army of Occupation to Britain in December 1818. The British Light Brigade remained in France with the Army of Occupation until the very end, as did a number of regiments that had served at the Battle of Waterloo some three and a half years earlier. Their return was hardly noticed, the euphoria after Waterloo had waned and the spectre of political unrest and the 'Peterloo Massacre' had changed public attitudes dramatically. As always happens, the British public soon forgot the bravery and heroism of their troops and of their suffering and privations. Soldiers, and particularly those returning maimed or mentally scarred by the scenes they had witnessed, returned to a land where they were often forced to live out their lives in penury or on a pitiful pension from the medical board. Many of these men could not settle, however, and soon took up arms again as paid mercenaries in the wars of independence that flared up across Southern America or back in Portugal and Spain during the Carlist Wars. Britain was no land 'Fit for Heroes'.

Henry Clinton's life was also unfortunately to suddenly change for the worse. His beloved Susan, who appears to have been sickly for some time, died on 17 August 1816. This seems to have had a profound effect on Henry, whose health rapidly deteriorated and he became a virtual recluse. It is very marked that from this date, there are few entries in his diary and his correspondence becomes sparse. He was reported to be at Lyons in the spring of 1817 'very ill' and by 1818 his brother William was extremely concerned for his health. With the return of the Army of Occupation, Henry returned home with the 2nd Division, but he was a broken man – a sad ending for a great soldier.

Henry eventually died on 11 December 1829, aged fifty-eight, at his country seat of Ashley Clinton near Lymington in Hampshire and was buried with his wife at the Church of St Mary Magdalen at Barkway in Hertfordshire.

The 2nd Division,as we have seen, played a very significant part in the defeat of Napoleon at the Battle of Waterloo. It is a part that has been ignored or misunderstood for far too long and it is hoped that this study has shown, for the first time, their major contribution to that victory, and also that their achievements that day cannot simply be summed up by the actions of one battalion alone, supposedly unsupported, in one glorious movement by which they swept the field clear.

The actions of the 2nd Division at Waterloo should be ranked equally with those other formations that are celebrated for their efforts on 18 June and not viewed as a 'reserve' formation which merely performed the *coup de grâce* to an enemy already beaten by the efforts of others.

I hope, instead, that I have shown that all of the troops within this division fought bravely and that all had a profound influence on the ultimate success on that fateful day.

Appendix 1

Evidence of Colonel Hugh Halkett's Capture of General Cambronne

Descriptions by witnesses, with explanatory text[1]

By an unknown author

> A French general, whose name is Cambronne, I believe, was with the French Guards as they were retiring, and who made strong efforts to bring the battalions to a halt and back to order … Our Brigadier, Colonel Halkett, noticed this, and, with unequalled intrepidity, rode through the French tirailleurs, who provided cover to the retiring columns, to this general and brought him along, despite his strong resistance, before the length of the line through the enemy tirailleurs to make him his prisoner.

Ensign Heinrich Bergmann, 2nd Line Battalion, KGL

> It was 8 o'clock … the Hanoverian Infantry Bataillon Osnabrück, which under the leadership of Colonel Hugh Halkett had assisted the brigade (Adams) by protecting the latter's flank, met, when arriving at the plateau of Belle Alliance, the First Chasseur Regiment of the French Imperial Guard under General Cambronne's command which retreated in good order.
>
> Halkett, at the head of the Osnabrückers, called upon the French to surrender, but as Cambronne, who accompanied the last company of his regiment on foot urged his men to resist, Halkett gave orders to fire. The French there upon accelerated their steps, but General Cambronne, probably too proud to run, was overtaken and made prisoner by Halkett who rode up to him at full speed.

Lieutenant Richers, Osnabrück Landwehr Battalion

An officer of the Osnabrück Battalion, Lieutenant Richers, later colonel and commander of the 2nd Hanoverian Infantry Regiment, reports:

I was now in front, and was able to observe, and the following has vividly been impressed in my memory ... A high-ranking officer, accompanied by two other mounted officers, was particularly active in his efforts to bring the Old Guard again to a halt. He could be seen encouraging them while riding back and forth and our men had already repeatedly been told to fire at those riders. The horse of the high ranking officer eventually fell down after being struck by a bullet. The rider was lying under the horse and was not immediately able to free himself. We now shouted at Colonel Halkett who was riding between our front ranks that the particular officer in the distinctive uniform, on whom he had kept his eyes, had fallen. As soon as the colonel had seen this, he drew his sabre, set the spurs to his horse, and rushed at the gallop towards the rider on the ground, leaving fugitives to his right and left, and thus in fact, being in the middle of the enemy. As the colonel approached the fallen rider, he had already freed himself from the horse and stood upright, I believed to have seen how the colonel slashed at him. All our men nearby and I myself ran towards the scene because the colonel was obviously in the greatest peril, as he could be killed from all around by a bullet or the thrust of a bayonet. Still, none of the Frenchmen had any time left to save their general, and the words '*sauve qui peut*' were of the utmost significance here, because even the general's mounted companions had galloped off. At the moment that the general had become the colonel's prisoner, the colonel gripped him by the collar and dragged him alongside his horse in our direction. I and three or four privates were the first to approach them. As we reached them, the colonel halted with his prisoner, turned him loose, and asked him who he was. The general was bleeding copiously from a head wound, blood was flowing all over his face, and after wiping the blood from his mouth with his hands he answered: '*Je suis le général* Cambronne.' I am unable to say whether Cambronne's wound was caused by a slash from Colonel Halkett or by a bullet; we just halted there for a brief moment, and then at the colonel's command, all of us rushed forward. Late in the evening, after the battalion had come to a halt, I heard that Sergeant Führing and three men had escorted General Cambronne to Brussels. Führing had later often told us about this escort episode, and that Cambronne had given him his watch and money pouch; he had also asked that his epaulettes be taken off because he was well known in Brussels and would not want to be recognised there as a prisoner.

Sergeant Führing, Osnabrück Landwehr Battalion

Sergeant Führing of the Osnabrück Battalion, later a janitor at the consistory or church council in Osnabrück, to whom Halkett had handed over his prisoner for transportation, no officer being available, has also recorded his experiences at Waterloo. I have selected the following from his narrative:

> Alerted by repeated shouts, I saw at a distance our brave and bold Colonel Halkett, who always stayed near us, engaged in a fight with the enemy general; I hurried there, held the tip of my Hirschfänger [short sabre] against the chest of our colonel's adversary, who immediately dropped his sword to the ground, shouting, 'Pardon Monsieur!' The prisoner had been wounded above one of his eyes, and I heard from our colonel's conversation with the general that the latter said that he was a Brigade General [Major General] of the Imperial Old Guard.
>
> In this way, the general became our prisoner due to the boldness of the brigadier colonel who surveyed everything with his calm and imperturbable determination and personally hurried to the spots of greatest danger. It was obvious that the prisoner could not be freed by his own men if one takes into account that they were heavily pressed in their battle with us and the Scottish infantrymen.
>
> Being put in charge [of him] by Colonel Halkett, I then took away the prisoner, together with three of our men whom I myself had selected. We might just have left the range of the firing, when the prisoner handed me his watch and money pouch; he later gave me his golden epaulettes and his aiguillette. I kept the watch, the money I shared with my comrades and the other objects I returned to the prisoner on the advice of other officers even though he refused to accept them ... with the words 'Tenez, Monsieur'.

He follows with a description of how an unauthorised individual, 'an officer with a detachment of 30 men', tried to take the prisoner away from him, how he refused to surrender him and how two Brunswick hussar officers came to his assistance in this critical situation. He then continues:

> Towards 11 to 12 o'clock in the evening, I delivered the prisoner to the hussars near Brussels who were in charge of collecting prisoners and, after taking leave from General Cambronne, returned with my three comrades to our brothers-in-arms, whom we met the next morning on the victory exalted battlefield near the farm of Belle Alliance.

Ensign Lyra, Osnabrück Landwehr Battalion

Ensign Lyra was his company's only remaining officer, who led it during the last phase of the battle, and he has commented on, and confirmed, Führing's account. But he believes that he had to insist on his authority as company commander, as he writes:

> It may be true that Führing held his Hirschfänger against General Cambronne's chest, whose head had been wounded by a grazing bullet, whereas the latter had been arrested by Colonel Halkett and then been turned over to me. Although I will not dispute that Colonel Halkett had chosen the very brave and dependable Sergeant Führing to transport the prisoner, in as much as he had been of help in this bold feat, I nevertheless must object that Führing, without my knowledge and permission as his company commander, had gone off and had selected on his own three men to accompany him. Even a civilian would understand, moreover, a non-commissioned officer and soldiers may leave their company only if this is with the company commander's prior knowledge and permission, of which no exception can be made under any circumstances. I am therefore compelled to amend Führing's relation with respect to the full truth and in regard to this point that Colonel Halkett brought the prisoner to the left flank of our battalion, at whose outermost division I happened to be. It was from there that Sergeant Führing took the prisoner away with the men assigned by me and after he had received my permission.

In supplementing the above descriptions it will not be without interest to learn more about Cambronne's watch and seal since they constitute important evidence regarding the present question. The watch was later sold to Registrar Lyra upon his repeated requests. Richers explains this, saying:

> I have often seen Cambronne's watch, both while it was in Führing's possession as well as after it was acquired by Ensign Lyra, who was later a chancellery registrar. It was a silver watch with an enamelled clock face, and Cambronne's coat of arms had been engraved on its exterior.

Lyra had been forced by health reasons to retire from military service in 1816 and had been employed as a chancellery registrar in Osnabrück. In his book *Letters in Low German, etc.* (Osnabrück 1845) he writes:

> The watch as well as the appended seal of this brave hero of the pyramids are my lawfully and deservedly acquired property, by which I believe to possess one of the most interesting relics of the great day of the Battle of Waterloo. Both are provided with the coat of arms conferred by Napoleon, an upright standing lion surrounded

by nine burning grenades in a blue field; in its honorary escutcheon, at the right an honourary sword, a crown at the top of the escutcheon; the casing carrying the decoration of the Légion d'honneur.

General Freiherr Hugh von Halkett

The editor of Lyra's book, Dehnel, makes the following observation:

> Regarding the following relation of the capture of General Cambronne, known worldwide, the editor of these pages has received the special permission of General H. Halkett who gave it with the particular intention 'to respond to the many requests that he received, and to put an end to the doubts and uncertainties that still are raised from time to time about the memorable incident and that primarily have had their origin in France'. The simple and humble relation by the general himself, most of it written here in dictation and then confirmed by his signature, runs as follows:
>
> General Hugh Halkett
>
> The Hanoverian Infantry Brigade under my command on the day of the Battle of Waterloo, consisting of the Osnabrück, Salzgitter, Bremervörde and Quakenbrück Battalions, was employed, besides other troop bodies, in the defence of the orchards surrounding Chateau Hougoumont for a long period of time. We were involved there in some hot engagements.
>
> After the last major, but completely unsuccessful, attack by the Imperial Guards upon the British position, I received orders to have my brigade advance together with the English one of Colonel Adam.
>
> At that moment, I had only the Osnabrück Battalion near me, which stood next to the eastern hedge in an open field, the other battalions were still situated between the hedges in the orchards of Hougoumont. I followed Adam's Brigade, but sent my Aide de camp, Captain August von Saffe of the 1st Line Battalion of the German Legion, to the other battalions to bring them the order to follow us without delay. During our advance, Captain von Saffe was killed before transmitting the order to the other battalions. These then did not follow.
>
> In the meantime, I had advanced with the Osnabrück Battalion, about in line with Adam's Brigade, against three battalions of Napoleon's Old Guard. These fired at us and we returned the fire while we moved closer to them. They turned about and retired, we followed. They turned around once more and fired another volley that we did not leave unanswered.

In this contest we had approached within 200 paces of the old veterans of the French Emperor. Several times I shouted at them: 'Rendez-vous mes amis!'

While I could hear that my challenge was answered, I did not understand their words.

The enemy continued to retire. Their commanding officer was at first on horseback and urged them energetically to stand fast, but in vain. I saw him somewhat later with two aides-de-camp about 150 paces behind the column, but now on foot after the loss of his horse.

Riding in front of the Osnabrück Battalion, I might have been only about 100 paces away from this officer of superior rank when I made the decision to attack him in person. I put the spurs to my horse, galloped at him, and menaced him with my sabre raised high.

He at once threw away his sabre and shouted: Je me rends! [I surrender] and let me know that he was General Cambronne. He then walked ahead of me in the direction of our line. After a few steps my horse that had already been wounded was struck again by a ball and collapsed under me. While I quickly tried to free myself from the saddle, the exceptionally strong animal jumped up again with me on it, and I now noticed that my prisoner attempted to escape. I hurried after him, held him by his aiguillette, led him to our troops, and handed him over to a sergeant.

Immediately after this incident, the Osnabrück Battalion captured a French battery located to its left near the Guards, and then followed the long disorderly, tightly pressed enemy masses to the first houses of Genappe. We there let a column of Prussian cavalry pass by, which hurriedly pursued the French, and we then occupied a few houses and spent the night among wounded French soldiers.

A day later, Lord Hill gathered the officer corps of the now reunited brigade at Nivelles and thanked them for their distinguished performance.

Appendix 2

The Controversy of the 52nd

Throughout this book there has been an 'elephant in the room', so to speak. I have until this point wanted to avoid delving into the great controversy of which regiment did most to win the Battle of Waterloo. For those not steeped in the mass of contradictory evidence and the spurious claims by those involved, I will attempt a dispassionate reappraisal of the argument.

I must start by stating that I am rarely a fan of the modern penchant for conspiracy theories. However, I hope that I have described fairly and without favour the roles of the 2nd Division in the battle and the achievements of each regiment. I do believe that the 52nd was unfairly treated in the aftermath of the battle, but was it caught up in part of some grand conspiracy? I'm not so sure.

During the Victorian era, Colonel Gawler and later Mr Leeke, both ex-52nd men who had fought at Waterloo, sought to prove that their regiment deserved all of the credit for defeating the Imperial Guards, not the British Guards. More recently the same cudgel has been picked up again by Nigel Sale, another ex-light infantryman, who has expounded exactly the same arguments as made over a hundred years ago; unfortunately the debate has hardly moved on.

Let us, therefore, look at the actual evidence.

Immediately after the battle of Waterloo ended, the Duke of Wellington, despite the physical and mental exhaustion he had undoubtedly suffered over the previous four days, sat down to write his report or despatch. He sat down at a desk at his headquarters in Waterloo[1] in the early hours of the morning, having had little rest, to pen a succinct account of the Waterloo campaign including the final battle itself. When he went to Brussels that morning he completed his report and despatched it that afternoon for London in the capable hands of his aide-de-camp Major the Honourable Henry Percy.

Wellington was not renowned for his writing style and he had often been criticised before for not giving enough credit to one regiment or another in the aftermath of battles. This was to be no exception, for having hardly mentioned any specific regiment or their actions in detail, except the 1st Life Guards at Genappe, Byng's Division of Guards at Hougoumont, the heavy cavalry brigades of Ponsonby and Somerset, the Guards division of Cooke for the example they set, and of course the Prussians for their timely assistance.

He did not actually mention the attack of the Imperial Guard specifically at all, nor did he describe how and by whom they were defeated. However, Earl Bathurst on 23 June announced in the House of Lords that, 'Towards the close of the day Bonaparte himself at the head of his Guards, made a desperate charge on the British Guards, and the British Guards immediately overthrew the French.' Soon after, the Prince Regent announced that the 1st Foot Guards were to be known as the 'Grenadier Guards' in honour of their defeating the French 'Old Guard' at Waterloo – and the arguments began.

So let us try to look dispassionately at the merit of each of the claims:

1. Who told Bathurst that the Guards had defeated the Imperial Guard?

Nigel Sale claims that either a second letter was carried by Henry Percy from the Duke of Wellington to Earl Bathurst or Percy was instructed to impart the information verbally from the Duke or used his own opportunity to forward the case for the Guard.

There is absolutely no evidence for a second letter. Nigel Sale uses the fact that it cannot be found to insinuate that this helps prove the conspiracy. It proves nothing of the sort; the lack of a letter proves nothing either way. Verbal messages were possible, but Percy fails to mention it. He was not required to give his own account of the battle by either the Prince Regent or Earl Bathurst, he simply handed over the despatch, which they read. It should also be pointed out that Percy was an officer of the 14th Light Dragoons with no affiliation to the Guards, nor is it clear what advantage Wellington hoped to gain by projecting their claim over any others.

Conclusion: The most likely option is that Bathurst got his information from others. On the night of the 18th and the morning of the 19th many officers penned a few words to reassure their families of their safety and some gave a short version of the battle before hurrying to get it added to the post bag just leaving.

Isn't it more likely that Earl Bathurst received a short note home from his son, Ensign the Honourable T. Seymour Bathurst,who fought at

Waterloo? Isn't it just possible that he told his father that his regiment was instrumental in the defeat of the Imperial Guard? And his son served in which regiment? Why, the 1st Foot Guards, of course!

2. Did the British Guards defeat any part of the Imperial Guard?

Even the officers of the 52nd admit that the 1st Foot Guards did drive some of the Imperial Guard away – see Leeke, for example. Their contention is that this was merely a large cloud of skirmishers preceding the advance of the Imperial Guard which they drove off. The 1st Foot, however, claim that they were in a firefight with formed units of Imperial Guardsmen.

Recent evidence, including a great deal of material from survivors of the Imperial Guard, suggest that there were three waves of attacks by the Imperial Guard, consisting of ten battalions in total. The first, consisting of four battalion squares of the chasseurs of the Guard, struck the area around the position of the present Lion Mound. There they came in contact with Halkett's Brigade, which was forced to give some ground, along with Maitland's Guards. It would appear that this attack was pushed back by the Guards. The second and third attacks were virtually simultaneous but separated by a large distance and were hidden from each other by the lay of the land. The attack near La Haye Sainte struck the line in front of Kielmansegge's, Vincke's and Kruse's men, which were all forced back and there was a great danger of a real collapse. This situation was only saved by the fire of Krahmer's battery and a frontal attack by Detmer's Dutch/Belgians.

The British Guards seem to have charged down the hill until confronted by the third attack and were forced to retreat hastily. This, it appears, is the column of Imperial Guards, supported by elements of Bachelu's infantry.

Conclusion: The 1st Guards did defeat a part of the attack by the Imperial Guard, but so did the 52nd, and they should have gained some recognition for this. But so also should Detmer's Dutch/Belgian Brigade, which also pursued a campaign for many years to be recognised as due a portion of the glory of defeating the Imperial Guard. This claim, however, has dwindled.

3. Did Wellington both see and approve the movement of the 52nd?

It is claimed that Wellington was behind the Guards when the 52nd, on the volition of Sir John Colborne, made its flank movement and that he therefore downplayed the role of the 52nd as he was not personally involved.

Wellington was certainly behind the Guards when they drove back the first attack of the Imperial Guard, and Leeke is a witness to a host of skirmishers (disbanded squares?) of Imperial Guardsmen running down from the face of the ridge as they wheeled into position. The Guards apparently pursued these for a short distance before returning to the ridge line on the appearance of this further attack. Wellington was now free to observe what occurred and to react to it.

Captain Logan and Private Lewis of the 2/95th are both witnesses to the fact that Wellington ordered them personally to follow the movement of the 52nd. General Adam had sent Blair to enquire what Colborne intended and it is certain that he approved and immediately ordered the 71st and 3/95th to support it. We have further evidence that Wellington then rode down to the KGL battalions at Hougoumont and ordered them to further support this movement, as witnessed by 1st Line Battalion KGL. This is also confirmed by Major Blair, who met Wellington here:

> After the repulse of the squares of the Old Guard … Sir Frederick Adam desired me to ride on the prolongation of our right in order to observe if any part of the enemy seemed to threaten our right flank – then apparently quite unprotected. Having gone some distance, I met the Duke of Wellington moving at a quick pace, followed by one individual to whom I spoke. His answer was *'Monsieur, je ne parle pas un seul mot d'Anglais.'* [Sir, I do not speak a word of English] I told him in French the order I had received. He replied, *'Le Duc lui-meme a ete voir, il n'y a rien a craindre'* [There is nothing to fear, the Duke is here]. I rejoined the brigade.[2]

Conclusion: Wellington was close enough that if he had wanted he could have cancelled the movement very quickly. In fact, the Duke appears to have immediately appreciated the movement, and the evidence shows that he personally ordered up all the other units he could find in the vicinity to support it.

4. Were the corps and divisional senior officers, namely Lord Hill and General Clinton, absent from this part of the front and therefore failed to appreciate the significance of the actions of the 52nd?

We have two eyewitnesses, both Hill's aides-de-camp, that Lord Hill was in the vicinity when the 52nd advanced and indeed was so close to the action that his horse was shot and he took a heavy fall, by which he was believed killed for some time. Sir Henry Clinton was also near enough to have witnessed the movement and we know that he rode over personally to order the Hanoverian Brigade and the 23rd Fusiliers to advance (although only the Osnabrück Battalion received the order).

Conclusion: Every senior officer in this part of the field was in the vicinity of the Guard attack and quickly became apprised of Colborne's movement and readily ordered up units to support it. In fact, they attempted to get the entire 2nd Division on the move in support and, in addition, as much of the 4th Brigade as possible.

Indeed, Clinton's private writings immediately after the battle were positively glowing with regard to the performance of the Hanoverian troops. It would appear that the manoeuvre was supported by Clinton but was not regarded by him as anything especially outstanding for experienced British troops and he simply expected it of them.

5. Did Wellington suppress General Adam's report?

It is claimed that the report from General Adam regarding the actions of his Light Brigade was ignored by the Duke of Wellington and that it was somehow lost, as it is not to be found in the archives. This is thought to indicate that Wellington actively suppressed this report, which is presumed to have supported the case of the 52nd.

Henry Clinton refers to the report by Adam and attaches it to his report to Lord Hill. It is very noticeable, however, that Lord Hill's report to the Duke of Wellington only mentions attaching Henry Clinton's report. His letter dated 20 June 1815, from Nivelles at 08.00 hours, begins:

> My Lord Duke, Although your Grace witnessed the conduct of that part of the troops under my command which had the good fortune to be employed in the action of the 18th instant, still I think it my duty to transmit the accompanying report from Lieutenant General Sir H. Clinton, commanding the 2nd Division, and beg leave to express my entire concurrence with the Lieutenant General's sentiments respecting the gallant conduct of the troops on this occasion.[3]

Conclusion: Lord Hill did not forward Adam's report, possibly quite simply because the report from Clinton covered the same material. There is no evidence of a suppression of evidence by the Duke of Wellington.

6. Was the 52nd's entry into Paris designed to placate them and was their long service in the Army of Occupation designed to keep them quiet?

When the troops arrived at Paris, the only allied brigade to receive the honour to march into Paris, camp on the Champs Élysées and mount guard at the Tuilleries was the Light Brigade. If Wellington wished to honour the Guards over everyone else, would they not have expected this honour to be bestowed on them?

As to the troops who remained as the Army of Occupation until 1818 along with the 1/52nd, it is a fact that the 4th, 43rd, 71st and 79th Foot also remained until 1818. Were these being punished as well? Henry Clinton remained in command of the 2nd Division throughout – was he also being silenced?

It is also known that Wellington had very little influence on the regiments allocated to him; the Duke of York guarded that privilege very tightly.

Conclusion: The honour of being the only British brigade to march into Paris was clearly a significant honour and a clear sign to everyone of Wellington's pleasure with this brigade. The fact that the regiment remained until 1818 in France was nothing to do with an attempt to silence them; many regiments remained throughout the entire period of the Army of Occupation. There was a clear attempt to honour the brigade and no evidence of an attempt to keep the regiment from home for any other reason than normal duty requirements.

7. Wellington actively refused to discuss the merits of the 52nd's movements, does this prove that he suppressed the evidence?

Wellington does appear to have been cagey about talking about the action in detail in later years. For example, Colonel Bentham wrote:

> I met Gurwood in London about 1828 … and I asked him why he never drew the Duke out about the catastrophe [crisis] at Waterloo. He said that he had repeatedly made the attempt, but that it was a subject which always created great impatience. On the last attempt the Duke said 'Oh! I know nothing of the services of particular regiments: there was glory enough for us all!' [4]

Rumours of the Duke's being surprised on the 15/16 June 1815 soon surfaced and a number of units were unhappy with their lack of a mention in Wellington's despatch. What of Picton's Division against d'Erlon, Vivian's and Vandeleur's light cavalry charges at the end of the battle, the heroic defence of La Haye Sainte by Major Baring, to name but a few?

Conclusion: Wellington does appear to have been tetchy over requests to discuss the battle or at any attempt to write the history of the campaign and this is likely to have been because he did not want his own actions questioned, but more so regarding his poor showing on

15/16 June than his actions on the 18th. However, attempts to prove that Wellington actively blocked such attempts (as per the supposed campaign against Siborne) have been generally shown to be wide of the mark. See the author's *Letters from the Battle of Waterloo* for full details.

8. Were the generals who commanded in the 2nd Corps silenced by honours?

Nigel Sale claims that a greater number of honours were bestowed upon those officers that would need to be kept silent to avoid the unfair treatment of the 52nd getting out. He names these officers so rewarded as Uxbridge, Hill, Clinton, Maitland and Adam. Why Uxbridge and Maitland are included is very unclear – they could gain no advantage personally or to their corps by favouring the 52nd's claims.

Bob Burnham and Ron McGuigan[5] show that no officers gained baronetcies. Three officers got the Knight Commander of the Bath for Waterloo: Cooke, Maitland and Adam. One other got the Knight Grand Cross, Kempt. These were awarded by the Prince Regent. Regarding thanks from the Houses of Parliament, twenty were granted this distinction, all were at least brigade commanders at Waterloo.

Sale also refers to the award of foreign medals, the issue of which was in the prerogative of those various monarchs. As to the Order of Maria Theresa, twenty-three officers were granted the award of either Commander or Knight, amongst them were Uxbridge, Hill, Clinton (Byng and Adam were not, although Sale claims they were), but these honours were also granted to Colborne and Reynell of the 71st.

Regarding the Russian Orders of St George, St Wladimir or St Anne, which Nigel Sale shows separately, officers gained one or the other, nobody gained both. In total sixty-six officers gained one or other in one of the three classes of this award. Amongst the recipients were indeed Uxbridge, Hill, Clinton and Adam, but so again were Colborne and Reynell.

Regarding the Netherlands Order of Wilhelm, there were twenty-four recipients, including Clinton and Maitland. Finally, regarding the Bavarian Order of Maximilian Joseph (not mentioned by Sale), there were eleven recipients, these included none of these specific officers, but did include Norcott of the 95th.

Conclusion: With regards to honours granted by the Prince Regent or foreign heads of state there is no evidence that any officers gained a significantly higher number of awards than others. There is no clear evidence therefore that these awards had been manipulated by anyone, including the Duke of Wellington.

9. Is it true that Clinton's report lacked any comment on the actions of the 52nd due to the fact that he was ignorant of events?

Leeke claims that Clinton had not been near the regiment throughout the day as he had been busy with the rest of his division. He says that Clinton's diary:

> may appear to carry weight with it, is of no weight at all, because he can only have received it as one of the reports current in the Army on the 19th of June and afterwards. Clinton could not have seen what the 1st Guards did at Waterloo, for the right of his command was two-thirds of a mile from the right of the Guards, and all his troops except Adam's Brigade, were stationed at that time to the rear of Hougoumont …
>
> Clinton therefore, was fully employed in that important portion of the battlefield, and it was often mentioned in the 52nd, that he was never seen amongst them at Waterloo; much less could he have seen what happened to the 1st Guards.[6]

This, as we have seen, is contradicted by the evidence from Clinton's diary and letters which shows that he witnessed the attack and immediately rode to the Hanoverian troops to send them off in support.

Conclusion: It is clear that Clinton was in the vicinity and acted quickly to support the attack. Although I have much sympathy with the claims of the 52nd, one has to be honest and conclude that Clinton was not so much interested in the individual actions of one regiment but saw that the decisive movement of most of his division as much more important.

10. Did the 52nd advance alone without support and therefore deserve all the laurels?

It has been shown, despite claims to the contrary from the 52nd, that the 2/95th moved with them and that the 71st and 3/95th followed quite quickly but were a few hundred yards behind. Claims that the 71st deviated so far from the 52nd, and that there was a huge gap have, however, been proven incorrect. They remained within a hundred yards or so of each other and the gap was largely filled by the 3/95th. When the 52nd halted to allow the 23rd Light Dragoons to clear their front the 71st also caught up. The Osnabrück Battalion drew close behind. The attack by the light cavalry to the east also had a very significant effect on the collapse of the French army.

Conclusion: The further claim that the 52nd drove the French army beyond La Belle Alliance unsupported is shown to be false.

The overall conclusion must be that although the 52nd were not recognised officially as much as they possibly should have been, this appears to have been an accident of circumstances rather than a concerted effort to prevent them receiving this acclaim. With regard to the Duke of Wellington, it is clear that he resisted all attempts to rewrite his despatch with a better history of the battle in later years. However, the charges that he deliberately favoured other regiments, actively sought to conceal or destroy evidence to the contrary and bought the silence of everyone around, is entirely without substance.

Indeed who was given the honour of marching triumphantly into Paris? None other than the brigade which swept the field clear.

Final conclusion: There was no conspiracy.

NOTES

Preface

1. A quote from Pierre Antoine Noël Bruno, Comte Daru although not referring to Waterloo *per se*.

Introduction

1. Many British ex soldiers emigrated to Commonwealth countries, and their records and memoirs travelled with them. A number from all sides also emigrated to the United States of America and American universities have since purchased some very important collections of papers regarding this period in history.
2. Published by Pen & Sword in September 2014.
3. The war with America, known generally as the War of 1812 had ended in January 1815.

Chapter 1

1. Maxstoke Castle is still privately owned (by the Fetherston-Dilkes family). It is in Warwickshire about 8 miles directly east of Birmingham.
2. Perceval (Holland) mss 23, ff. 87, 88; *Glenbervie Diaries*, ii. 317.
3. The North Devonshire Regiment.
4. Friedrich Adolf Riedesel, Freiherr zu Eisenbach (1738 –1800), had commanded the German contingent at Saratoga.
5. The Yorkshire East Riding Regiment.
6. The Berkshire Regiment.
7. On 22 August, nearly two months after the main Irish uprisings had been defeated, about 1,000 French soldiers under General Humbert landed in the north-west of the country, at Kilcummin in County Mayo. Joined by up to 5,000 local rebels, they had some initial success, inflicting a humiliating defeat on the British at the Castlebar (and setting up a short-lived 'Republic of Connacht'). This force was defeated at the Battle of Ballinamuck, in County Longford, on 8 September 1798. The French troops who surrendered were repatriated to France in exchange for British prisoners of war, but hundreds of the captured Irish rebels were executed.
8. William Wickham (1761–1840) was a British civil servant and politician who was the founder of British foreign secret service activities during the French Revolution.

9. 'Proceedings of a general court martial ... on charges preferred by Brigadier General Henry Clinton ... against the Hon. W. E. Cochrane (1809) statement of the service of Brigadier General Henry Clinton', The National Archives (TNA), WO 25/744 2768.
10. H. Clinton, *A Few Remarks Explanatory of the Motives which Guided the Operations of the British Army during the Late Short Campaign in Spain* (London, 1809).
11. The Royal American Regiment had no fewer than eight battalions during the Napoleonic Wars.
12. The 3rd (East Kent) Regiment of Foot were known colloquially by the epithet 'the Buffs' because of the colour on the collars and cuffs of their red tunics.

Chapter 2

1. Lieutenant General Sir Thomas Graham, Lord Lynedoch had led these British forces in the unsuccessful assault on the fortress of Bergen op Zoom on 8 March 1814.
2. Major General Henry Bunbury was actually Under Secretary of State for War and the Colonies.
3. Henry Clinton's diary dated 30 August 1814.
4. There were two General Alten's in the Netherlands at this time; Major General Victor, Count von Alten and Lieutenant General Charles, Count von Alten, who commanded the 3rd Division at Waterloo. The latter is the von Alten referred to here, who at this period commanded the 16,000 Hanoverian troops present in Holland and Belgium.
5. Henry Clinton's diary dated 1 September 1814.
6. Henry Clinton's diary dated 2 September 1814.
7. Colonel Edward Gibbs, brother of Major General Sir Samuel Gibbs.
8. Henry Clinton's Inspection Report dated 14 September 1814.
9. Henry Clinton's Inspection Report dated 17 September 1814.
10. This must be Sympher's Troop.
11. Lieutenant Colonel Adolphus von der Beck was slightly wounded at Bayonne on 14 April 1814, he retired on half pay on 25 May 1815.
12. Beck is recorded as having been slightly wounded at the Sortie of Bayonne 14 April 1814 and actually was placed on half pay in May 1815.
13. Major Frederick Breymann.
14. Lieutenant Colonel Rudolphus Bodecker, in Beamish, *History of the King's German Legion* (London 1832–37) (hereafter Beamish), No. 375, p. 570.
15. Henry Clinton's Inspection Report dated 24 September 1814.
16. Lieutenant Colonel Frederick von Wissell 3rd Line Battalion KGL, No. 470 in Beamish, p. 470.
17. Major General Heinrich von Hinuber commanded the KGL Division in the Netherlands. Beamish No. 469, p. 470.
18. Henry Clinton's letter to Major General Sir Hudson Lowe dated Bruges, 23 September 1814.
19. Henry Clinton's Inspection Report dated 11 October 1814.
20. Brevet Colonel Charles du Plat, who commanded 1st Brigade King's German Legion at Waterloo.
21. More usually known as the 2nd Duke of York's Osnabrück Landwehr Battalion.
22. Henry Clinton's Inspection Report dated 16 September 1814.
23. Brevet Colonel Hugh Halkett.

24. Henry Clinton's Inspection Report of 16 September 1814.
25. Lieutenant Colonel Friedrich von der Schulenburg.
26. Henry Clinton's Inspection Report dated 17 September 1814.
27. Although the report states it refers to the 2nd Duke of York, from later comments it is clear that this is a mistake and that it should read the 3rd Duke of York (Quakenbrück) Battalion.
28. Major Carl Friedrich von Bülow.
29. Henry Clinton's Inspection Report of 29 September 1814.
30. Henry Clinton's diary entry for 1 October 1814.
31. Letter of Henry Clinton dated 25 September 1814
32. Letter date Brussels 4 October 1814, Henry Clinton to Major General Sir Henry Torrens, Military Secretary.
33. This letter is clearly dated August but appears in his letter book in October, the August date also agrees much better with the content.
34. Letter from Henry Clinton to Major General Sir James Willoughby Gordon, Quartermaster General, dated Brussels 15 October 1814.
35. Henry Clinton's letter to Major General Gordon dated Brussels 4 December 1814.
36. Henry Clinton's letter to Major General Halkett dated Antwerp 21 December 1814.
37. Henry Clinton's Inspection Report dated Ypres 6 January 1815.
38. Henry Clinton's Remarks on Major General Mackenzie's Brigade dated Tournai 8 January 1815.
39. Henry Clinton's diary entry dated 8 January 1815.
40. Henry Clinton's Inspection Report dated Mons 7 March 1815.

Chapter 3

1. Letter of Henry Clinton to Henry Calvert dated 21 March 1815.
2. Henry Clinton's diary entry for 22 March 1815.
3. Henry Clinton's diary entry dated 25 March 1815.
4. Henry Clinton's letter to Sir John Colborne dated 26 March 1815.
5. Charles Stuart, 1st Baron Stuart de Rothesay (1779–1845), known as Sir Charles Stuart between 1812. and 1828, was Ambassador to Holland at this time.
6. Henry Clinton's diary entry for 28 March 1815.
7. Henry Clinton's letter to Henry Torrens dated 31 March 1815.
8. Henry Clinton's diary entry dated 1 April 1815.
9. Henry Clinton's letter to Sir Hudson Lowe dated 3 April 6 pm.
10. *Ibid.*
11. Captain Digby Mackworth 7th Foot, diary entry for 2 April from the author's *Waterloo Archive* 6 Vols (Barnsley 2010–14),volume IV, pp. 7–25.
12. Frederick Adam's letter to Sir Henry Clinton undated but annotated 'Tuesday morning'. Believed to have been sent on 4 April.
13. The Cathedral of St Michael and St Gudule in Brussels.
14. Henry Clinton's letter to Sir Hudson Lowe dated 4 April 1815.
15. Letter of Henry Clinton to his brother William dated 7 April.
16. This is an error; the 55th Foot only ever consisted of one battalion.
17. Letter of Henry Clinton to his brother William dated 7 April.
18. Letter from Henry Clinton to Sir Hudson Lowe dated 4 April 1815.

Chapter 4

1. Dated Horse Guards 27 March 1815.

2. *Historical Record of the Fifty Second Regiment 1755–1858*, by William Moorsom, (London 1860).
3. *The life of John Colborne, Field-Marshal Lord Seaton, G.C.B., G.C.H., G.C.M.G., K.T.S., K.St.G., K.M.T., &c., compiled from his letters, records of his conversations, and other sources*, by G.C. Moore Smith (London 1903), p. 212.
4. Returns of the Army in Holland September 1814, *Napoleon Series website* by Andrew Bamford.
5. *The Hanoverian Army of the Napoleonic Wars* by Peter Hofschröer and Bryan Fosten (London 1989), pp. 37–8.
6. Peter Hofschröer *1815: The Waterloo Campaign*, 2 Vols, (Greenhill, London 1998), Vol 1, p. 75 states that the corps arrived during 'the winter of 1814/15', but it is clear from Clinton's reports that they were in the Netherlands well before September.
7. Henry Clinton's Inspection Report dated 15 April 1815.
8. Oliver Schmidt was kindly able to confirm that Schulenburg had served in the Garde du Corps in 1806–07 and left as a Major. He was promoted to Lieutenant Colonel when he took command of the Hanoverian Battalion. Reference *Das Geschlecht der von der Schulenburg* by Johann Friedrich Danniel, (Salzwedel 1847).
9. *Waterloo Archive* volume II, p. 66.
10. Henry Clinton indicates that the battalion was only formed 'for the duration of the war' and should have been disbanded in 1814.
11. Henry Clinton's Inspection Report dated 16 September 1814.
12. *Waterloo Archive* volume II, p. 67.
13. Henry Clinton's Inspection Report dated 6 May 1815. Peter Hofschröer indicates that the Salzgitter Battalion arrived with the 'Subsidiary Corps' but it is clear from Clinton's records that they only arrived in the Netherlands some three months later.
14. *Ibid.*
15. As per his obituary of 1842. Kane's List mistakenly shows him as a cadet in 1776 but this would mean he was a cadet for fourteen years.
16. Augustus Sympher's Horse Artillery Troop KGL should not be confused with Captain Frederick Sympher's Foot Battery KGL which fought throughout the Peninsular War until Sympher was killed at the Battle of Orthes in 1814.

Chapter 5

1. Letter of Henry Clinton to his brother dated 13 April.
2. Lieutenant Colonel Hamlet Wade.
3. Henry Clinton's Inspection Report dated Villers St Amand 14 April 1815.
4. Letter from Sir John Colborne to Henry Clinton dated Brussels 16 April 1815.
5. Henry Clinton's letter to Sir John Colborne dated 18 April 1815.
6. Henry Clinton's diary entry of 23 April 1815.
7. Henry Clinton's Inspection Report dated 1 May 1815.
8. Henry Clinton's letter to General Adam dated 18 May 1815.
9. General Adam's letter to Henry Clinton dated 21 May 1815.
10. Henry Clinton's letter to Lord Somerset dated 9 June 1815.
11. Letter from General Adam to Henry Clinton dated 10 June 1815.
12. Henry Clinton's letter to General Adam dated 11 June 1815.
13. Henry Clinton's Inspection Report dated 12 June 1815.
14. Diary of Digby Mackworth dated 13 May 1815, *The Waterloo Archive* vol. IV p. 17.

15. Henry Clinton's Inspection Report dated 17 April 1815.
16. Henry Clinton's letter to Colonel du Plat dated 4 May 1815.
17. Henry Clinton's letter to Colonel du Plat dated 18 May 1815.
18. Henry Clinton's diary entry dated 1 June 1815.
19. Henry Clinton's diary entry for 8 June 1815.
20. *Ibid.*
21. Henry Clinton's diary entry for 9 June 1815.
22. Henry Clinton's Inspection Reports dated Tournai 14 April 1815.
23. *Ibid.*
24. Henry Clinton's Inspection Report dated Tournai 15 April 1815.
25. Henry Clinton's letter to General Hinuber dated 18 April 1815.
26. General Hinuber's letter to Henry Clinton dated 19 April 1815 at 5.30am.
27. Hinuber's letter to Henry Clinton dated 24 [April?].
28. Henry Clinton's diary entries of that date.
29. Henry Clinton's Inspection Report dated 6 May 1815.
30. Henry Clinton's detailed remarks dated 6 May 1815.
31. Letter from General Hinuber to Henry Clinton dated 4 May 1815.
32. Henry Clinton's letter to Colonel Halkett dated 7 May 1815.
33. Henry Clinton's letter to Henry Torrens dated 29 May 1815.
34. The Saxon contingent was then with the Prussian army under Blücher but was due to transfer to Wellington's army. However, a heavy-handed approach to the division of the Saxon troops into those coming from lands now held by Prussia and those still held by the King of Saxony led to a mutiny and the troops being disarmed. Their use was therefore lost to the allies for the ensuing campaign.

Chapter 6

1. Henry Clinton's letter to Commissary General Drummond dated 13 April 1815.
2. The Journal of Commissar Tupper Carey published by the author in *Waterloo Archive* volume VI.
3. Henry Clinton's letter to Colonel Halkett dated 5 May 1815.
4. Henry Clinton's letter dated Ath 15 April to Sir Hudson Lowe.
5. Letter from Sir Hudson Lowe to Henry Clinton dated 10 May 1815.
6. Letter from Adjutant General Barnes to Henry Clinton dated 21 May 1815.
7. General Adam's letter to Henry Clinton dated 21 May 1815.
8. Henry Clinton's diary entry for 22 May 1815.
9. General Alten's letter to Sir Henry Clinton dated 25 May 1815.
10. Henry Clinton's diary entry dated 2 April 1815.
11. Henry Clinton's letter to Sir Hudson Lowe dated 4 April 1815.
12. Henry Clinton's letter to William Clinton dated 7 April 1815.
13. Henry Clinton's letter to General Hinuber dated Ath 10 May 1815.
14. The family home was at Rhue, north of Ullapool.
15. Letter of Lieutenant John McDonald 23rd Fusiliers dated 13 June 1815 published in the author's *Waterloo Archive* volume III.
16. Henry Clinton's letter to his brother dated Ath 16 April 1815.
17. Reference Henry Clinton's diary entry for 19 April 1815.
18. Memoirs of Lieutenant Henry Dehnel 3rd Line Battalion KGL translated and published in the author's *Waterloo Archive* volume V, p. 26.
19. Digby Mackworth's diary entry for 20 April 1815, *Waterloo Archive* volume IV, p. 12.
20. Sir Henry Clinton's letter to Sir George Wood dated 19 May 1815.

21. Henry Clinton's diary entry dated 20 April 1815.
22. The author's *Waterloo Archive* volume V, p. 207.
23. Memoirs of Lieutenant Henry Dehnel 3rd Line Battalion KGL translated and published in the author's *Waterloo Archive* volume V, p. 26.
24. Lord Hill's memorandum dated Grammont, 2 May 1815.
25. Henry Clinton's letter to Sir Hudson Lowe dated 3 May 1815.
26. Henry Clinton's letter to Lord Hill dated 3 May 1815.
27. Letter from Lieutenant Colonel Charles Broke to Henry Clinton dated 9 May 1815.
28. Henry Clinton's letter to Charles Broke dated 10 May 1815.
29. Henry Clinton's letter to Charles Broke dated 11 May 1815.
30. Henry Clinton's diary entry for 26 May 1815.
31. Henry Clinton's letter to his brother dated 28 May 1815.
32. Wellington's letter to Baron Alten dated 16 May 1815 in the *Wellington's Dispatches* volume XII, p. 392.
33. Letter from the Duke of Wellington to General Decken from J. Gurnwood, *The Dispatches of Field Marshall the Duke of Wellington 1799–1815*, volume XII, p. 401.
34. Undated letter from General Adam to Henry Clinton, but its position in the letter book would indicate it was written on 1 June 1815.
35. Henry Clinton's diary entry for 13 June 1815. It is very interesting, as this was the actual day that Napoleon attacked.
36. Surgeon John Maling of the Medical Staff.
37. Letter to Colonel Halkett dated 13 June 1815 9 ½ am.
38. Henry Clinton's letter to General Adam dated 15 June 1815.
39. Henry Clinton's diary entry for 15 June 1815.

Chapter 7

1. Letter of Henry Clinton to the Duke of Wellington dated Ath 16 June, it therefore was written before he rode with his troops to Enghien.
2. Nivelles was clearly understood by Wellington and Blücher as his point of concentration against an attack in the vicinity of Charleroi or Mons. Although it left the road to Brussels via Quatre Bras open, the allies were certain that Napoleon could not march upon the capital with their two armies concentrating so close on either flank of such an advance.
3. *Wellington's Dispatches* volume XII, p.474.
4. It has been assumed that Hill attended the ball because it appears that Digby Mackworth did (see David Miller's *The Duchess of Richmond's Ball, 15 June* (Staplehurst 2005), but Colonel Mitchell states that he received the news at Grammont at dinner with Lord Hill.
5. Letter from Charles Broke to Henry Clinton dated 16 June 1815 (no time given).
6. Henry Clinton's diary entry for 16 June 1815.
7. Henry Clinton's letter to General Sir Thomas Graham dated 23 June 1815.
8. This is a particularly late notification, it is likely actually to have been a little earlier.
9. Report of the 1st Line Battalion of the [King's] German Legion on its participation in the Battle of Belle-Alliance translated into English in the author's *Waterloo Archive* volume II, p. 58.
10. This confirms the receipt of late orders by this brigade.
11. Cambron-casteau.
12. Report of the 3rd Line Battalion KGL on its participation in the Battle of Belle-

Alliance, translated from German and published by the author in his *Waterloo Archive* volume II.
13. Memoirs of Lieutenant Henry Dehnel 3rd Line Battalion KGL, in the author's *Waterloo Archive* volume II, p. 62.
14. Five kilometres north-east of Ath.
15. Report of the Hanoverian Landwehr Battalion Bremervorde on its participation in the Battle of Belle-Alliance by Captain F. Scheuch, published in English by the author in his *Waterloo Archive* volume II, p. 66.
16. *Wellington's Dispatches* volume XII, p. 474. The Duke was going to Waterloo on his way from Brussels towards Quatre Bras.
17. Letter of 2nd Lieutenant Richard Cocks Eyre, 2nd Battalion 95th Foot, published in the author's *Waterloo Archive* volume III, p. 114.
18. Henry Clinton's letter to General Sir Thomas Graham dated 23 June 1815.
19. Memoirs of Lieutenant Henry Dehnel 3rd Line Battalion KGL, in the author's *Waterloo Archive* volume V, p. 27.
20. Letter of Private John Lewis of the 2nd Battalion 95th Foot in the author's *Waterloo Archive* volume I, p. 160.
21. Journal of Private Thomas Jeremiah 23rd Fusiliers from the author's *Waterloo Archive* volume IV, p. 183.
22. Henry Clinton's letter to his wife Susan Clinton dated Braine le Comte 16 June at 5.30pm.
23. Report of the 3rd Line Battalion KGL on its participation in the Battle of Belle-Alliance, translated from German and published by the author in his *Waterloo Archive* volume II p. 63.
24. Actually the Bois de la Houssiere.
25. *ibid*
26. *The History of Lord Seaton's Regiment (52nd Light Infantry) at the Battle of Waterloo* by Reverend William Leeke, 2 vols (London 1866) volume I, (henceforth referred to as Leeke), p. 38.
27. The Journal of Commissariat Tupper Carey published by the author in *Waterloo Archive* volume VI, p. 233.

Chapter 8

1. *Wellington's Dispatches* volume XII, p. 475.
2. Henry Clinton's diary entry for 16 June 1815.
3. Sir Henry Clinton's letter to Sir Thomas Graham dated 23 June 1815.
4. Report of the 1st Line Battalion of the KGL on its participation in the Battle of Belle-Alliance, translated and published in the author's *Waterloo Archive* volume II. p. 58.
5. Report of the 3rd Line Battalion of the KGL on its participation in the Battle of Belle-Alliance, translated and published in the author's *Waterloo Archive* volume II, p. 63.
6. Sir Henry Clinton's letter to Sir Thomas Graham dated 23 June 1815.
7. Report of the 1st Line Battalion of the KGL on its participation in the Battle of Belle-Alliance, translated and published in the author's *Waterloo Archive* volume II, p 58.
8. Henry Clinton's diary entry dated 17 June 1815.
9. Private Thomas Jeremiah 23rd Fusiliers published in *Waterloo Archive* volume IV, p. 183.

10. Leeke, p. 13.
11. Letter of Private John Lewis 95th Foot published in *Waterloo Archive* volume I.
12. Leeke, p. 13.
13. Report of the 1st Line Battalion of the KGL *Waterloo Archive* volume II, p. 58.
14. Report of the 3rd Line Battalion of the KGL on its participation in the Battle of Belle-Alliance *Waterloo Archive* volume II, p. 63.
15. Letter from Henry Clinton dated Le Cateau, 23 June 1815 to his brother Lt. General Sir William Clinton.
16. Report of the Hanoverian Landwehr Battalion Osnabrück, 2nd Battalion, on its participation in the Battle of Belle Alliance by Major L. von Dreves from the author's *Waterloo Archive* volume II, p. 68.
17. It is interesting to learn of the loss of so many stores, which is glossed over in histories of the campaign.
18. Storekeeper James Robinson's letter to Sir Henry Clinton dated 31 August 1815,from the author's *Waterloo Archive* volume VI, p. 225.
19. Report of the 1st Line Battalion of KGL on its participation in the Battle of Belle-Alliance from the author's *Waterloo Archive* volume II, p. 59.
20. Ensign Jack Barnett, 71st Foot, published in the author's *Waterloo Archive* volume VI, p. 150.

Chapter 9

1. Report of the 1st Line Battalion of the KGL on its participation in the Battle of Belle-Alliance from the author's *Waterloo Archive,* volume II, p. 59.
2. An interesting comment relative to the free flow of troops through the forest. It is clear that off road the going was very difficult, but it is true that there were a number of good roads that traversed the forest.
3. Tupper Carey, *Waterloo Archive* volume VI, p. 234.
4. Colville records receiving the orders at 6am.
5. Lieutenant Colonel F. S. Tidy (by his daughter) from the author's *Waterloo Archive* volume I, p. 171.
6. *Fifty Years of my Life*, by George, Lord Albemarle, (London 1876) volume II, p. 16.
7. Leeke p. 15.
8. *Fifty Years of my Life*, by George, Lord Albemarle, p. 17.
9. Private Conrade Geige, 3rd Line Battalion, KGL.
10. Captain Diedel was killed at Waterloo.
11. Henry Dehnel of the 3rd Line Battalion KGL, published in the author's *Waterloo Archive* volume V p. 29.
12. Private John Smith 71st Foot from the author's *Waterloo Archive* vol III, p. 113.
13. Letter of Major von Hammerstein, Battalion Commander, to Colonel Hugh Halkett. Report of the Salzgitter Battalion at the Battle of 18 June from the author's *Waterloo Archive* volume II, p. 70.
14. Private John Lewis of 2nd Battalion 95th Foot from the author's *Waterloo Archive* volume I, p. 160.
15. An interesting comment, given the usual assertion by modern historians that Wellington maintained such a tight discipline on the troops that only the French, Belgian and Prussian forces looted. It is clear from a number of sources that in his Belgian campaign Wellington was unable to exert the same level of discipline on the troops, presumably because of the massive change in his Staff, and that both plundering and excessive baggage were actually problems for the British

troops as well once campaigning began in Belgium. There is some reason to believe, however, that the tight control reasserted itself on the march to Paris because of a fear of aggravating the population, and the British troops seem to have behaved themselves.

16. 2nd Lieutenant Richard Cocks Eyre 2nd Battalion 95th Foot from the author's *Waterloo Archive* volume III, p. 115.
17. Army slang for food.
18. Journal of Private Thomas Jeremiah 23rd Fusiliers from the author's *Waterloo Archive* volume IV, pp. 185–7.
19. Ensign Jack Barnett 71st Foot from the author's *Waterloo Archive* volume VI, p. 151.

Chapter 10

1. Actually one battalion was of Nassau troops, these are often misnamed by eyewitnesses as until recently Nassau had formed part of Brunswick.
2. Lieutenant General Sir Henry Clinton's letter to General Sir Thomas Graham dated 23 June 1815.
3. Diary of Digby Mackworth from the author's *Waterloo Archive* volume IV, p. 23.
4. Ensign Ferdinand von Uslar-Gleichen 4th Line Battalion KGL from the author's *Waterloo Archive* volume V, p. 35.
5. Report of the 2nd Line Battalion of the KGL on its participation in the Battle of Belle-Alliance by Lieutenant Colonel G. von Muller from the author's *Waterloo Archive* volume II, p. 60.
6. Report of the Hanoverian Landwehr Battalion Bremervorde on its participation in the Battle of Belle-Alliance by Captain F. Scheuch, from the author's *Waterloo Archive* volume II, p. 66.
7. Leeke, p. 19.
8. Sir Henry Clinton.
9. Commissary Tupper Carey from the author's *Waterloo Archive* volume VI.
10. Leeke, p. 19.
11. This statement is fully corroborated by Ensign Leeke of the 52nd, who says, 'I saw our general of division, Sir Henry Clinton, and some of his staff coming towards me. He looked all the more formidable from a fashion he had adopted of wearing his cocked hat, not in the usual way, 'fore and aft' but with the small ends over each shoulder.'
12. Lieutenant Henry Dehnel 3rd Line Battalion KGL, from the author's *Waterloo Archive* volume II.
13. Lieutenant Henry Lane's letter (no. 69) in H. T. Siborne's *The Waterloo Letters,* (London 1983) p. 143.
14. Journal of Private Thomas Jeremiah 23rd Fusiliers from the author's *Waterloo Archive* volume IV, p. 187.

Chapter 11

1. Private Thomas Jeremiah 23rd Fusiliers from the author's *Waterloo Archive* volume IV, p. 188.
2. 2nd Lieutenant Richard Cocks Eyre 2nd Battalion 95th Foot from the author's *Waterloo Archive* volume III, p. 115.
3. Report of the Hanoverian Landwehr Battalion Osnabrück, on its participation in the Battle of Belle Alliance by Major L. von Dreves from the author's *Waterloo Archive* volume II, p. 68.

4. General Adam's Letter (no. 120) in Siborne's *Waterloo Letters*, p. 276.
5. Report of the 3rd Line Battalion of the KGL on its participation in the Battle of Belle-Alliance from the author's *Waterloo Archive* volume II, p. 64.
6. Captain Joseph Logan 2nd Battalion 95th Foot from the author's *Waterloo Archive* volume I, p. 157.
7. Leeke, p. 24.
8. Report of the 2nd Line Battalion of KGL on its participation in the Battle of Belle-Alliance by Lieutenant Colonel G. von Muller from the author's *Waterloo Archive* volume II, p. 60.
9. Lieutenant Henry Dehnel 3rd Line Battalion KGL from the author's *Waterloo Archive* volume V, p. 31.
10. Private John Smith 71st Foot from the author's *Waterloo Archive* volume III, p. 113.
11. Letter of Major von Hammerstein, to Colonel Hugh Halkett. Report of the Salzgitter Battalion at the Battle of 18 June, from the author's *Waterloo Archive* volume II, p. 70.
12. *Fifty Years of my Life*, by George, Lord Albemarle, p. 29.
13. Probably the 15th Hussars who had one squadron on the Nivelles road.
14. Lieutenant Colonel F. S. Tidy (by his daughter) from the author's *Waterloo Archive* volume I, p. 171.

Chapter 12

1. Lieutenant Henry Dehnel 3rd Line Battalion KGL, from the author's *Waterloo Archive* volume V, pp. 31–2.
2. Report of the 3rd Line Battalion of the KGL on its participation in the Battle of Belle-Alliance from the author's *Waterloo Archive* volume II, p. 264.
3. Report of the 2nd Line Battalion of the KGL on its participation in the Battle of Belle-Alliance by Lieutenant Colonel G. von Muller from the author's *Waterloo Archive* volume II, p. 61.
4. Ensign Ferdinand von Uslar-Gleichen 4th Line Battalion from the author's *Waterloo Archive* volume V, p. 36.
5. Report of the 1st Line Battalion of the KGL on its participation in the Battle of Belle-Alliance from the author's *Waterloo Archive* volume II, p. 59.
6. Colonel Hepburn's letter (no. 117) in Siborne's *Waterloo Letters*, p. 267.
7. Lieutenant Henry Dehnel 3rd Line Battalion KGL, from the author's *Waterloo Archive* volume V, p. 32.
8. These were probably Hanoverians or Nassauers; asat the time, no Brunswick troops were yet involved in the action at Hougoumont.
9. Report of the 2nd Line Battalion of the KGL on its participation in the Battle of Belle-Alliance by Lieutenant Colonel G. von Muller from the author's *Waterloo Archive* volume II, p. 61.
10. Ensign Ferdinand von Uslar-Gleichen 4th Line Battalion from the author's *Waterloo Archive* volume V, p. 36.
11. Ensign Jack Barnett 71st Foot from the author's *Waterloo Archive* volume VI, p. 151.

Chapter 13

1. Undated letter of Lieutenant General Adam, No. 120, from Siborne's *Waterloo Letter*.
2. Private John Lewis 2nd Battalion 95th Foot from the author's *Waterloo Archive* volume I, p. 159.

3. Captain Joseph Logan 2nd Battalion 95th Foot from the author's *Waterloo Archive* volume I, p. 157.
4. *Ibid.*
5. Captain Joseph Logan now commanded the battalion.
6. Private John Lewis 2nd Battalion 95th Foot from the author's *Waterloo Archive* volume I, p. 159.
7. Private John Smith 71st Foot from the author's *Waterloo Archive* volume III, p. 113.
8. Report of the 1st Line Battalion of the KGL on its participation in the Battle of Belle-Alliance from the author's *Waterloo Archive* volume II, p. 59.
9. Private John Smith 71st Foot from the author's *Waterloo Archive* volume III, p. 113.
10. Leeke, p.33.
11. Letter of Lieutenant Colonel Eeles (Major at Waterloo) of the 3rd Battalion 95th Foot, Siborne's *Waterloo Letters*, no. 129.
12. Ensign Jack Barnett 71st Foot, from the author's *Waterloo Archive* volume VI, p. 151.
13. I have found no mention of this attack on the 14th Foot elsewhere; it is true they were very inexperienced and could have been caught out of formation by the cavalry, but their casualties that day (only thirty-six casualties of which seven rank and file killed) indicate that nothing too serious befell them.
14. Private Thomas Jeremiah 23rd Fusiliers from the author's *Waterloo Archive* volume IV.
15. Lieutenant Colonel Ellis was severely wounded by a carbine shot in the chest and further was thrown from his horse whilst being led to the rear. He was placed in a hovel, which caught fire on the 19th, from which he was rescued by Assistant Surgeon Munro. He died of his wounds on 20 June and was buried at Braine l'Alleud.
16. Lieutenant John McDonald 23rd Fusiliers from the author's *Waterloo Archive* volume III, p. 129.
17. Report of the Hanoverian Landwehr Battalion Bremervorde on its participation in the Battle of Belle-Alliance by Captain F. Scheuch from the author's *Waterloo Archive* volume II, p. 67.
18. Letter of Major von Hammerstein, Battalion Commander, to Colonel Hugh Halkett. Report of the Salzgitter Battalion at the Battle of 18 June from the author's *Waterloo Archive* volume II, p.71.
19. Report of the Hanoverian Landwehr Battalion Osnabrück, on its participation in the Battle of Belle Alliance by Major L. von Dreves from the author's *Waterloo Archive* volume II, p. 68.
20. This refers to Ensign Charles Fraser who exchanged into the 3rd Foot Guards a month later. This is confirmed by G. Albemarle, *Fifty Years of my Life*.
21. Lieutenant Charles Myler Brannan.
22. The 14th Foot.
23. Memoirs of Lieutenant Colonel Tidy, in the author's *Waterloo Archive* volume I, p. 172.
24. Lieutenant Henry Dehnel 3rd Line Battalion KGL, from the author's *Waterloo Archive* volume V, p. 31.
25. Lieutenant Colonel F. S. Tidy (by his daughter) from the author's *Waterloo Archive* volume I, p. 172.

26. General Cavalie Mercer's *Journal of the Waterloo Campaign* (London 1870), p. 169.
27. Diary of Captain Digby Mackworth 7th Foot, aide-de-camp to General Hill from the author's *Waterloo Archive* volume IV, p. 23.
28. From later comments, it is clear that this 'favoured' division was Clinton's 2nd Division, which had remained in reserve for much of the battle, but contributed significantly to the defeat of the Imperial Guard.
29. Captain Horace Churchill, 1st Foot Guards, aide-de-camp to Lord Hill from the author's *Waterloo Archive* volume VI, p. 4.
30. Colonel Colborne explains that the battalion was actually formed in two lines of the two wings behind each other. Some have misinterpreted this as remaining in a two-rank line formation. However, each wing consisted of troops in two actual ranks, therefore the two wings in line behind each other effectively meant they they were in four ranks.
31. Sir John Colborne's memorandum (no. 123) in Siborne's *Waterloo Letters*, p. 280.
32. Bull's and Ramsay's batteries were virtually alongside each other here and it is possible he mistook them for a single strong battery of twelve guns.
33. Report of the Hanoverian Landwehr Battalion Osnabrück on its participation in the Battle of Belle Alliance by Major L. von Dreves from the author's *Waterloo Archive* volume II, p. 69.
34. General Adam's letter (no. 120) in Siborne's *Waterloo Letters*, p. 276.
35. Sir John Colborne's memorandum (no. 123) in Siborne's *Waterloo Letters*, p. 280.
36. Leeke, p. 38.
37. 2nd Lieutenant Richard Cocks Eyre, 2nd Battalion 95th Foot, from the author's *Waterloo Archive* volume III, p. 116.
38. Lieutenant General Sir Henry Clinton to General Sir Thomas Graham dated 23 June 1815 from the author's *Waterloo Archive* volume I, p. 151.

Chapter 14

1. Sir John Colborne's memorandum (no. 123) in Siborne's *Waterloo Letters*, p. 280.
2. Major Hunter Blair's letter (no.122) Brigade Major to General Adam in Siborne's *Waterloo Letters*, p. 279.
3. Lieutenant General Sir Henry Clinton's letter to General Sir Thomas Graham dated 23 June 1815, from the author's *Waterloo Archive* volume I, p. 152.
4. Lieutenant General Sir Frederick Adam's memorandum (no. 120) in Siborne's *Waterloo Letters*, p. 275
5. Captain Powell's letter (no. 109) in Siborne's *Waterloo Letters*, p. 255.
6. Lieutenant Pringle's letter (no. 96) in Siborne's *Waterloo Letters*, pp. 227–8.
7. Captain Powell's letter (no. 109) in Siborne's *Waterloo Letters*, p. 255.
8. Sir John Colborne's memorandum (no. 123) in Siborne's *Waterloo Letters*, p. 280.
9. Lieutenant General Sir Frederick Adam's memorandum (no. 120) in Siborne's *Waterloo Letters*, p. 275.
10. 'The Guard dies but does not surrender.' This is an extremely interesting use of this famous phrase, often attributed to General Cambronne, General Michel or cited as the invention of a French journalist in later years, but this appears to be in a letter written on the very night of the battle. However, without the ability to view the original it cannot be established beyond doubt that it is not a later addition.
11. Diary of Captain Digby Mackworth 7th Foot, aide-de-camp to General Hill from the author's *Waterloo Archive* volume IV, p. 24.

12. Captain Horace Churchill, 1st Foot Guards, aide-de-camp to Lord Hill from the author's *Waterloo Archive* volume VI, p. 5.
13. Diary of Captain Digby Mackworth, 7th Foot, aide-de-camp to General Hill from the author's *Waterloo Archive* volume IV, p. 24.
14. This incident is not recorded so fully elsewhere, to the editor's knowledge. Orlando Bridgeman, a fellow aide-de-camp does confirm that a horse was killed under Lord Hill and that there were a number of shot holes through his cape. See his account in *Waterloo Archive*, Volume IV, pp. 25–31.
15. Captain Horace Churchill, 1st Foot Guards, aide-de-camp to Lord Hill from the author's *Waterloo Archive* volume VI, p. 6.
16. Captain Joseph Logan, 2nd Battalion 95th Foot, from the author's *Waterloo Archive* volume I, p. 157.
17. Private John Lewis, 2nd Battalion 95th Foot from the author's *Waterloo Archive* volume I, p. 160.
18. Leeke, vol.1, p. 79.
19. 2nd Lieutenant Richard Cocks Eyre, 2/95th *Waterloo Archive* volume III, p. 116.
20. Sir John Colborne's memorandum (no. 123) in Siborne's *Waterloo Letters*, p. 280.
21. Corporal Aldridge letter (no. 128) 2nd Battalion 95th in Siborne's *Waterloo Letters*, p. 303.
22. Leeke, vol.1, p. 49.
23. Sir John Colborne's memorandum (no. 123) in Siborne's *Waterloo Letters*, p. 280.
24. Lieutenant Gawler's Letter (no. 124) in Siborne's *Waterloo Letters*, p. 287.
25. Captain Powell's letter (no. 109) in Siborne's *Waterloo Letters*, p. 255.
26. Lieutenant General Sir Frederick Adam's memorandum (no. 120) in Siborne's *Waterloo Letters*, p. 275.
27. Letter from Henry Clinton dated Le Cateau, 23 June 1815 to his brother Lieutenant General Sir William Clinton.
28. Report of the 3rd Line Battalion of the KGL on its participation in the Battle of Belle-Alliance from the author's *Waterloo Archive* volume II, p. 64.
29. Report of the 1st Line Battalion of the KGL on its participation in the Battle of Belle-Alliance from the author's *Waterloo Archive* volume II, p. 59.
30. Report of the Osnabrück Battalion by Major Dreves in *Waterloo Archive*, volume II, p. 69.
31. The evidence is clear and strong that Cambronne was captured and did not utter the immortal phrase (this even appears to be a later invention). 'The Guard dies but never surrenders'.
32. Report of the Osnabrück Battalion by Major Dreves in *Waterloo Archive*, volume II, p. 69.
33. Sir Hussey Vivian's letter (no. 70) in Siborne's *Waterloo Letters*, p. 149.
34. Ensign Leeke records the words of Wellington as 'Well done, Colborne! Well done, Go on; don't give them time to rally'.
35. General Adam's letter (no. 120) in Siborne's *Waterloo Letters*, p. 276.
36. Sir John Colborne's memorandum (no. 123) in Siborne's *Waterloo Letters*, p. 280.
37. Captain Reed, 71st Foot, letter (no. 126) in Siborne's *Waterloo Letters*, p. 298.
38. Report of Major L. von Dreves from the author's *Waterloo Archive* volume II, p. 69
39. *Supplementary History of Lord Seaton's Regiment* by W. Leeke (London, 1871), p. 32.
40. Ensign Jack Barnett, 71st Foot, from the author's *Waterloo Archive*, volume VI, p. 151.
41. Sir John Colborne's memorandum (no. 123) in Siborne's *Waterloo Letters*, p. 280.

42. Lieutenant General Sir Henry Clinton's letter to General Sir Thomas Graham dated 23 June 1815 from the author's *Waterloo Archive* volume I, p. 148.
43. 2nd Lieutenant Richard Cocks Eyre, 2nd Battalion 95th Foot, from the author's *Waterloo Archive* volume III, p. 116.
44. Private John Smith, 71st Foot, from the author's *Waterloo Archive* volume III, p. 113.
45. Report by Major L. von Dreves from the author's *Waterloo Archive* volume II, p. 70.
46. Only two eagles were captured, although one other may have been temporarily in British hands before being recaptured.
47. Captain Horace Churchill, 1st Foot Guards, aide-de-camp to Lord Hill from the author's *Waterloo Archive* volume VI, p. 6.
48. Report of the 3rd Line Battalion of the KGL on its participation in the Battle of Belle-Alliance from the author's *Waterloo Archive* volume II, p. 355.
49. Ensign Jack Barnett 71st Foot from the author's *Waterloo Archive* volume VI, p. 151.
50. Lieutenant Henry Dehnel, 3rd Line Battalion, from the author's *Waterloo Archive* volume V, p. 34.
51. The calibre of the British Brown Bess muskets being larger than that of the French muskets permitted the use of their cartridges.
52. Letter of Major von Hammerstein to Colonel Hugh Halkett. Report of the Salzgitter Battalion at the Battle of 18 June, from the author's *Waterloo Archive* volume II, p. 71.
53. N.N. in German is a customary abbreviation for the Latin 'Nomen Nescio' which translates as 'I am ignorant of the name'. The description would seem to indicate Genappe, but it is very unlikely that they proceeded this far that night.
54. Report of the 2nd Line Battalion of the KGL on its participation in the Battle of Belle-Alliance by Lieutenant Colonel G. von Muller from the author's *Waterloo Archive* volume II, p. 62.
55. Lieutenant George Horton, 1st Battalion 71st Foot, from the author's *Waterloo Archive* volume I, p. 154.
56. Report of the Hanoverian Landwehr Battalion Bremervorde on its participation in the Battle of Belle-Alliance by Captain F. Scheuch from the author's *Waterloo Archive* volume II, p. 67.
57. Diary of Captain Digby Mackworth, 7th Foot, aide-de-camp to General Hill from the author's *Waterloo Archive* volume IV, p. 25.

Chapter 15

1. From Susan Clinton to William Clinton dated Brussels 20 June 1815.
2. Susan Clinton's letter to William Clinton dated 19 June
3. From Susan Clinton to William Clinton dated Brussels 20 June 1815.
4. Lieutenant Henry Dehnel, 3rd Line Battalion, from the author's *Waterloo Archive* volume V, p. 35.
5. This figure is taken from the State of the Division taken on 11 June 1815 minus about twenty men taken prisoner on 17 June.
6. Lieutenant William Woolcombe, 71st Foot, from the author's *Waterloo Archive,* volume II, p. 156.
7. 2nd Lieutenant Richard Cocks Eyre, 2nd Battalion 95th Foot, from the author's *Waterloo Archive,* volume III, p. 117.

8. Major John Humphrey Edward Hill, 1st Battalion 23rd Foot, from the author's *Waterloo Archive* volume VI, p. 153.
9. Susan Clinton's letter dated Brussels 22 June 1815 to Sir William Clinton.
10. Letter of Major von Hammerstein to Colonel Hugh Halkett. Report of the Salzgitter Battalion at the Battle of 18 June from the author's *Waterloo Archive* volume II.
11. Report of the Hanoverian Landwehr Battalion Bremervorde on its participation in the Battle of Belle-Alliance by Captain F. Scheuch from the author's *Waterloo Archive* volume II, p. 67.
12. Sir Henry Clinton to Lord Hill dated Nivelles 19 June 1815.
13. Letter from Henry Clinton to Lord Hill dated Nauroy 26 June 1815.
14. This sometimes causes confusion as the commander of the Quakenbrück Battalion was Baron Clamor Wilhelm von dem Bussche-Hunefeld.
15. Letter of Henry Clinton to Colonel Sir F. Hervey dated Neuilly 5 July 1815.
16. Leeke, p. 67.
17. From Beamish's *History of the King's German Legion* and Lieutenant von Wissel's *Glorious Feats of Arms Performed in the Recent Wars by Non-commissioned Officers and Soldiers of the English-German Legion and the Hanoverian Army* (Hanover 1846).
18. From Beamish, volume II, p. 515.

Chapter 16

1. Leeke, p. 75.
2. Lieutenant General Sir Henry Clinton to General Sir Thomas Graham 23 June 1815 from the author's *Waterloo Archive* volume I, p. 153.
3. Commissary Tupper Carey from the author's *Waterloo Archive* volume VI, p. 238.
4. *Waterloo Archive* volume VI, p. 239.
5. Private John Smith, 71st Foot, from the author's *Waterloo Archive* volume III, p. 113.
6. Lieutenant George Horton, 1st Battalion 71st Foot, from the author's *Waterloo Archive* volume I, p. 154.
7. Letter of Sir Henry Clinton dated Le Cateau 24 June 1815.
8. Henry Clinton's letter to William Clinton dated originally 27 June although not completed until 2 July.
9. Henry Clinton to Susan Clinton dated Sarcelles 2 July 1815.
10. Henry Clinton to Lord Hill dated Neuilly 6 July.

Chapter 17

1. Sir John Colborne Lord Seaton from Siborne's The *Waterloo Letters*, no.123, p. 280.
2. Captain Joseph Logan, 2nd Battalion 95th Foot from the author's *Waterloo Archive* volume I, p. 158.
3. Private John Lewis, 2nd Battalion 95th Foot, from the author's *Waterloo Archive* volume I.
4. Henry Clinton to Colonel Halkett, dated [Bois de] Boulogne 7 July.
5. Henry Clinton's Inspection Report dated 8 July 1815.
6. *ibid.*
7. *ibid.*
8. *ibid.*
9. Henry Clinton's Inspection Report dated 10 July 1815.
10. *ibid.*

12. *ibid.*
13. *ibid.*
14. Henry Clinton's Inspection Report dated 17 July 1815.
15. *ibid.*
16. *ibid.*
17. Henry Clinton's Inspection Report dated 18 July 1815.
18. Sir Henry Clinton to Colonel Bodecker dated Boulogne 26 August 1815.
19. General Clinton to Colonel Halkett dated Beauregard 7 December 1815 from the author's *Waterloo Archive* volume V, p. 23.

Appendix 1

1. All of the quotes in this Appendix are from the author's *Waterloo Archive* volume V, pp. 191–5

Appendix 2

1. It should be noted that Wellington should not be blamed for calling it the Battle of Waterloo, when it was nearer and more apt to use La Belle Alliance (as the Prussians referred to it) or Mont St Jean (which the French preferred), but having dated his report from Waterloo, that is the name it was then given in London and it stuck.
2. Major Hunter Blair's letter (no. 121) Brigade Major to General Adam in Siborne's *Waterloo Letters*, p. 278.
3. See *Supplementary Despatches and Memorand of Field Marshal Arthur, Duke of Wellington* (John Murray, London 1872) volume X, p. 544.
4. Letter of Colonel Bentham dated November 1853 quoted by Leeke, Vol. I, p. 414.
5. *The British Army Against Napoleon* by Robert Burnham and Ron McGuigan, (Barnsley 2010).
6. Leeke, *Supplementary History of Lord Seaton's Regiment*, p. 29.

Select Bibliography

Anonymous *Particulars of the Battle of Waterloo, also of Ligny and Quatre Bras, with Circumstantial Details, by a Near Observer* (2 Vols), (London 1817).
Adkin, M. *The Waterloo Companion* (London 2001).
Albemarle, G. *Fifty Years of my Life* (London 1876).
Anglesey, Earl of, *One Leg; The Life and Letters of Henry William Paget, First Marquess of Anglesey K.G., 1768–1854* (Oxford 1961).
Anglesey, Marquess of, *The Capel Letters 1814–17* (London, 1955).
Barbero, A. *The Battle, A New History of the Battle of Waterloo* (London 2005).
Batty, Capt. *An Historical Sketch of the Campaign of 1815* (London 1820).
Beamish, L. *History of the King's German Legion* (London, 1832–7).
Bentley, N. *Selections from the Reminiscences of Captain Gronow* (London 1977).
Bernard, G. & Lachaux, G. *Waterloo Relics* (Paris 2005).
Black, J. *The Battle of Waterloo* (New York 2010).
Booth, J. *The Field of Waterloo* (London 1817).
Brett-James, A. *The Hundred Days; Napoleon's Last Campaign from Eye-Witness Accounts* (London 1964).
Burnham, R. & McGuigan, R. *The British Army Against Napoleon* (Barnsley 2010).
Caldwell, G. *Rifles at Waterloo* (1995).
Clark, Major F. *Borne to the Grave by Heroes; The Story of William Martin Middleditch of the First Foot Guards* (Suffolk 1994).
Colby, R. *The Waterloo Despatch* (London 1965).
Colville, J. *The Portrait of a General* (Salisbury 1980).
Coppens, B. *Waterloo, Critical Account* (Brussels 2004).
Cotton, E. *A Voice from Waterloo* (London 1849).
Crook, J. *The Very Thing – Memoirs of Drummer Richard Bentinck 23rd Foot* (Barnsley 2011).
Crosthwaite, J.F. *Brief Memoir of Major Gen. Sir John Woodford* (London 1881).
Dalton, C. *The Waterloo Roll Call* (London 1904).
Eaton, C. *Narrative of the Battle of Waterloo from a Near Observer*, 2 Vols (London 1816).
Franklin, J. *Waterloo Netherlands Correspondence* (Ulverston 2010).
Franklin, J. *Waterloo Hanoverian Correspondence* (Ulverston 2010).
Glover, G. *Letters from the Battle of Waterloo* (London 2004).
Glover, G. *Reminiscences of Waterloo The Correspondence between Henry Leathes and Alexander Mercer of G Troop RHA* (Huntingdon 2004).
Glover, G. *Recollections of My Life including Military Service at Waterloo, G. Blathwayt*

23rd Light Dragoons (Huntingdon 2004).
Glover, G. *A Narrative of the Battles of Quatre Bras and Waterloo; with the Defence of Hougoumont by Matthew Clay* (Huntingdon 2006).
Glover, G. *Waterloo Letters: The 1815 Letters of Lt John Hibbert, 1st King's Drag. Gds.* (Huntingdon 2007).
Glover, G. *From Corunna to Waterloo, The Journals and Letters of Maj. Edwin Griffiths & Capt. Frederick Philips 15th Hussars 1801–16* (London, 2007).
Glover, G. *A Short Account of the Life and Adventures of Private Thomas Jeremiah Royal Welch Fusiliers 1812–37* (Huntingdon 2008).
Glover, G. *The Waterloo Diary of Capt. James Naylor 1st King's Drag. Gds. 1815–16* (Huntingdon 2008).
Glover, G. *A Young Gentleman at War, the Letters of Capt. the Hon. Orlando Bridgeman 1st Foot Guards 1812–25* (Huntingdon, 2008).
Glover, G. *A Guards Officer in the Peninsula and at Waterloo, The Letters of Capt. George Bowles Coldstream Guards* (Huntingdon, 2008).
Glover, G. *'It All Culminated at Waterloo' The Letters of Capt. John Lucie Blackman 2nd Batt. Coldstream Guards* (Huntingdon 2009).
Glover, G. *Recollections of Which I was a Witness … The Journal and Letters of the Rev. George Stonestreet 1814*–16 (Huntingdon 2009).
Glover, G. *The Waterloo Archive* (Barnsley 2010–14).
Glover, G. *Eyewitness to the Peninsular War and Waterloo: The Letters and Journals of James Stanhope 1808–15* (Barnsley 2010).
Glover, G. *Letters of an Officer of the Corps of Engineers 1813–16. 1st Lt John Sperling* (Huntingdon 2012).
Glover G. *Wellington's Voice, The Candid Letters of Lt Col John Fremantle Coldstream Guards 1808–21* (Barnsley 2012).
Gurwood, J. *The Dispatches of Field Marshal the Duke of Wellington 1799–1815*, Vol. XII (London 1838).
Hill, J. *Wellington's Right Hand, Rowland, Viscount Hill* (Stroud 2011).
Hofschröer, P. *1815: The Waterloo Campaign*, 2 vols, (London 1999).
Kelly, C. *A Full and Circumstantial Account of the Battle of Waterloo* (London 1830).
Lachouque, H. *The Anatomy of Glory* (London 1997).
Leeke, Rev. W. *The History of Lord Seaton's Regiment (The 52nd Light Infantry) at the Battle of Waterloo*, 2 Vols, (London 1866).
Leeke, Rev W. *Supplementary History of Lord Seaton's Regiment (The 52nd Light Infantry) at the Battle of Waterloo* (London 1871).
Mercer, Gen. C. *Journal of the Waterloo Campaign Kept Throughout the Campaign of 1815 by the Late General Cavalie Mercer of the 9th Brigade Royal Artillery* (London 1870).
Miller, D. *The Duchess of Richmond's Ball 15th June* (Staplehurst 2005).
Mockler-Ferryman, A.F. *The Life of a Regimental Officer during the Great War 1793–1815* (London, 1913).
Mudford, W. *An Historical Account of the Campaign in the Netherlands in 1815* (London 1817).
Moore Smith, G. *The Life of John Colborne Field-Marshal Lord Seaton* (London 1903).
Sabine, Maj. Gen. E. *Letters of Colonel Sir Augustus Simon Frazer* (London 1859).
Sale, N., *Wellington's Waterloo Secret* (Georgia 2005).
Siborne, H.T. *The Waterloo Letters* (London 1983).
Siborne, W. *History of the Waterloo Campaign* (London 1848).

Index